Advance Praise for *An Everyone Culture*

"Among the deluge of books on leadership and culture that are published every year, only a few stand out as truly revolutionary. This book is one of them. It should be required reading for anyone in the field of talent management who is interested in dramatically accelerating the individual and collective capabilities of people at work. I highly recommend it!"

— **WILLIAM H. HODGETTS**, Vice President, Enterprise Coaching and Assessment, Fidelity Investments

"Kegan and Lahey's book *Immunity to Change* fundamentally improved my life when I first went through its exercises years ago, so I was eager to read their new book. It didn't disappoint. A thought-provoking and inspiring read, *An Everyone Culture* shows how small changes can help organizations, and individual leaders, reap huge rewards."

— **EMILY LAWSON**, Chief People Officer, Kingfisher

"This is a most provocative and challenging book in asking us to consider seriously how organizations can create workplace cultures that are effective as economic entities and, *at the same time*, develop all of their leaders, managers, and employees as human beings. If you want a book that will make you think differently about what an organization could be and how you could lead people differently, this book is for you."

— **EDGAR H. SCHEIN**, author, *Humble Inquiry*

"In this remarkable book, Kegan and Lahey prescribe a radically new paradigm of organizational life. They examine in detail three organizations—each an exemplary performer in its field—that valorize the emotional growth of every organizational participant and engage in unrelenting discipline to make every aspect of organizational life a forcing bed for that growth. Not since Deming extinguished Taylorism has anyone offered such a profound challenge to our conventional notions of how to achieve exceptional organizational performance."

—**HARRY SPENCE**, Court Administrator, Massachusetts Trial Court

"In a world of constant change and ever-increasing challenges, companies need to learn how to unleash the full potential of their employees. Kegan and Lahey explain how organizations can become 'deliberately developmental' to boost employee satisfaction while also achieving great business results."

—**DANIEL VASELLA, MD**, former Chairman and CEO, Novartis AG

AN
EVERYONE
CULTURE

AN EVERYONE CULTURE

Becoming a Deliberately Developmental Organization

ROBERT KEGAN

AND LISA LASKOW LAHEY

with Matthew L. Miller, Andy Fleming,
and Deborah Helsing

Harvard Business Review Press

Boston, Massachusetts

Copyright 2016 Harvard Business School Publishing
All rights reserved
Printed in the United States of America
10 9 8 7 6 5 4 3 2 1

The web addresses referenced in this book were live and correct at the time of the book's publication but may be subject to change.

Library-of-Congress cataloging information forthcoming

ISBN 978-1-62527-862-3
eISBN 978-1-62527-863-0

The paper used in this publication meets the requirements of the American National Standard for Permanence of Paper for Publications and Documents in Libraries and Archives Z39.48-1992.

For our children and grandchildren, our nieces and nephews, and their children—in hopes the future is filled with many more workplaces built for flourishing

Contents

AN
EVERYONE
CULTURE

Introduction

Culture as Strategy

In an ordinary organization, most people are doing a second job no one is paying them for. In businesses large and small; in government agencies, schools, and hospitals; in for-profits and nonprofits, and in any country in the world, most people are spending time and energy covering up their weaknesses, managing other people's impressions of them, showing themselves to their best advantage, playing politics, hiding their inadequacies, hiding their uncertainties, hiding their limitations. Hiding.

We regard this as the single biggest loss of resources that organizations suffer every day. Is anything more valuable to a company than the way its people spend their energies? The total cost of this waste is simple to state and staggering to contemplate: it prevents organizations, and the people who work in them, from reaching their full potential.

The organizations you will meet in this book, taken together, point the way to a qualitatively new model for *people development*—the single most powerful way we know of, as developmental psychologists, for an organization to unleash the potential of its people.

And with what result? These exemplar organizations, taken as a whole, show us a picture of the following benefits:

- Increases in profitability, improved employee retention, greater speed to promotability, greater frankness in communication, better error detection in operational and strategic design, more effective delegation, and enhanced accountability

- Reductions in cost structures, political maneuvering, interdepartmental strife, employee downtime, and disengagement

- Solutions to seemingly intractable problems, such as: how to convert the familiar team of leaders (each looking out for his own franchise) into the more valuable, but elusive, leadership team; how to anticipate crises no one in the company has experienced previously and to successfully manage through them; how to invent and realize future possibilities no one has experienced previously

In short, this book is as much about realizing organizational potential as it is about realizing human potential. Most of all, this book describes a new model for the way each can contribute to the other—how organizations and their people can become dramatically greater resources to support each other's flourishing.

Now let's return to the ordinary organization where everyone works a second job of hiding imperfections. Consider it from the employer's point of view. Imagine you're paying a full-time wage for part-time work to every employee, every day. Even worse, consider that when people are hiding their weaknesses they have less chance to overcome them, so you must continue to pay the cost of these limitations as well—every day.

Consider the second job from the employee's point of view. What does it cost you to live a double life at work, every day, knowing you're not the person you present yourself to be? As human beings we're set up to protect ourselves—but it is just as true that we're set up to grow psychologically, to evolve, to develop. In fact, research shows that the single biggest cause of work burnout is not work overload, but working too long without experiencing your own personal development. Now consider the drag or cap on personal development we create by hiding our weaknesses rather than having a regular opportunity to overcome them.

In an increasingly volatile, uncertain, complex, and ambiguous world (the so-called VUCA world)—a world of new challenges and opportunities—organizations naturally need to expect *more*, and not less, of themselves and the people who work for them. But our familiar organizational design fails to match that need.

How did we come to this observation about everyone in the ordinary organization doing a second job? Was it by staring hard at the ordinary organization? No. When you're staring very hard at the normal organization, it's hard to see anything but normal.

Normal began to look strange to us only after we stared hard at organizations where no one is doing the second job. Different as the companies in this book are in their look and feel, they share a striking commonality: they are the most powerful settings in the world we have found for developing people's capabilities, precisely because they have created a safe enough and demanding enough culture that everyone comes out of hiding. This is what we call the deliberately developmental organization: the DDO.

An Everyone Culture

We (your lead authors) have devoted our professional lives to the study and advancement of adult-developmental theory, which illuminates the gradual evolution of people's meaning-making systems and psychological capabilities. Developmental practitioners have known for years how to provide expert support to individuals on a one-to-one basis. However, little attention has been given to applying these principles and methods to an entire organization.

From the start of our research team's investigation of the three DDOs at the heart of this book, we were struck by three things. First, all of them are doing what the science of human development recommends, and they are doing so in ingenious and effective ways (even though only one of the organizations explicitly studied the science). They seemed to have an intuitive, practical grasp of how to accelerate people's development.

Second, these organizations are taking these concepts to scale so that everyone in the organization—workers, managers, and leaders alike—has the opportunity to develop. In the pages ahead, not only will you meet three unusual organizations, but you will also learn an explicit theory of human development that will help you better understand how these organizations' cultures impact their members. The theory will help you see under the organizations' practices to the way they help people uncover, engage, and ultimately transcend the limiting assumptions and defensive routines that prevent us from developing our capabilities beyond our own expectations.

In this way, should you have an interest in fostering, or working in, a deliberately developmental organization, you will have something more to guide you than a set of exemplary practices you may think to copy. You will have a crack-the-code understanding that may enable you to create practices that do not yet even exist.

Finally, all three companies intentionally and continuously nourish a culture that puts business and individual development—and the way each one supports the other—front and center for everyone, every day. Delivered via their homegrown, robust, daily practices, their cultures constitute breakthroughs in the design of people development and business strategy.

A Twenty-First-Century Design for Development

One way to look at this book is to see it as a twenty-first-century answer to the question, "What is the most powerful way to develop the capabilities of people at work?" Executive coaching, high-potential programs, mentoring, corporate universities, off-sites, retreats, and leadership development programs may sound like widely varying approaches, but they actually share enough common (and problematic) features to be seen as a single, twentieth-century answer to the way we might best develop human capabilities.

What are the features common to these approaches? First, they give people punctuated inputs, delivered from time to time rather than continuously. By themselves they may not occur often or intensely enough. Given how daunting the project is to help people grow in fundamental ways, the application of the intervention may be too thin.

Second, they constitute "something extra"—something beyond and outside the normal flow of work, an approach that raises the vexing problems of transfer and cost. Even if these activities support powerful learning in a context outside work, how do you ensure that employees transfer their new knowledge to the stubbornly durable context of business as usual? And how do you sustain the double costs of external inputs and employees' time away from the job?

Third, these types of programs are provided only for a few, generally for the 5 to 10 percent of employees who are designated "high potentials" (to say nothing of the way such a label indirectly writes off the potential of 90 to 95 percent of your workers).

Finally, and above all, notice that the twentieth-century answer to developing potential, in all cases, makes the individual and not the organization the point of dynamic entry. If the organization wants to significantly impact people's capabilities, it should apparently find something new, outside the organization itself, some additive: give them a coach, a program, a course, a mentor. The organization itself does not change. We might soup up the fuel through these additives, but the engine remains what it has always been.

What is the alternative? Imagine so valuing the importance of developing people's capabilities that you design a culture that itself immersively sweeps every member of the organization into an ongoing developmental journey in the course of working every day.

Imagine making the organization itself—and not separate, extra benefits—the incubator of capability. Imagine hardwiring development into your bottom line so that, along with asking whether your culture is fostering the other elements of business success (such as profitability or the consistent quality of your offering), you ask—demand—that your culture as a whole, visibly and in the regular, daily operations of the company, be a continuous force on behalf of people overcoming their limitations and blind spots and improving their mastery of increasingly challenging work.

Imagine finding yourself in a trustworthy environment, one that tolerates—even prefers—making your weaknesses public so that your colleagues can support you in the process of overcoming them. Imagine recapturing the full-time energies of your employees now joined to the mission of the enterprise.

You're imagining an organization that, through its culture, is an incubator or accelerator of people's growth. In short, you're imagining a deliberately developmental organization.

Being a DDO does not present a choice between focusing on individuals or focusing on the organization as a whole. In a DDO, coaching, leadership programs, and the like do not disappear; instead, they become figures on the ground of a more comprehensively developmental culture. Development is not an additive. Instead, both the fuel and the engine are developmentally enriched.

In this book, we show you the twenty-first-century way to create a robust incubator for people's development.

A Strategic Approach to Culture

The intention of every DDO leader in the pages ahead is crystal clear: he or she is working hard on the culture every day as much to enhance the business as its employees. These leaders do not see two goals or two missions, but one. The relationship between realizing human potential and organizational potential in these companies is a dialectic, not a trade-off. We believe these companies have something provocative to teach about a new route to business success.

You will see not only how a DDO helps its people develop but also how the DDO culture enables it to come up with original and effective means to meet its most vexing challenges—and capitalize on its most promising opportunities. One of these companies, for example, is in an industry with an annual turnover of 40 percent, but this organization figured out a way, year after year, to get that figure into the single digits. Another entered a whole new industry in record time. A third may be the only company to have anticipated the economic crisis of 2008—and manage through it successfully.

The distinctive quality of business challenges in a VUCA world is that they are as often adaptive as technical. Technical challenges are not necessarily easy, but they can be met by improvements to existing mind-sets and organizational designs. Adaptive challenges can only be met by people and organizations exceeding themselves. We believe the DDO may be the single best means for meeting adaptive challenges.

In short, in the pages ahead you'll get a good look at culture as itself a business strategy.

Planning Your Route through This Book

Let's look at what you may want to consider as you choose the best sequence through the book. Chapter 1 drops you immediately into a ground-level experience of a DDO. As we guide you through the three organizations, we're trying to let you swivel your head in all directions to take in as many impressions as possible. The goal is not to be comprehensive or systematic but to let the novelty jump out at you. "Toto, I've a feeling we're not in Kansas anymore."

Chapters 2 and 3 give you an aerial view of the deliberately developmental organization, including its conceptual underpinnings and its common features across companies. Chapter 2 drills down into what we mean by *developmental* when we speak of a deliberately developmental organization. Chapter 3 takes you through twelve common features of a DDO, grouped according to their developmental aspirations, practices, and sense of community.

If you're a "part to whole" learner and want to experience the particular look and feel of something before you consider it more generally and conceptually, you'll probably most appreciate the inductive sequence through the first three chapters as we have laid it out. But if you prefer to see the big picture before you look at living instances (as "whole to part" learners do), you may prefer a more deductive sequence, beginning with chapters 2 and 3 and then moving to chapter 1.

Chapter 4 is a deep dive into the practices that the exemplar companies have created to support their deliberately developmental cultures. You will understand these practices better after you've read the chapter on developmental theory (chapter 2), but if you're most interested in an on-the-ground account of life in a DDO, you may want to go directly from chapter 1 to chapter 4 and then to chapter 5.

Chapter 5 addresses the strictly business value of a DDO. "Yes, I see how such an organization may be a fantastic experience for the employee," you might say, "but is this really any way to run a business?" This chapter addresses whether the exemplar businesses succeed *despite* the attention they give to personal development or *because* of it.

Chapter 6 gives you a direct experience of your own growing edge so that you might consider firsthand the kind of personal learning a DDO would collectively encourage and support for you. (If, after finishing chapter 4 on DDO practices, you find yourself wondering about your own blind spot or about the kind of discomfort you would have to manage were you in a DDO, you might want to go directly to chapter 6 and then come back to chapter 5.)

If all the preceding chapters have created in you an interest in moving your workplace—your team, department, or whole enterprise—more in the direction of becoming a DDO, then chapter 7, the final chapter, gives you pictures of the ways we have seen organizations choose to get started.

The Rise of the New Incomes

We live in unprecedented times. Alongside the seismic shifts of the VUCA world are equally significant shifts in what people are looking for when they go to work each day. Gone are the days when payoffs to Economic Man alone—to the material self, to greater agency in the external world—were enough. In those days, conventional incomes—such as paychecks, health benefits, and limits to the hours in a workweek—sufficed.

Now we're seeing the pursuit of *new incomes*: personal satisfaction, meaningfulness, and happiness. These are payoffs to the Psychological Person, to the intangible self, to fulfillment in the interior world. Paychecks, bonuses, and benefits will always matter, of course, but, increasingly, they're not enough for many of us. The rise of the new incomes may represent the biggest shift in the work-reward equation since the emergence of the labor movement in the nineteenth century. That whole countries, and even the United Nations, are now exploring the development of measures like GNH (gross national happiness, a qualitatively different way of measuring success) as well as GNP is evidence of the robustness of the new incomes.

But what is happiness? The definition most in vogue, fueled by the positive psychology movement, is one of happiness as a state, characterized by pleasure; a banishing of pain, suffering, and boredom; a sense of engagement and meaning through the experience of positive emotions and resilience. This is the dominant version of the new incomes sought and paid in the most widely celebrated "great places to work." Think of flexible work hours, pool tables and dart boards, dining areas run by chefs serving fabulous and nutritious food at all hours, frequent talks by visiting thought leaders, spaces for naps, unlimited vacation time.

However, the research literature on happiness suggests another definition, one that is overlapping but significantly different. The second definition sees happiness as a process of human flourishing. This definition, whose roots go back to Aristotle and the Greeks' concept of *eudaemonia*, includes an experience of meaning and engagement but in relation to the satisfactions of experiencing one's own growth and unfolding, becoming more of the person one was meant to be, bringing more of oneself into the world.

Just as labor pains are a part of bringing new life into the world, the process of human development, of seeing and overcoming one's previous limitations, can involve pain. Unlike happiness as a state brought on by experiencing only the so-called positive emotions, happiness as a process of development includes the experience of loss, pain, and suffering (rather than standing in contrast to it).

This other kind of happiness may be less fashionable in a world entranced with pleasure, stimulation, and the avoidance of pain, but for anyone who has tasted it, as our DDO informants testify, it is a treasured income of surpassing value. People find themselves experiencing pleasure and aliveness in new, unexplored terrain, with a heightened sense of awareness and presence even as they engage their most difficult moments.

The workplaces we call deliberately developmental organizations are delivering this second kind of new income in settings that expressly attend to the process of human development. Their cultures include everyone in this process—everyone experiencing their own unfolding but, equally important, everyone witnessing, supporting, and at times even provoking this unfolding in others. Although it is occasionally difficult or unsettling for individuals to face old, unproductive patterns or vulnerabilities, people experience an overall sense of shared excitement and energy, forward movement and growth—of themselves, their colleagues, and the organization.

It is far too soon to settle, in the reorganization of work, for what amounts to experiments confined to a single conception of happiness. As an experiment in new ways to organize work, the workplace built for flourishing stands shoulder to shoulder with the workplace built for well-being. These workplaces may one day marry, or they may not, but they should be mutually supporting, each taking an interest in and cheering for the other as together they lead a common movement to repay, with a new income, the gift of our labor.

The workplace built for well-being has already begun to claim a space in the public imagination. We believe this is only half the mansion. We invite you to take a grand tour of the workplace built for flourishing, the other half of the house of human happiness.

Meet the DDOs

You know how there are people, when they realize that vulnerability is important, they kind of walk right toward it? Well, first—that's not me; and, second—I don't even hang out with people like that! . . . Vulnerability is at the core of shame and fear and our struggle for worthiness, but it appears it is also the birthplace of joy, of creativity, of belonging, of love.

—Brené Brown, University of Houston

I n this chapter, you'll get inside three deliberately developmental organizations (DDOs). You'll meet some of the people who call them home—leaders, new recruits, and experienced employees. Some of these people will appear again in later chapters. You won't get a comprehensive, top-down introduction to the companies or to the general idea of the DDO. Instead, you'll get the closest thing, in book form, to a quick immersion: what you might see if you were plunked down in the middle of one of these companies.

Before we enter, a few words of preparation: Are you the rarer kind of person Brené Brown (author and researcher at the University of Houston) describes as valuing the experience of your own vulnerability and running right toward it?[1] If you are, your only risks in the pages ahead are being too sure you understand fully what you're seeing or too quick to suspend your critical faculties and automatically endorse what you think these people are trying to do.

But if you are, like most people, more wary of feeling vulnerable, ashamed, and unworthy—especially at work—you might find yourself feeling alarmed soon after you enter. That might be the case especially if you happen to be a leader in an organization and you feel you don't have the luxury of being vulnerable ("I have people counting on me, people who need me to have it together"). In any case, none of us chooses or decides to be alarmed. It happens automatically. Once alarmed, any of us will, as the neuroscientists have taught us, just as automatically protect ourselves.

If you feel alarmed, you might protect yourself by "fleeing"— perhaps by putting down the book and finding something else to do. But more commonly, you'll flee, while continuing to read, by distancing yourself from what you're reading. Your mind might begin looking for reasons to conclude there is actually nothing novel here: "This sounds a lot like what we're already doing" or "I've heard all this before." Or you might find yourself thinking, "This manner of working is the most exotic of rare flowers, unlikely to grow in any other soil, and thus not really worth thinking any more about, since it would be impossible for most people or organizations."

Or you might protect yourself by "fighting," finding yourself on the attack without a declaration of war. Somehow, before you know it, your mind is doing whatever it can to take apart what is being built in front of you. "These people are crazy," your mind might say. Or, "This is too extreme." Or, "This is too X." Or, "This violates my belief that Y, or my value for Z."

All these reactions are fine. Many of your thoughts that come up in this chapter deserve careful consideration, and we've made space in future chapters to do that. The important thing is for you to realize that when these thoughts arise automatically, you're *not* considering them. You're not even "having" them. Rather, they are having you. They are taking over.

All we ask is that you keep track of these automatic reactions, know that you will explore them in future chapters, and not let them be your whole experience as you try to stay present in the places we invite you to explore.

In a sense, it will be wonderful if you do find yourself having these reactions, because you will begin to experience the first kind of work everyone must do in a DDO: to take responsibility for the workings of our minds so that we can stay present, so that we can stay at work.

It's also important to say that the exemplar companies are, in many respects, very different from one another. Each does business in a different industry: entertainment and real estate; e-commerce; and hedge-fund investing. There are striking differences in the "feel" and operation of each company. If Bridgewater Associates might be glibly characterized as a cross between business and the Navy SEALs, then The Decurion Corporation might be seen as a cross between business and the wisdom traditions of the East and the West. Next Jump Inc., has a "no firing" policy and an explicit commitment to stand by employees through thick and thin ("You wouldn't fire your children from your family," Charlie Kim, its leader, often says). But Bridgewater is equally explicit in saying, "We are up to *growing* people, not *rehabilitating* them; some people have to go." In thinking about its operations, Bridgewater makes continuous use of the metaphor of the machine, an analogy you would never hear at Decurion. Next Jump is in some ways proudly nonexceptionalist (the two top leaders talk about *not* being the stars growing up in their own families or schools); Bridgewater's leaders believe you become a one-in-ten-thousand company by hiring one-in-ten-thousand-type people.

In short, a DDO can come in many flavors. But even though each DDO may have its own feel, may have taken a different path to its current culture, and may have evolved its principles and practices independently, it's striking how much they have in common. There's no single right way to be a DDO—no simple recipe of programs, policies, incentives, and perks—but there are deep assumptions that run through all the DDOs: assumptions about the possibility and value of growing in adulthood, ways of structuring people's growth directly in their work, ways of helping people get the most out of giving and receiving feedback and coaching, ways of making people development and business development all one thing.

DDO work settings are built for human development. They support people in overcoming their limitations as part of contributing to the profitability of the business. It's just as true that DDOs seek profitability so that they can stay in business to help people overcome their limitations and grow. (Please note, too, that these companies are not our clients; we formed a research relationship, and not a service relationship, with each of them.)

Finally, it is possible, perhaps inevitable, that at the same time you learn about these DDOs, through your reactions you will also begin learning about some aspects of yourself. This, too, is exactly in keeping with the spirit of a DDO. As Bryan Ungard, COO of Decurion, says, "There is no way, really, to be a spectator here. You become a participant the second you enter. And welcome!"

The Next Jump Story

There is no way to "get better" other than to first do it, however poorly you do. So get started; go out and fail! We have become good at getting better because we are so good at failing.

—Charlie Kim, Next Jump

It is an early Saturday morning in New York, and the Next Jump conference room is packed with twenty-somethings. Most are graduating college seniors, completing their engineering or business degrees from prestigious universities such as MIT, Carnegie Mellon, and Georgia Tech. The young people are chatting nervously. They have been flown in the night before and are dressed up for a full day of demonstrating their thought processes in repeated interviews, presentations, and team challenges.

It's Super Saturday at Next Jump, an e-commerce tech company, which devotes two Saturdays per year to interviewing, testing, and choosing new employees. Greg Kunkel, senior vice president and cofounder, squeezes to the front of the room to welcome the applicants. Kunkel lets everyone know that of the thousand candidates screened on campus, forty-four have made the cut and accepted the chance to come for interviews. They are about to experience a unique approach to hiring, one that will give them a taste of the Next Jump culture.

"You will learn about yourself today, as well as about Next Jump," Kunkel says. "Think of today as a nine-hour blind date, one that is long enough for the truth to come out." Candidates smile nervously and exchange glances. "It will be a long day, and you will be tired by the end," Kunkel continues. "But remember, it takes twice as much energy to fake and hide who you really are than it does to just be honest, to just be your real self."

Kunkel then introduces software engineer Nayan Busa to share a little of his own work experience at Next Jump. Calmly and quietly, Busa begins.

"I have been here since 2010," he tells the packed room. "When I first started, I lacked confidence. I was insecure. I was scared about how I was portrayed by my peers. This has not been easy to overcome. I had to practice a lot. I realized I lacked confidence in all parts of my life, even when it came to choosing furniture in my home or going to a restaurant." Busa explains how he has been working on becoming more confident through his job. "I practiced by speaking in front of the company about my growth. I am practicing right now in front of you. When you start improving, it impacts revenue and business. And I still have a long way to go."

Busa's tone and content illustrate how Next Jump operates differently from the other companies where candidates are interviewing. "All this growth is for a reason," he explains. "Our goal is to build a top-ten global technology company. And we want to change the world by changing workplace culture."

Next Jump generates billions of dollars in annual sales by using a unique distribution channel to employees in their workplaces. Through its PerksAtWork.com platform, Next Jump built a marketplace connecting 30,000 merchants with 70,000,000 employees from 4,000 large businesses (including 700 of the *Fortune* 1,000) and more than 100,000 small businesses. By aggregating the buying power of jobholders, Next Jump offers employee discounts and privileges for all types of products and services.

Busa leads the PerksAtWork e-commerce marketplace, and his position comes with a great deal of responsibility, something he knows is unusual for someone so young (he is twenty-eight) and relatively inexperienced. "I graduated from Cornell in 2009 doing my master's," he tells the applicants. "A lot of my friends went into Amazon, Google, Bloomberg, etc. And they're still doing the same thing they did five years ago. They still do the same code. Yes, their projects might have expanded. Maybe now a couple of them are leading one or two people. But none of them is in some way running a company. Charlie [Kim, Next Jump CEO and cofounder] relies on us to come up with strategies for the company. And even when we attended the board meeting, I was like, 'Shit! Which company allows such a young engineer to be sitting in front of the board talking about strategy?'"

Like the two other DDOs, Next Jump challenges employees by moving them into roles for which they're not yet prepared to succeed and then provides them with steady streams of feedback to help them grow into those roles. In all three companies, if you're completely able to perform your role, it's no longer the right role for you; it has no "stretch" left. Once, at a retreat for MV21, Next Jump's twenty-one-person, peer-chosen leadership team, Busa told a long and rambling story to the other leaders; then he heard the feedback that he needed to improve his storytelling and presentation skills. Since then, he has looked for any chance to develop this skill, pushing himself to present regularly in front of the company, asking for and learning from the feedback he receives.

This occasion—speaking to the forty-four applicants on Super Saturday—is no different. At the end of the remarks, as the candidates file out to prepare for their first interviews, Busa receives lengthy, detailed feedback from, among others, CEO Kim. "I could feel your angst," Kim tells him. "You were too focused on yourself. Focus more on them." Another listener reminds Busa of material he omitted.

Busa remains calm, nodding, agreeing, and finally thanking them for their help—a common response to receiving tough feedback at Next Jump. Busa sees these opportunities to practice and receive feedback as opportunities to learn. "It's basically an 'investment in loss,'" he says in an interview. The phrase is a touchstone at Next Jump, borrowed from performance coach Josh Waitzkin. When we take risks and experience "loss" or failure, says Waitzkin, we create the conditions for learning and enhance our flexibility. Winning, in this sense, is less valuable than what we learn by losing in the pursuit of excellence.[2]

But Busa didn't always feel this way. When he first started working at Next Jump, he thought that all the talk of self-improvement and helping each other by giving feedback was only talk. The turning point came when he began to see that feedback was a way people were showing him they cared for him. Then, he says, he began "accepting that I can do more and that I have weaknesses. The day I accepted that—that was a turning point for me at Next Jump."

The Hiring Process at Next Jump: Super Saturday

Next Jump began recruiting engineers at colleges in 2006, alongside technology heavyweights such as Google, Facebook, and Microsoft, companies with far greater resources to invest in college recruiting. "We recruited for similar characteristics that others do—for who was the smartest, the most driven," explains Kim. "We looked for the most competitive and driven people. We ended up hiring what we later called 'brilliant jerks.'"

The workforce the company built had too many solo players, people with raw smarts and plenty of arrogance. Next Jump leaders faced a choice. Would they continue to hire the brilliant jerks, whom they would probably lose to poaching anyway? Or would they make a bigger bet on a different kind of workplace culture—and on selecting a different kind of employee? "One day in 2008," Kim recalls, "we fired literally half of our engineering staff."

The company's founders had made a brazen choice. Super Saturday was born soon thereafter.

Throughout the day on Super Saturday, seventy-five Next Jumpers walk around with a custom app on their mobile devices for gathering impressions and ratings about the applicants. Team members try to be as inconspicuous as possible as they record green lights and red flags, thumbs-up and thumbs-down ratings. Even in informal settings, the Next Jumpers gather data about how well applicants listen or whether they seem blatantly rude or self-absorbed. The evaluators continuously send comments as well as quick candidate ratings.

As the day goes on, a composite picture of each candidate comes into focus. In the Super Saturday War Room set aside for synthesizing the incoming data, the recruiting team gets a clear sense of how the applicants stack up on the qualities that matter most.

- Everyone at Super Saturday looks technically strong based on the earlier rounds of recruitment screening. But do they have the hard skills in real-life settings?

- Are they humble? Are they willing to learn from others in order to grow?

- Do they have grit—the persistence to see themselves through challenging times and setbacks rather than give up?

- Are they takers? Are they in it only for themselves, or do they have the ability to be givers (helping others grow)?

Next Jump leaders say they're looking to understand each applicant's character. As with all companies, the leaders are certainly looking for the right fit between the applicant and the company's culture and purpose. But like other DDOs, Next Jump is also looking for something more: the kind of person who will grow in an environment of constant practice, failing, and feedback.

When officials have made their selection, based on analyzing and debating the results collected on Super Saturday, the recruiting team will offer jobs only to those candidates who gained unanimous thumbs-up ratings, perhaps one-tenth to one-third of the candidates. As the new Next Jumpers come on board, they will be given their interview profile data from Super Saturday. On their first day of work, they're provided with concrete feedback about areas in which they can begin improving right away.

Congratulations! Welcome to Boot Camp

The onboarding process gives new employees an intense introduction to Next Jump's culture. Because the culture differs markedly from that of other organizations, Next Jump has found that helping people adapt as soon as they enter is the easiest time to accelerate their growth.

For their first three weeks, all new employees—including those who come with years of experience and success and are moving into senior leadership positions—attend Personal Leadership Boot Camp (PLBC for short). The program starts with participants learning to identify their character weaknesses—what Next Jump calls their "backhands." The metaphor comes from tennis: everyone has strengths (our forehand), but to be a great tennis player, you must also work on your backhand, the areas where you feel less comfortable, less natural, less skillful.

After trying to identify people's backhands by using long lists of psychological and character traits, the company found that most people's deeper limitations circled back to struggling with being overly confident (for shorthand, the company refers to this, without deprecation, as "arrogant") or being overly humble ("insecure"). At Next Jump, overcoming an "imbalance of character" in either direction is something everyone is assumed to be working on, from the cofounders to the newest engineer.

Everyone knows everyone else's backhand, or, if they don't, it is commonplace to inquire. Working on your backhand might mean, for someone who is on the arrogant side, trying to wait until the forty-five-minute mark to make a first comment in an hour long meeting. In contrast, someone on the insecure side, in that same meeting, might work on offering a contribution in the first fifteen minutes. Either move represents working on one's backhand—practicing to overcome a deep-seated mind-set.

In the boot camp, participants spend the three weeks in customer service—the bread-and-butter work of maintaining relationships with individual customers. Inquiries managed by the customer service team can include everything from security and log-in issues to ordering to almost any question a customer might have for an e-commerce company.

New Next Jumpers are given daily targets for customer engagement. They are expected to take risks, to reflect on what they're learning, and to practice their backhands. They're also expected to engage in a "plus-1 project": they identify a way to contribute to improving the customer service process. This personal project becomes a key practice ground that lets new workers exercise leadership in a team setting. Boot campers receive regular feedback from others (peers and managers) to help them identify weaknesses and build their leadership effectiveness.

At the end of the three-week boot camp, each employee shares her learning and experience in front of colleagues and a senior leadership committee, describing the powerful, if often painful, learning of the past weeks. The committee, based on the feedback from peers, coaches, and leaders, decides whether the employee will graduate from boot camp. If you're voted a graduate, you receive a custom Next Jump team jacket embroidered with your name. Then your journey in the company takes its next steps.

If you don't graduate, it's likely because the evidence from your stint in boot camp suggests you haven't been engaging fully and authentically. Most often, those who don't graduate are judged to be faking it or not demonstrating that they're striving to learn about themselves. They fail to have a "face the truth" moment, as Greg Kunkel explains. If the consensus is that you have only been going through the motions, you can accept an offer of $5,000 to leave the company, or you can return to boot camp until you graduate.

After facing their inadequacies and experimenting with new ways of working, Next Jumpers return to their primary job with a practice plan for working on their backhands. Everyone leaving boot camp develops such a plan, highlighting targeted situations to actively practice. They're given peer mentors, who coach them, hold them accountable, and help them stick to the practice plan. And if they fail, after all this support, to keep working on their backhand? If they choose to continue, they can look forward to a new round of boot camp.

Better Me + Better You = Better Us

Next Jump sums up the belief system behind its culture with an equation:

Better Me + Better You = Better Us

Better Me signals the importance of constant improvement. You've seen it in action in the boot camp experience. Next Jump expects its employees to face their limitations directly and practice to overcome them. When you visit the company's headquarters, it's clear that the consistent work on self-improvement extends to supporting healthy lifestyles, in addition to transcending the mind-set you bring to the office. With nutritious free snacks and meals, as well as an on-premises gym and trainers, employees are expected to make a habit of good health.

Better You is about the meaning people derive from work through helping others, inside and outside the company. Next Jump's leaders are struck by the research suggesting human beings are wired to serve others. When jobs are not meaningful, employees are more likely to volunteer outside work to derive that sense of purpose. The Next Jump response? Build service to others, and the resulting meaningfulness people derive from it, into the job. "Bake it into the culture," says Kim.

As part of their work, Next Jumpers lead and participate in dozens of giving-back initiatives. For example, they can donate their expertise through a range of programs. Engineers can code for a cause, offering up to two weeks a year to help nonprofits in need. But cultural initiatives that lead to a Better You also serve the company's own employees. They give everyone at Next Jump opportunities to practice leadership in settings that give employees more room to fail and learn with less risk to profitability.

Better Us is the payoff for a company, the community, and ultimately the world, built around both Better Me and Better You; it's the outcome for everyone in the company of being more fulfilled and better off in a deeper sense. At Next Jump, the organizing belief behind these programs is that when we feel our own growth and when we engage in activities that also help others (including helping our colleagues grow), we can experience true wealth in the form of long-term, sustained happiness. This form of wealth cannot be obtained from a paycheck.

To be sure, Next Jump pays its employees well, but the outcome of sustained happiness, executives insist, can come only from a culture that makes work meaningful. To that end, in the salary review process, contributions to revenue are weighed at 50 percent and contributions to culture at 50 percent.

Next Jump leaders also note that you don't have to be a charitable or nonprofit organization to give people opportunities for meaningful work. The company's culture initiatives create opportunities as well as recognition for helping others. Programs range from a team that serves breakfast to Next Jump colleagues, to creating internal engineer skill-development newsletters, to hosting a Vendor Appreciation Day. In addition to giving meaning to work, cultural initiatives provide a place for workers to practice self-improvement and program leadership and even to fail big in circumstances where failure is less risky than it would be on the revenue-generating side of the corporate perks business.

FLO: Growing Leaders

To accelerate people's growth, Next Jump has a system of clearly defined roles in the leadership teams that implement cultural initiatives. They call this model the *follower-leader organization* (FLO).

FLO involves four key roles: captain, coach, right hand, and left hand. Heading up a culture initiative is the role of the *captain*. At the heart of FLO's design is the role of the *coach*, which is filled by the person who most recently captained the same initiative. Her job, above all else, is to coach the captain in leadership and provide feedback that will help the captain develop his backhand.

The *right hand* is the team member who works closely with the captain, knowing that she will someday soon take over as the next captain as the roles rotate. Finally, the *left hand* is another team member who can contribute to the success of the initiative and is next in line to succeed the right hand.

Meghan Messenger, a Next Jump cofounder, identifies what is unique about the FLO model: the coach role. "You're sacrificing your number one player and moving them from the *doing* to *coaching*," Messenger explains. After all, the new coach has only just learned how to lead the initiative. Wouldn't things go better if you let captains keep running a program, to get the benefit of all their experience just when they're getting good at the role?

This seeming sacrifice of expertise makes sense when you recognize that the main purpose of FLO is not to help people learn the ins and outs of leading a specific initiative or program. Instead, each project is a practice ground for working on your blind spots as a leader. Initiatives come and go, in a constant process of experimenting with new ways to strengthen the culture. For example, rather than develop captains to handle Super Saturdays—people who would then get better and better at leading Super Saturdays—FLO is about developing everyone's capabilities of captaining and coaching generally.

"The work goes more slowly at first" when there's a new captain of an initiative, Messenger acknowledges. But the trade-off is another "investment in loss." Coaches, before rotating off an initiative entirely, develop another captain into a coach and must leave the program itself better off than when they started. Messenger has seen FLO produce consistent results over time, noting, "In the long run, we have a stronger organization with deeper bench strength."

Jackie's Journey

Jackie knows the backhand she is working on at Next Jump. But that wasn't always the case.

A ten-year veteran of the company, Jackie had risen to be leader of the marketing group. Competitive and focused, she excelled in situations when she could contribute individually, such as landing a big sale. She was especially successful working with merchant partners for the company's corporate perks program and had built a solid track record of accomplishment in sales.

But several months before we first met her, Jackie had been shocked to learn that she had been voted off MV21, the company's leadership group. The group's members are not selected by executives but rather are elected by peers, and people are voted off when they either fail to get enough votes or are nominated for removal by their peers. Sitting at the MV21 table is an honor that reflects the perception across the company that a Next Jumper can be counted on to help others succeed. The company's senior leaders talk about valuing "linebackers over quarterbacks"—rewarding those who help others win rather than the star players identified as formal leaders. Jackie may have been a star negotiator of deals, but increasingly she was seen as someone who didn't do enough to support others.

Hearing that she was voted off MV21 was "a crushing blow," Jackie says. But feedback from others about her patterns of work had been accumulating. She was seen by her peers as working entirely for herself. She wasn't someone you could count on to reach out and offer help. She would answer questions or respond, but she didn't make time to give to others.

At first, Jackie tried to make sense of her rejection by her peers in ways that kept the focus off herself. She initially resisted introspection, deflecting the impact of the vote by thinking, "Oh, those newbies on MV21? They'll fail. I'll probably be back in three, six, ten months, tops." But soon she saw that the new MV21 group was thriving without her.

It took a lot of reflection, coaching by company executives and peers, and the practice ground provided by working on several culture initiatives for Jackie to see the limitations of her own deep-seated mind-set. Jackie had heard others tell her what her backhand was—not helping others—but they "were others' words, not mine." One source of support was her boss, David. The two of them opened up to each other about their weaknesses, giving Jackie another context at Next Jump to question her patterns of behavior. Jackie began to describe her backhand in her own words rather than others' terms.

> What is the thing that is more meaningful, that is actually painful to say, that is embarrassing to say? I think that's when you really get to your true backhand. And for me, it was that I put my own success before anyone else's. I tend not to want to help others. I want to see myself move forward, and I am not so generous always with sharing things that may help other people.

At an event called 10X—an all-staff meeting for presenting and getting live feedback on one's contributions to the company (which you will learn more about in chapter 4)—Jackie shared with all of Next Jump her realization about what she was focusing on in her work of self-improvement.

> I realized I needed to face the truth. I am selfish, and I put my success above everyone else's. In fact, I spent the last ten years trying to get to the top. When I looked at the reality, I saw I left hundreds of Next Jumpers behind in my quest to get to the top.
>
> Now that I'm becoming more self-aware, I'm doing deliberate practice—practice to become a steward leader.
>
> There is a driving force for me. There is a fear instilled in me. It's about my two children [her voice breaks here, and

she takes a moment to compose herself]. My biggest fear in life is that they are going to develop the same backhand that I have—that they are going to help themselves before they help other people.

I need to help develop others because I know it is integral to my own growth. The old Jackie would have just said, "Get back on MV21 as soon as possible."

After making this presentation to the company, Jackie started putting herself into more situations where she could practice helping others be successful. She started small at first, coaching others once a month. "Even that was painful for me at first," she admits. Pretty soon, she was doing it weekly for offices and people outside her immediate group, such as the London office—peers she wouldn't have made time for before.

After a while, as Jackie increased her coaching to all-day sessions on Mondays, her peers started to see her taking risks and extending herself regularly for her colleagues and for the good of the company. Jackie says, "People saw where I was spending my time. And still getting my job done, which I didn't think was possible. I really thought that if I spent too much time with other people, I wouldn't be successful." Less than a year later, members of MV21 voted her back onto the group, something she had thought could never happen. She is confident she knows why: it is because she is starting to demonstrate a qualitatively different kind of success. Not only is she spending time developing others, but also she and other Next Jumpers can see the benefits to people across the company that are flowing from her new way of working.

Jackie's story is one of many similar ones at Next Jump. Running through each is a common thread. People are working on themselves at work as part of improving the company. Jackie sums up the reasons she is growing because of the company and believes that others are as well.

Some days are better than others, but I think that's what is so great. And this may sound cliché, too, but Next Jump really does give you this platform to constantly practice. And if I have bad days, then the next day can be a good day. I don't really have to have that fear of failure.

Decurion: Creating Places for People to Flourish

Feast on your imperfections, or starve on your ego.

—Bryan Ungard, Decurion

It's early in the morning on the top floor of the ArcLight Hollywood cinema multiplex. Colleagues are milling around the main conference room, laughing, talking about the 101 Freeway traffic, and pouring coffee and grabbing a muffin before the meeting gets under way. Nora Dashwood, chief operating officer, is bringing together key leaders from the home office with the general managers of each of the locations. The occasion is a regular meeting known as the theater work group.

If you watch television coverage of the entertainment industry, you may have seen ArcLight Hollywood as the backdrop for a star-studded event. The flagship location—which anchors a shopping complex near the corner of Sunset Boulevard and Vine Street in the heart of historic Hollywood—is owned by the real estate arm of its parent company, The Decurion Corporation. The multiplex, with its soaring glass lobby, is fronted by an entrance plaza large enough to accommodate red carpets for a film premiere or welcome lines of sneak-peek fans for major preview screenings. Hollywood is an industry town, and ArcLight is known as Hollywood's favorite place to enjoy a movie.

Joining the Community: The Theater Work Group

There is no meeting table this morning for the twenty or so theater work group attendees. Instead, the chairs are arranged to form a large circle so that everyone can see all the faces. As you will see, creating the conditions for people to feel joined together in a community as they work is the foundation of every meeting at Decurion.

Around the room, posters remind employees of the beliefs and values of the company. Decurion calls these its "axioms"—statements of the company's "fundamental beliefs about people and work."

1. We believe that *work is meaningful*, that work gives meaning to people's lives. For us, meaning comes from three things: developing oneself, creating something excellent and enduring, and contributing to other people.

2. We believe that *people are not only means but also ends in themselves*. Most businesses view people (employees, customers, suppliers, and others) as a means to some end, such as completing a transaction or meeting a goal. We feel that reducing people to a role in a process dehumanizes them. While honoring the roles they play, we approach people as fellow human beings, as ends in themselves.

3. We believe that *individuals and communities naturally develop*. Much of the literature on development ends with the teenage years. But we know that adults continue to develop. Our structures and practices create conditions that pull people into greater levels of complexity and wholeness.

4. And while we did not begin with this belief, our experience has shown us that *pursuing profitability and human growth emerges as one thing*. They are part of a single whole, not two things to be traded off or two elements of a "double bottom line." We capture this axiom by saying that nothing extra is required.

These axioms offer a common language and touchstone for the company's bedrock principles. No member of the company (and *member* is the preferred term for an employee here) is required to believe that these axioms are true. But each member, and especially each manager, is expected to act in accordance with the axioms as part of his job responsibilities.

In the discussion this morning, these beliefs will be put into service. Dashwood knows that the theater work group must join in a challenging conversation. As people take their seats, the room grows quiet. Around the circle, people look comfortable. No one is peeking at mobile devices or laptops. Some are visibly relaxed, settling into a moment of silent reflection, and making a transition from the bubbly chat over coffee a moment before.

Dashwood brings everyone together by inviting them to *check in*. At Decurion, most meetings begin with a practice of checking in that can take up to an hour with a group this large.

What goes on during a check-in? First, when people choose to speak (all speaking is voluntary), they often begin by saying their name ("Hi, I am Carlos"), even though it would be rare for anyone not to know the name of another team member. They do it to remind themselves, and their teammates, that they seek to stand fully in whatever they're about to say, that it comes from their person and not their role.

They then say whatever they need to, to bring themselves fully, as whole people, into the work space. They may share an internal state, such as feeling excited or nervous, or they may report where they are on an interior goal—for example, how they see this meeting as a chance to engage their efforts to listen better to others' competing ideas. Or they might let the group in on something that is happening at home that is inevitably part of how they are "showing up at work" that day—that the celebration of a daughter's first Communion is coming up or that visiting family members are wearing out their welcome. COO Bryan Ungard explains the practice: "It's about what the individual needs to do to be fully present—it can't be scripted. As soon as you script it, you drive the meaning out. Our full humanity is required, and to have that, you need authentic engagement."

Check-ins are part of honoring Decurion's axioms. If people are to be treated as more than a means to an end and are worthy of unconditional regard as developing adults, then check-ins present constantly threaded opportunities to bring that humanity—and each member's interior life—to the foreground. The culture as a whole places inner experience in bounds rather than out-of-bounds in the life of the workplace. Decurion exposes and overturns the assumption that work is public and the personal is private, and so the personal should not be part of work. In the same way, Decurion rejects the idea of work-life balance as a simple goal or mantra. After all, if your life is everything *outside* the workplace, then that leaves a bleak notion of what work is—something that we're forced to trade off against joyful living.

Everyone who has ever worked anywhere knows that work is intensely personal, with daily opportunities to experience pain, exhilaration, self-doubt, and meaning. We all bring our whole selves to work every day: "Wherever you go, there you are." In a DDO such as Decurion, practices like check-ins openly welcome the whole person into work every day.

And at the end of any meeting, there is a check-out as well. Checking out is routinely briefer but an important ritual. As they check out—again speaking as they are moved to speak—members share personal reflections or feelings that allow them to end well. Whether it's an expression of excitement about the work ahead, a sense of having broken through on something challenging, or even a need for greater support from others, check-out brings closure through another moment of focusing on people's individual presence and humanity. By building checking in and checking out into every meeting, Decurion members ensure that focusing on individual mind-sets and growth becomes a habit. More than that, the habit is part of creating and maintaining a sense of strong community.

In the meeting that day in Hollywood, as people connect to one another and the conversation moves forward, Dashwood continues to create the conditions for authentic and productive dialogue. Decurion members call this "setting the field," borrowing a term from Joseph Jaworksi, Kaz Gozdz, and Peter Senge that has deeply influenced the company.[3] This practice, which is also a part of most meetings, involves taking the time to help people see how the present business challenge is connected with their individual sense of meaning about the work and with the collective power of the group to do the work as a community.

Dashwood speaks with authority but in a spirit of invitation. Her engagement appears total, and she calls people to lean in together for the work ahead.

> This morning we are going to be practicing with one another. We've got a real-life work situation, and we need to work through it as a community. And I think we can use this to

keep developing the level of competency we need as a business to meet our top-line goals for the coming year.

This really ties to what we were talking about at the most recent DBL [Decurion business leadership, a companywide meeting]. These are the requirements that we have as a company—that the business is flourishing, that we are getting superior results, that we are doing the adaptive things we need to do, that our guests in the theaters are having their lives changed for the better through the quality of the experience they have. We are developing an offering with a distinctive impact in the market—and if it disappeared, you just couldn't get it anywhere else.

As we do this, we are working to be more autonomous, experiencing our own well-being, advancing personally and professionally, and moving toward what we each want out of our own lives. So, we've got an important business initiative, our customer loyalty program. It's key to unlocking three million dollars in additional revenue we need moving into the next year. But we don't seem to be having a singular conversation at the leadership level and as a community about how that work is going.

Dashwood's work of setting the field for this conversation is designed to create a space for several things to emerge. There is no doubt on the part of the theater work group members that their COO is calling them together to work as a community. But how does that experience at Decurion differ from merely having a clear agenda, or reaffirming the goals of a meeting?

In this case, members of IT and marketing, as well as theater-operations leaders in the division, are working to retire the existing membership loyalty program and develop a new offering, including revitalizing all aspects of the customer loyalty experience. But communication in the organization has ruptured, and it needs to be addressed collectively. Status updates from all sides, a dressing-down, a directed solution—these wouldn't help meet the developmental goals that Dashwood has just invited everyone in the room to hold on to together.

In the Fishbowl

Instead, Dashwood is doing something that's common at Decurion. Rather than jump to solve the problem, the group members will try to let the problem solve them, exposing issues and patterns of thinking that go much deeper than the immediate circumstances. Dashwood invites Bob, a senior leader on the operations side, to facilitate a "fishbowl" conversation, and she asks several individuals (whom she has asked in advance to participate) to step forward. These four people—those most directly implicated in the pattern of conflict and misunderstanding in the work-group circle—pull their chairs into a small, tight circle-within-a-circle at the center of the room. This small group includes the head of the loyalty program from the marketing side, the technology lead, one of the general managers from theater operations, and Bob.

Their colleagues remain seated in the outer circle, bearing witness and participating by their active listening and presence and, if required, joining in the inner-circle dialogue spontaneously. Whether sitting inside or outside the fishbowl, everyone is expected to get better at spotting and fully stepping into opportunities for overcoming limiting behaviors and the underlying mind-sets that generate them.

Bob begins the fishbowl by reminding everyone of the shared norms for these conversations. They are a learning community, and he spotlights several ground rules to create healthy dialogue, including speaking from your own experience and not leaping to inferences about what others believe. He frames this dialogue as a discussion of whether people are aligned: "I'm concerned. I can't tell whether this initiative is on track or not. There are conflicting reports, depending on who I talk to."

Bob focuses everyone on uncovering data—not quantitative metrics, but the kind of evidence from multiple perspectives that will help the group sort out what is going on and why: "How can we know whether we are on track through looking at the data? A place we can start is to ask what we think is working well and what's not working well, both in and outside of the circle. Let's start by surfacing what's true for each of us."

As the conversation develops, Bob leans in close, and the four people in the fishbowl seem to be trying to focus on each other's eyes. Those in the outer circle seem to feel the intensity and vulnerability of those in the fishbowl. This is not a shark tank but rather a respectful and brave space. For everyone in the room, there is nowhere else in the world right now but here.

The fishbowl brings to the surface a range of complicated feelings and candid insights. The marketing manager shares her view that the design and development process of the loyalty program has left her feeling isolated. "For months," she says, "I felt like I was being tested, pointed at, like I was sent off to a desert island, and I didn't feel like I had any support of a community in this. When I tried to raise issues, I felt like I didn't make a lot of headway." But she also acknowledges her own part in the dynamic—that she herself didn't do an effective job of communicating clearly what was going on for her. "I should have stood my ground," she says.

The theater general manager admits that his interactions with the technology lead feel "off." He says that their phone conversations are rushed, and they're not getting to the point where he is able to provide his ground-level, operational input to enhance the theater guest's journey through the loyalty program. He, too, acknowledges his own role and needs in the situation. Working directly with major vendors, he says, is new for him. He feels he needs to ask questions, and he needs his questions to be heard. He also needs to feel joined in a common effort, and he realizes how frustrated he becomes when he is not experiencing that kind of alignment.

The technology lead, for his part, shares his sense of pressing urgency to get the technical work done. He's trying to navigate the tension between meeting his responsibilities and keeping the theater manager closely involved. In talking about the quality of their phone conversations, the technology lead has his own take. "I'm stuck. Do we push 'reset' on the project to bring you in, or do we help you come up alongside us where we already are?" He concedes that he has more to do to build trust. He wants to better understand whether he's not structuring their check-in calls appropriately or if he's not listening to others well, despite having the right work structure and routines.

Dashwood has been a silent listener as the dialogue unfolds, taking her place among the other work group members in the outer circle. Now she stands and pulls her chair into the heart of the circle. "I felt the need to join," she says. "I've been trying not to be a bull in a china shop here," she adds, laughing as she acknowledges how hard it was to listen to the fishbowl without intervening. As you become better acquainted with Dashwood's inner work in chapter 6, one piece of her personal "curriculum" as a leader is knowing when to exert authority and when to release control and responsibility to others.

Now she is coming to a conclusion. "I'm hearing that we have not structured ourselves effectively to make the best loyalty program. Was anyone pulling the alarm bell here and saying, 'We've got a problem?'" She continues, before the conversation closes, to ensure that everyone agrees that additional customer testing of the online experience needs to happen immediately.

As the fishbowl discussion comes to an end, a marketing manager calls on her colleagues to look more deeply at what has been going on in this fishbowl: "We sometimes think we should keep our heads down and think we are working with intention, but that can be disruptive for the business. This discussion felt like it was doing the right thing for the business. The loyalty program is a huge developmental opportunity for me and for the whole group. But there is something for us to take away about involving the right parties in the right way *from the start.*"

Another theater manager closes the conversation with a similar reflection: "I felt leadership here. We were dealing with a difficult issue, but we need to do that in order to take the next step that the business needs."

Decurion's Approach to Business

Decurion has come to operate in this way more fully only in the past decade, under the leadership of its current president, Christopher Forman. The company is a relative rarity in the business world: a family-owned business that has made a successful transition to a third generation of leadership and growth. Based in Los Angeles,

Decurion employs about eleven hundred members and is the parent company of a set of subsidiary businesses that span several industries: movie exhibition, real estate, and senior living.

The movie exhibition business provided the seed corn. Pacific Theatres, founded in 1946 and for decades the name of the company, was a major regional exhibitor on the West Coast and in Hawaii, even recognized with a technical Academy Award (an "Oscar") for its pioneering practices. The company was a leading owner-developer of drive-in movie theaters as well as cineplexes. As the business for drive-in movies declined and the company invested in growing its walk-in theaters, it held on to enviable real estate assets: large former drive-in parcels in the heart of California's metropolitan landscape, the Pacific Northwest, and Hawaii. These properties allowed Decurion's Robertson Properties Group to grow. In 2011, *Retail Traffic* magazine named it one of the one hundred largest shopping center owners in the United States.

ArcLight Cinemas, launched in 2002 as a new subsidiary, was founded to provide a structure for rethinking the quality and experience of going to the movies. The guest's experience from start to finish is central in every way—from the quality of personal engagement in guest service, to reserved seating for every show, to the concessions, bar, and restaurant offerings. ArcLight's success was not immediate, but Forman and his senior team (including Dashwood) stuck by the concept to see it take off. Revenues grew by 72 percent, to $81 million, from 2009 to 2013. Pacific and ArcLight combined now have the highest gross per screen in North America, and in 2012 *Forbes* magazine named the ArcLight Hollywood location one of the ten best movie theaters in the country.

Forman describes those early days of creating ArcLight as similar to the origins of Saturn Corporation, which was protected from the culture of General Motors. In ArcLight, Forman was attempting to create a place to practice a new way of doing business, distant from the gravitational drag of the Pacific Theatres group. The way of doing business in the family company in 1989, when he took an increased role in its leadership, lacked the compass it needed, Forman explains.

> I returned to the company from business school with shiny
> new tools, things like budgeting (which the company had never

done), strategic planning, and statistical analysis. With much enthusiasm, I deployed them, and then with equal disappointment, I saw them rejected. The people at the company just didn't see the point. And there were really two aspects to that. They didn't see that these tools would necessarily help us be more profitable. And they also pointed to a lack of context. *Why* should we do these things? What's the bigger picture that these fit into? The second question was really the more important one.

Over time, I came to formulate my purpose as providing contexts for people to flourish . . . And it is the animating purpose of Decurion. I love movies like *Brazil* and *The Hudsucker Proxy*, because they capture and warn us of the dehumanizing reality in too many businesses. Decurion is a place of wholeness, of connection, of excellence, and of meaning . . . but that didn't happen overnight. [In those days], the values were present at the company, but I wasn't happy with the ways we were expressing them. Caring about people showed up as paternalism. I saw a lot of loyalty to my family and to people, rather than loyalty to principles. And so, I thought, I'm not comfortable with that. It has to change.

COO Ungard echoes Forman in describing the change that took place. Caring for people would no longer be about loyalty between company and employees, about protecting people. Rather, Decurion's purpose—its reason for existence and its deepest "why?"—is to create places for people to flourish. But flourishing isn't about having fun or keeping people sheltered from threat, challenge, or risk to the self. Ungard explains.

People entering Decurion have an idea about what it's going to be like, but three or four months later everyone thinks, "It's not what I thought it would be."

When people hear "flourishing," they think of appreciation and good feelings. But growth and development does not always equal "feeling good." Our culture is not about maximizing the minutes you feel good at work. We don't define flourishing by sitting-around-the-campfire moments. We ask people to do seemingly impossible things.

We've learned, also, when we are onboarding people to our culture, we have to manage their expectations. We say, "It will be hard, but it will be rewarding. You won't get it right away. And you won't be given any time to sit on the sidelines and just observe. You will be part of our practice from the start, asked to jump in right away, even when you are thinking, 'But I don't know anything yet!'" No one is an observer. You must include yourself. Building community means inclusion—new entrants are welcomed, affirmed.

Working life at Decurion is organized around this idea of community. There still is a hierarchy; this is a profit-making, privately held business, and not a cooperative. There must be accountability in individual roles for decisions that affect the business.

That said, what's different at Decurion? Members of the company participate in communal governance structures such as the theater work group because they provide a setting for deep personal learning and improved business decisions for the company. These structures are not only a necessary support for individual growth but also a form of collective wisdom. The groups share responsibility for the success of the business, even if individual business leaders hold accountability. Communities have a say; they're expected to help seize opportunities and spot problems at their source.

The collective wisdom in a community, Decurion executives say, also grows and develops over time. People still report to one another, people are let go, and people are overruled on decisions, but the structure of a learning community like the theater work group pushes every member to "hold the whole of the business" and to be "businesspeople first," looking at the wider success of the company, rather than being trapped myopically in a particular role or function.

Ungard underscores the power of community at Decurion, and he cautions that outsiders may be tempted to reduce this idea to the familiar concepts of "team" or "committee." That would miss something.

When authentic community forms in groups, learning happens: a collective intelligence. A learning community is such a different animal than a "committee." It's greater than the sum of its parts and can handle far greater complexity than a group of brilliant individuals. Something magical and important happens in a learning community that we use as a foundational element everywhere in the company. Community has a method. There is a way of building it. It has particular phases it goes through, and there are ways of practicing it—principles, practices, guidelines of a learning community . . . We use community to be simultaneously communal and hierarchical.

This emphasis on learning communities enables another feature of Decurion's culture. Because people are joined together in common responsibility for running the business, it's possible for people to be more detached from titles and roles. When you attend meetings, you generally don't hear references to titles. It's not that roles and titles don't exist but that Decurion's strong ethos pulls against attachment to one's expert role, particularly in the context of learning communities.

A saying at Decurion is that you should always be "giving your job away." Rather than stand on the authority of expertise or title, everyone should try to share hard-earned wisdom. It's an alternative to the view that an individual's knowledge is power and that one should take advantage of information asymmetries to gain the advantage in a corporate jungle. That framing, however apt a description for many business contexts, is anathema to Decurion's leaders—even a description of organizational failure to live up to the beliefs that undergird the company. But it's not collective naïveté about power and status that motivates this view. Rather, the company wants to help every member break with the instinct to hoard information, to seek advantage by protecting one's base of authority and power, and to squander time managing others' favorable impressions. Jobs here are designed not to be "person-dependent."

Dashwood, for her part, sees the power for achieving business results in weaving together peer-to-peer communities with hierarchical leadership, as everyone sheds the safety of being the indispensable expert.

It gets at a lot of the energy and the waste that's spent in people not being fully engaged in the work, and feeling like they are healthy in what they're doing. It's about the effect on the business, the customer, and the working environment. But it has the effect of people making better decisions. It's a healthier environment. I've never experienced that in my career before Decurion. That's a whole different way of being. It is a work environment that requires managers, senior managers, directors, VPs, to work on building trust in each other, to work on not being tied to their roles, identities, fiefdoms, or to protecting themselves over the needs of the business or the effectiveness of others and the group.

Dashwood's Challenge

During the theater work group meeting that we joined, Dashwood was conscious of the individual growth she is seeking for herself as a leader. To her credit, she strives to develop her capabilities even after nearly four decades in the exhibition industry. It is a consistent mark of the DDOs we studied that the senior people are as deeply engaged in the personal growth journey as the newest hires. Working at Decurion has helped Dashwood explore the mind-set driving her day-to-day actions, and, in settings where there is a learning community to help her, she frequently practices new ways of being and seeing. In some ways, the very things she is working on with the greatest clarity are the shadow side of the confidence that led her to Decurion.

Hired in 2000 to lead Pacific Theatres and shortly thereafter asked to launch ArcLight Cinemas, Dashwood came to Decurion from a major national theater chain where she had worked for twenty-three years, rising from her first high school job behind a concession stand to become a senior operations executive. She was brought to Christopher Forman's attention by someone who referred to Dashwood as the best theater operations executive in the country, and that's the kind of person Forman wanted to oversee the company's theater business.

Within a couple of years of joining Decurion, when ArcLight was the proving ground for creating a new kind of culture in the company, Dashwood was getting feedback about her limitations.

I started bumping up against some walls. I started hearing feedback from Chris, and from others around me, that the way I was leading was actually holding people back. And at forty-two years old, and it is humbling for me to say this, I had never gotten feedback that anything I was doing in business wasn't just beyond reproach. So, I've got to tell you, I was kicking and screaming, and I would have fired myself five times in terms of how I resisted the feedback and the coaching. I mean, I listened to it all, but I literally couldn't *see* it. I didn't know what to do with it.

She recalls one exchange, in a community setting much like the theater work group, that marked a turning point for her in a moment of insight.

I was in a meeting, and a theater assistant manager in his early twenties said to me that he felt that when things weren't going the way I wanted them to go, he could feel the air in the room turn cold.

She chokes up a little and then continues.

He never would have been able to say that if it hadn't been for Decurion not only allowing but requiring its members to give feedback to each other regardless of position or tenure so that we can form effective business communities. I call that assistant manager my "canary in a coal mine." This manager's observation shifted my ability to see and understand that there was another way, that aspects of how I led were creating bar-riers for others. That what he felt as the room going cold was me withdrawing my goodwill and closing my heart to others because things were not going the way I thought they should.

I didn't know if I could do it, but I now knew that to be more effective as a leader and more of who I wanted to be as a person, I needed to *be* with the people as they engaged in their work. That for people to be able to flourish, they would need to do it in their own way, and not the way I thought was the way. The business requirement and practices of Decurion allowed me to become aware of my deeply held assumptions and beliefs about what it means to be a leader, to be a mentor, to be with a community, and to count on other people.

Growing up with very loving, strong-willed, independent, immigrant parents, I absorbed a consistent, powerful message. The message was that you need to take care of yourself because no one else will. That if you want all that life has to offer you, you need to count on yourself and take charge. That if you are not leading, you might as well be failing. I became very good at taking charge and counting on my abilities to get what I wanted. But you can only go so far with that mind-set.

Now, I can see more and I am a better listener. I am more aware. I have a community that supports and challenges me. What I have learned at Decurion is that I can be a part of something that produces results much bigger than I can produce on my own. It was the hardest thing I've ever done and it has been the most meaningful growth and development I've ever experienced.

As she creates the fishbowl space for the theater work group community, Dashwood continues her own work on leading others without "withdrawing her goodwill" when they don't see the world her way. In other words, the question she struggles with is, "How can I keep holding high standards for excellence in the business while at the same time allowing others to step forward with their own ideas and solutions, even if they are at odds with my instincts and preferred pathway for getting the work done ('the way Nora would do it')?"

Dashwood has been testing her assumptions—that others won't get it right unless they do it her way and that she can rely only on herself—in other situations, too. One opportunity arose from her growing frustration with the design of a company website. Her first instinct was to gather everyone together and get into the thick of designing a better site, and then get everyone working fast on implementing it. But she resisted that impulse. Instead, she took the problem as an opportunity to delegate and empower a group to produce the new design.

She had a conversation with her colleagues, discussing her expectations and standards but without doing the work for them. Empowering the team, she realized, didn't mean that she wouldn't give feedback on the evolving work. In fact, when the first site design was "just OK," Dashwood again resisted jumping in, instead working to help guide the group on how they could discover a better solution. They came back with a much better result, something she admits surprised her, given her habitual pattern of thinking she couldn't trust others to get to a good solution on their own.

What did Dashwood discover about herself? She learned she could let others take up the work with accountability, rather than feeling that the only viable option, when something important is facing the business, was to take charge of doing it herself.

The fishbowl, then, is another "practice field," in Decurion's term, for everyone involved, including Dashwood. It's both a way to move the business ahead—removing roadblocks to collaboration—and a way to work on helping people grow. For her own growth, Dashwood is using the fishbowl to explore navigating the balance between, on the one hand, having a clear vision as a leader and being accountable for the business and, on the other hand, allowing the members of the theater work group to step into individual and collective responsibility for an excellent loyalty product. She is creating a context for them to grow by tackling the live problems of the business, as individuals and as a learning community. They, in turn, are providing her with a setting to keep pushing beyond her own limits as a leader.

This is what the company means by taking a "nothing extra" approach (a term introduced by Kaz Gozdz, a trusted adviser whom Forman sees as the architect of its transformation). People work on overcoming their limitations as an integrated part of working through active business dilemmas—the work sitting right in front of them—and as part of the pursuit of business excellence. This is the rhythm of daily life at Decurion. And this is what trying to create places for people to flourish looks like.

Bridgewater: Getting to Root Causes

*Do you worry more about how good you are—
or about how fast you are learning?*

—Ray Dalio, Bridgewater

If you sit in a meeting room at the Bridgewater headquarters in Westport, Connecticut, it's apparent that you're in an environment designed for transparency. Floor-to-ceiling windows let in sunlight and offer treetop views of the Saugatuck River, which flows through the middle of the campus. Meeting rooms have the same open windows onto the hallway. Anyone can see who's meeting, and there's no such thing as a private meeting. People at Bridgewater—the world's best-performing hedge fund—use sunlight as a metaphor for the kind of culture they value, one that prizes transparency as the best disinfectant.

As you meet some of the people at Bridgewater, you learn how an unrelenting search for truth—including the often painful truths about one's own limitations—is at the heart of every meeting, indeed every exchange of ideas. The company's leaders will tell you this search for radical truth and radical transparency is not merely an important aspect of the culture but the heart of the culture and the reason for the company's unparalleled success.

Sergio and the Failed Meeting

It's 9:00 a.m. on a bright Friday morning in winter. The Bridgewater training team is holding its daily meeting. This group of about a dozen people, which reports to founder Ray Dalio, creates case-study materials for everyone in the company, part of the stream of daily learning experiences people participate in here to strengthen the culture and reinforce its values. The interactive video cases and self-assessment tools the group is creating help employees, from the newest recruit to the most senior management committee members, interpret the core principles of the company and apply them to real-life situations. Most of the people on the curriculum team of sorts are in their early twenties and were recruited directly from Ivy League universities into their first postcollegiate jobs. They're using their Friday meeting, as they do each week, to diagnose a problem encountered within the team and for which it is worth understanding why the problem occurred. This task is called a diagnosis.

A diagnosis is part of a five-step process that is essential to the continuing personal evolution that Dalio sees as necessary for individuals to get what they want out of life. These steps are distinct and not to be blurred together—diagnosis of a problem is not the same as designing a solution—and they begin with setting goals based on your values:

1. *Setting goals.* You can have virtually anything you want, but you can't have everything you want . . . To achieve your goals, you have to prioritize, and that includes rejecting good alternatives.

2. *Identifying and not tolerating problems.* Most problems are potential improvements screaming at you . . . The more painful the problem, the louder it is screaming. In order to be successful, you have to (1) perceive problems and (2) not tolerate them . . . So push through the pain of facing your problems, knowing you will end up in a much better place.

3. *Diagnosing the problems.* You must be calm and logical . . . You must get at the root causes . . . the deep-seated reasons behind the actions that cause problems . . . Recognizing and learning from one's mistakes and the mistakes of others who affect outcomes is critical to eliminating problems . . . More than anything else, what differentiates people who live up to their potential from those who don't is a willingness to look at themselves and others objectively . . . The most important qualities for successfully diagnosing problems are logic, the ability to see multiple possibilities, and the willingness to touch people's nerves to overcome the ego barriers that stand in the way of truth.

4. *Designing the plan (determining the solutions).* Creating a design is like writing a movie script in that you visualize who will do what through time in order to achieve the goal . . . When designing solutions, the objective is to change how you do things so that problems don't recur—or recur so often. Think about each problem individually, and as the product of root causes—like the outcomes produced by a machine. Then think about how the machine should be changed to produce good outcomes rather than bad ones . . . Designing precedes doing!

5. *Doing the tasks.* Great planners who don't carry out their plans go nowhere. You need to "push through" to accomplish the goals . . . People who are good at this stage can reliably execute a plan . . . If they see that daily tasks are taking them away from executing the plan (i.e., they identify this problem), they diagnose it and design how they can deal with both the daily tasks and moving forward with the plan.

In the five-step process, diagnosing problems is the key to learning about the sources of your limitations. It's not enough at Bridgewater to recognize that you or someone else made a mistake, although that's a start (and it means you're at least showing some sign of "not tolerating badness," as Dalio puts it). Instead of identifying the mistake and jumping to solutions—solving the problem—you are pushed first to systematically unearth the limitations in your and others' thinking that lie behind the mistake. What can you learn about "the deeper whys," as people at Bridgewater say—focusing relentlessly on the root causes of behavior rather than the behavior itself?

The team's diagnosis of a problem this morning centers on Sergio. The entire group has just spent time discussing Sergio's most recent review. On any given day, all employees are getting and giving feedback from multiple sources about how they're doing their jobs. Nothing in a formal review comes as a surprise. But it's also expected that individual reviews will be discussed with the entire team and with total candor. Niko Canner, a former member of the company's management committee, is leading the meeting.

More than a year earlier, Sergio told Dalio that he was interested in leaving Bridgewater to go to medical school. Dalio shared his gratitude for Sergio's transparency but made sure to tell him that he could have a great career at Bridgewater, if that's what he chose to do. Sergio was candid. He couldn't help thinking, he said, that he would be disappointed in himself if he woke up at age forty-five and was managing people who were managing money.

In this morning's meeting, Sergio is sharing a related struggle. He admits that he "feels an acute need, almost at random, to please others. That could take me in a direction I don't want to go." He tells his teammates that he feels stuck, torn between a desire to please Dalio by staying at Bridgewater and the pull of going to medical school and taking on a new career.

Sergio opens up about his sense of being a people pleaser. "The thing I worry about," he says, "is pleasing whoever is in front of me."

As the diagnosis begins, the reasons for Sergio's recent actions in another meeting are the topic of discussion. Earlier in the week, Sergio was responsible for leading a meeting, and, in preparation, he delegated the task of creating the meeting slide deck to Virginia, a fellow team member. Sergio's teammates who attended the earlier meeting, which was organized around the slide deck, were not impressed. The meeting was "derailed" because the slide deck contained inadequate materials to help Sergio run the meeting successfully or to cope well in the moment.

Canner, the facilitator, asks whether Sergio realized how bad the deck was. "Did you even know what you needed?" he asks. "How much did you look at the deck as a deck?" Sergio's colleagues jump in to point out the ways the materials didn't serve the goals of the meeting. None of this is focused on improving the quality of Virginia's work. That's not the point right now.

Canner and the teammates continue to ask questions and make observations. Sergio acknowledges he spent his time in the earlier meeting justifying the slide deck, even though it was patently not good enough, something he realized after the meeting. "I found myself defending a document," he says. But to get to the deeper why, the group needs to discover what about Sergio made him do this.

Sergio offers a diagnosis. First, he didn't have an adequate mental map of what was required to move the work forward in the meeting. He also wasn't "in sync" (an important term at Bridgewater) with others about expectations, and he didn't get a clear and granular picture of what was required for success. "I lost sight of the goal of the meeting," Sergio says. "Ray [Dalio] talks about a choice between worrying if you're looking good and achieving your goals. And I was defending the intelligence of the deck." Now Sergio is getting to the root cause: his own need to look good and please others. It hijacked his behavior in the meeting.

The team meeting wraps up on time, just as Sergio asks for more opportunities to practice in similar situations. He tells Canner he wants to take a next step a little further down the developmental road and check in again with him, not so that Canner can "feed him fish," Sergio says, but so that he can learn to fish.

Coming full circle, Canner summarizes some takeaways, not only for Sergio but also for the team to hear. "These failures are fuel," Canner says. He praises Sergio for focusing on the "loops" of learning—being ready for more practice—and for now seeing clearly what the team members don't want to do (among other things, delegate a task without a clear sense of what a good outcome looks like that meets the need and the standard of excellence).

In parting words that are typical at the end of a meeting here, capping a high-energy Socratic dialogue designed to get to the truth, Sergio acknowledges, "We're probably in agreement."

An Idea Meritocracy

Bridgewater Associates manages approximately $165 billion in global investments in two hedge funds: Pure Alpha Strategy and All Weather Strategy. The company serves institutional clients, such as foreign governments, central banks, corporate and public pension funds, university endowments, and charitable foundations. Bridgewater began in Ray Dalio's two-bedroom apartment in 1975 and is still privately held. There are about fifteen hundred employees.

Throughout its nearly four decades, Bridgewater has been recognized as a top-performing money manager; it has won more than forty industry awards in the past five years alone. At the time of this writing, the Pure Alpha fund has had only one losing year and has gained an average of 14 percent per year since its founding in 1991. The All Weather fund, which is designed to make money during good times and bad, has been up 9.5 percent per year since its launch, in 1996, and delivered an astonishing 34 percent return from 2009 through 2011, even as the hedge fund industry as a whole underperformed the S&P 500. In both 2010 and 2011 Bridgewater was ranked by *Institutional Investor's Alpha* as the largest and best-performing hedge fund manager in the world. And in 2012, *Economist* credited the firm with having made more money for its investors than any other hedge fund in history.

Greg Jensen, co-CEO, explains that all this success derives from the company's approach to its principles, a source of "compounding understanding," much like compound interest, over time.

> The thing that we found . . . in our business, and I think for most businesses, you have to have better ideas than other people. That's basically what it comes down to. We're competing against everyone in the markets. The market price is a weighted-average view of what's going to happen in the future. The only way you can know something better is to have a better understanding of what can happen in the future. So, it's a perfect form of idea meritocracy. And for us the building blocks of that, of creating an idea meritocracy, is having a shared, transparent set of principles, so that everybody understands the roles, the constitution of the place . . . We have this notion about the constitution of the company that these are the principles. So that every decision, we are reflecting on, "What principles are at play? And how do you take this decision with respect to those principles?" . . . When we change our views, we'll change it there, so that people can keep learning from that compounding understanding and thirty-five years of running this business . . . If you disagree with the principles, you gotta fight like hell. There's no behind-the-corner talk.

In the algorithms of its proprietary systems, the company has recorded all its technical investment knowledge—a set of principles to guide investing. As many as 98 percent of Bridgewater's financial decisions are executed automatically based on that set of codified market decision rules. In contrast, the "Principles" document—the Bridgewater constitution, which all citizens of the company seek to uphold (or "fight like hell" to change, if they disagree)—is not about the laws of finance, the market economy, or investing. Instead, it's about the ways people act to foster and preserve a culture of truth and transparency. The principles set a clear bar of excellence for all decision making and are the common textual and conceptual reference for every Bridgewater employee seeking to act in a principled way.

The principles, which number more than two hundred, are organized in several categories, each building out to a core takeaway through a collection of related ideas. The following summarizes some of these foundational beliefs.

- *Trust in truth.* Be radically transparent, be extremely open, and don't tolerate dishonesty.

- *Create a culture in which it is OK to make mistakes but unacceptable not to identify, analyze, and learn from them.* Do not feel bad about your mistakes or those of others. Love them! Don't worry about looking good—worry about achieving your goals. When you experience pain, remember to reflect.

- *Constantly get in sync.* Talk about "Is it true?" and "Does it make sense?" Be assertive and open-minded at the same time. Don't treat all opinions as equally valuable. Consider your own and others' "believabilities." Spend lavishly on the time and energy you devote to getting in sync because it's the best investment you can make.

- *Get the right people.* Remember that almost everything good comes from having great people operating in a great culture. First, match the person to the design.

- *Recognize that people are built very differently.* Understand what each person who works for you is like so that you know what to expect from them. Don't hide these differences. Explore them openly with the goal of figuring out how you and your people are built so that you can put the right people in the right jobs and clearly assign responsibilities.

- *Manage as someone who is designing and operating a machine to achieve the goal.* Constantly compare your outcomes to your goals. Conduct the discussion at two levels when a problem occurs: (1) the "machine" level discussion of why the machine produced that outcome and (2) the "case at hand" discussion of what to do now about the problem. Hold people accountable and appreciate them holding you accountable. Logic, reason, and common sense must trump everything else in decision making.

- *Probe deep and hard to learn what to expect from your "machine."* Constantly probe the people who report to you, and encourage them to probe you. Remember that few people see themselves objectively, so it's important to welcome probing and to probe others. Don't "pick your battles." Fight them all. Make the probing transparent rather than private.

- *Evaluate people accurately, not "kindly."* Understand that you and the people you manage will go through a process of personal evolution. Help people through the pain that comes with exploring their weaknesses.

- *Train and test people through experiences.* Remember that everything is a case study. Teach your people to fish rather than give them fish.

- *Sort people into other jobs at Bridgewater, or remove them from Bridgewater.* When you find that someone is not a good "click" for a job, get them out of it ASAP. Do not lower the bar.

- *Know how to perceive problems effectively.* Understand that problems are the fuel for improvement. Don't tolerate badness. Don't use the anonymous "we" and "they," because that masks personal responsibility—use specific names.

- *Diagnose to understand what the problems are symptomatic of.* Recognize that all problems are just manifestations of their root causes, so diagnose to understand what the problems are symptomatic of. Remember that a proper diagnosis requires a quality, collaborative, and honest discussion to get at the truth.

- *Design your machine to achieve your goals.* Remember: you are designing a "machine" or system that will produce outcomes. Most importantly, build the organization around goals rather than tasks. Build your organization from the top down.

- *Recognize the power of knowing how to deal with not knowing.* Remember that your goal is to find the best answer, not to give the best one you have. Constantly worry about what you are missing.

- *Synthesize.* Understand and connect the dots. Avoid the temptation to compromise on that which is uncompromisable. Don't try to please everyone.

Bridgewater's commitment to radical truth, as elaborated in these principles, is anchored in a demand for excellence through constant improvement. The company leaders see all of its processes through the image of a machine—an inevitably imperfect but improvable system.

The economy is likewise described at Bridgewater as a machine that produces outputs, and, by any accounting, the company has developed penetrating insight into the workings of the machine. But human-designed processes within the company are also viewed as machines. Each process—from the hiring of new Bridgewater recruits, to the way the desktop technology support team manages software installation, to the approach to developing training case videos—delivers on specific goals and is designed to work in more or less effective ways to produce outcomes. Enhancing the functioning of the company's many processes—its machines—requires a constant search for the truth about how things are actually going and what needs to be learned by whom if there's a problem.

Probing and Transparency

"Probing" at Bridgewater is a way to understand the deeper whys. In probing, you ask someone questions about the design of a specific process, about a problem, or about the person's actions or inaction.

Probing also allows people, in an inquiry-based culture, to ensure that they're aligned in looking at the same data and zeroing in on shared causal explanations. It is the practice of figuring out what is true. It also reveals information about what people are like (the WPALs), which can help managers understand whether the source of a problem is a given person or the design of the machine—the definition of the role and workflow.

The company's other primary commitment—to radical transparency—goes much deeper than the glass office walls. Every meeting is recorded, and (unless proprietary client information is discussed) every recording is available to every member of the organization. Each office and meeting room is equipped with audio recording technology. For example, if your boss and your boss's boss are discussing your performance and you weren't invited to the meeting, the recording is available for you to review. And you don't have to scour every audio file to find out whether you were the subject of a closed-door conversation. If your name came up, you're likely to be given a heads-up, just so that you will review the file. In effect, there is no such thing as a closed-door conversation; everything is part of a "historical record of what is true."

Co-CEO Jensen says that in the beginning, the company's lawyers "went nuts" about recording meetings. But after Bridgewater was sued several times and used the tapes as evidence, Jensen explains, "We won every case. We won because the tapes made clear that we were operating consistently with how we say we are operating."

At any time, routine business conversations can shift into an opportunity for truth-telling and collective learning. It is common to pause for a "step-back moment" in the middle of a meeting to take stock of errors, to diagnose their root causes in people's habitual actions and thinking, and to identify what individuals can do to learn from their own defensiveness. A participant whose limitations are being scrutinized might also be encouraged to "design around" those ways of thinking rather than pretend they don't exist, using reliable peers or leaders or setting up processes that "guardrail" against failure—proactively compensate for one's inadequacies.

At Bridgewater, every day is a kind of after-action review, although the process goes much deeper than a typical postmortem. A given conversation of this sort doesn't stop until people have learned something about the person involved. What does what happened say about you—about how you think? And is there a higher vantage point that you can take, sitting above your own in-the-moment, reactive, defensive self—looking down to see the "you" that is messing up repeatedly and predictably? How are your actions, missteps, or successes, viewed by this "higher you," an expression of something deeper that's true about you? There is an urgency in asking this question each time, because if you (and others you work with) don't figure out the deeper whys, then you'll keep doing the same things, with similarly disappointing results.

As you might imagine, all this can be disorienting for people early in their tenure at the company—especially for people who have had professional careers at other firms where they were shining stars to be emulated and examples of what success typically looks like at work. At Bridgewater, people talk openly and honestly about the pain that can be triggered by looking closely at our own internal barriers and the root causes of things that happen at work. They refer to an equation to remind themselves and each other why they do this every day:

$$Pain + Reflection = Progress$$

Members even have an app—the Pain Button—that is standard issue on company-provided iPads. This tool allows employees to record and share experiences of negative emotions at work—especially when their ego defenses are activated by interactions with others. Open sharing of these experiences then triggers follow-up conversations among the parties, as they seek to explore the truth and identify what individuals might do to directly address the underlying personal causes.

This practice is aimed at helping people "get to the other side"—a Bridgewater phrase for working through ego defenses, neutralizing the sting of having your mind-set questioned, and coming to actively manage forms of emotional self-protection that otherwise would be barriers to personal growth. Because learning from one's mistakes is a job requirement, people who cannot get to the other side after sufficient time will either leave Bridgewater or be asked to go.

John Woody's Reliability Problem

John Woody (who goes by Woody) coleads Bridgewater's recruiting efforts. Now in his early thirties, Woody started working at the company on the team directly supporting Ray Dalio.

When we met Woody, who was also featured in a 2013 Harvard Business School case study of Bridgewater, he shared his story of growth.[4] Woody has by now gotten to the other side, where he can discuss his limitations directly with anyone in the company. But there was a time when Woody could not face what he was hearing about himself. After several years in the company, Dalio directly addressed what he called Woody's "chronic reliability issue." Because Bridgewater records all such conversations, we can share a portion of that conversation Woody had with Dalio.

> *Dalio:* He told you to deliver the daily updates. I told you to deliver the daily updates.
>
> *Woody:* I'm in agreement about the daily updates. No question.

D: And so there are two issues. Not only aren't you getting the daily updates, but we have a chronic reliability issue. You cannot be trusted to do the things you're asked to do.

W: Um . . . when you take it to that level, I disagree with you. But when we're talking about—

D: That's your problem.

W: Well, can we explore that?

D: Yes, of course!

W: Because I think I take on massive amounts of responsibility and deliver on all of them. There are certain things that—

D: No, you don't. It's become a joke, about your reliability, and your reliability grades. You're given assignments, you don't do it. You are given the daily updates. You're asked to do stuff. This is your problem. You don't embrace your problem.

Woody's reaction—in this meeting and in the weeks that followed— was to reject the harsh feedback. Dalio had "touched the nerve," in the phrase people at Bridgewater use. Woody in turn immediately grew defensive.

Here, we pride ourselves on being logical and facing the truth, but my initial response was, "You're wrong!" which is me already being illogical, because I'm not even asking him why he thinks I'm unreliable . . . I thought I was really open-minded, that I was [open to being] wrong in situations. And I came to realize very quickly that that wasn't the case. That when I was challenged, it would actually emotionally impact the way I interacted. I would get heated. I would lose my logic. I would feel like when people challenged my ideas, it was almost an affront [to] me.

But pushed by Dalio and others to continue exploring his behavior—"to get past his ego"—Woody began to see some patterns over time, rather than seeing his shortcomings as exceptions or situational. He started to "come to a realization that not only is it a problem for me professionally, but it's actually been a problem for me personally all the way back to the time where I'm eight years old."

> So then I have to ask myself, "How is it that something that has pervasively affected me since I was eight years old is something I can deny steadfastly when confronted on it as a thirty-year-old? . . . Who do I want to be?" I want to be the guy you give the ball to on the two-yard line. "We need to score, we've got to give it to the most dependable guy. You are the guy." That's who I want to be. [But] I am being confronted in the moment by someone saying, "You are not the guy. I don't even know if you are going to be there when I try to hand the ball to you." And that hurts, right?

Woody credits "a pretty powerful community" for helping him confront the fact that he was quick to anger and to get defensive, that he was chronically late to meetings and other commitments, and that he was someone people couldn't rely on to follow through. Now he is at a point in his journey at Bridgewater where he is trying to "become comfortable with it, and I'm trying to change certain bits about myself that are causing problems, but I'm also much more comfortable being conscious of it."

Woody sees the progress he's making on his reliability problem, but he insists he still has a long way to go. It is clear, though, that he has come quite a distance: "[Now] I prioritize more ruthlessly," he says, "pause longer and more thoughtfully before promising things to others, visualize more granularly how I will actually get something done, check in with those who ask things of me more frequently and with more questions, and lean on those around me much more explicitly now than I ever did."

For people like Woody, who thrive in Bridgewater's incubator for human performance, getting to the other side is not the end of a journey. But it's a richer vista from the other side, with the hard-won ability to see and understand much more about oneself. And for most, like Woody, Pain + Reflection [+ "a pretty powerful community"] = Progress.

Summing Up

One thing is clear: none of these companies is formally in the human potential business. They are not universities filled with professional educators, or clinics or personal growth centers staffed with psychologists. They aren't management consultancies. None of these three companies markets services related to helping people overcome their limitations. They manage hedge funds, movie theaters, and e-commerce transactions. Their businesses and products are as diverse as the companies are distant from being human services organizations. Macroeconomic investors, software engineers, and movie theater operators would probably not be your first choice of people to naturally take to the continuous levels of self-examination you've had a glimpse of here.

And that is the point. Although these companies develop their cultures as principled investments in their own business success, they also refuse to separate the people who make up the business from the business itself. Their big bet on a deliberately developmental culture is rooted in the unshakable belief that business can be an ideal context for people's growth, evolution, and flourishing—and that such personal development may be the secret weapon for business success in the future.

In each of these DDOs—Next Jump, Decurion, and Bridgewater—we see a seamless integration of two pursuits as if they were a single goal: business excellence and the growth of people into more capable versions of themselves *through* the work of the business. Each company has its own approach, but, interestingly, what each emphasizes can be found in the others as well. Next Jump's culture puts helping others explicitly at the forefront, including the central importance of coaching as a way to grow while serving others. Decurion builds the strength of next-generation learning communities (really, development communities) as a way to create conditions for people to both grow as individuals and seize business opportunities fully. Bridgewater stands for the pursuit of what is true, no matter how inconvenient, both as a business necessity in the financial markets and as a path for personal evolution and cultural integrity.

But underlying these approaches is a shared and surprising reversal of the most fundamental agreement in ordinary organizational life: the separation of the personal and the public. The ordinary organization is like the "old Brené Brown" as she described herself at the beginning of this chapter: it doesn't "do" vulnerability, and it doesn't hang out with those who do. The ordinary organization conspires with that part of its employees' psyches that believes the place for imperfection and vulnerability and shame and unworthiness is somewhere far away from work.

(The ordinary organization says, in effect, "If vulnerability does have to come into work from time to time, then we will make provisions for it: let it go on in a private room, with others who will keep whatever they see and hear to themselves, and let it be tended to as quickly as possible, and let us do the person the courtesy of pretending it never happened"—in other words, just the way some people think we should treat nursing mothers.)

No doubt you have had a variety of reactions to what you have seen in this chapter, but almost certainly, whatever those reactions are, at their core is one thing: the way you feel about vulnerability. Your reactions may be about the way you feel about experiencing vulnerability yourself in the company of others; the way you feel about being in the presence of others' vulnerability; and, especially, the way you feel about any of that going on at work. You can be assured that whatever your current thoughts and feelings are, every one of them has been shared—is currently being shared—by people working in a DDO. In that way, this chapter helps you meet a DDO in more ways than one.

Now that you've generated a variety of first impressions, the next two chapters create spaces to help you hold on to them, to turn them around in your hands, and to consider them in the context of the underlying theory of the DDO. We begin with an exploration of what development means in a deliberately developmental organization. There exists a well-worked-out theory about the trajectory of psychological development in adulthood, based on forty years of research, that we believe can help you understand the deep structure of a DDO. In essence, a DDO is working on ways to provide people the maximum exposure to those experiences likely to help them continue—when they are ready—the ongoing journey of adult development.

2

What Do We Mean by Development?

Words like *development* and *growth* are widely used in business and other professions. If you're the leader of a company or one of its shareholders, you want it to develop. As an employee, you want to work at a place where your career can develop over time.

When people refer to a company growing or developing, they are generally talking about an increase in revenue, profits, stock price, personnel, markets, lines of business, office locations, or subsidiaries—increases in the "size" of the business. When individuals talk about the growth or development of their career, they generally mean an increase in their seniority, their scope of responsibility, their authority, their compensation—increases in the "size" of their position. If deliberately developmental organizations did not also develop in this sense, and if their people did not find their careers also developing in this sense, it isn't likely they would last or find employees.

But when we talk about a DDO, we use the term *development* very differently. We mean, not the development of a career, but the

---

This is a significantly revised version of material first appearing in Robert Kegan and Lisa Laskow Lahey, *Immunity to Change* (Boston: Harvard Business Review Press, 2009).

development of the person having the career. We aren't first talking about the business becoming bigger, but becoming a better version of itself. Businesses expand and careers flourish within a DDO, but these changes are *consequences* of the kind of development we're talking about; they are not the development itself.

What is "the development itself"? For more than a hundred years, researchers have studied the ways human beings construct reality and have observed how that constructing can become more expansive, less distorted, less egocentric, and less reactive over time. They began with the study of children, teasing out, first, the underlying logic used by their young subjects to make sense of themselves and the world around them; then researchers discovered the principles and processes by which this logic gradually evolves to enable growing children to overcome their cognitive distortions and see more deeply and accurately into themselves and their worlds. Testing the robustness of this logic and the sequence of its development, researchers found that the basic patterns hold up across genders, cultures, and social classes.

Forty years ago this science took a significant, and controversial, turn with the investigation of adult development. Many theorists and researchers, ourselves among them (Kegan and Lahey), advanced an understanding of a succession of more-complex mental logics after adolescence. Informed by our research subjects whom we followed over many years, we began to see further possibilities in adulthood for overcoming limitations in the ability to understand oneself and one's worlds—even if not every adult traveled the full course of this trajectory.[1]

The Trajectory of Adult Development

When we began our work, the accepted picture of mental development was akin to the picture of physical development; human growth was thought fundamentally to end by our twenties. Most people don't get any taller than the height they reach in their twenties, and it was believed they didn't get any "taller" psychologically, either. If, forty years ago, you were to place "age" on one axis and "mental complexity" on another, and if you asked the experts in the field to draw the graph as they understood it, they would have produced something similar to figure 2-1: an upward sloping line until

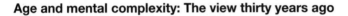

FIGURE 2-1

Age and mental complexity: The view thirty years ago

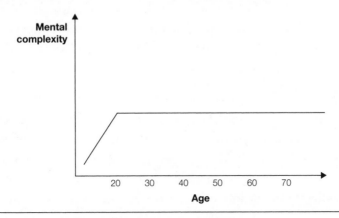

the twenties, and a flat line thereafter. And they would have drawn it with confidence.

In the 1980s we began reporting the results of our research, suggesting that some (though not all) adults seemed to undergo qualitative advances in their mental complexity akin to earlier, well-documented quantum leaps from early childhood to later childhood and from later childhood to adolescence. When we talked about these results on distinguished panels, our brain-research colleagues sitting next to us would greet them with polite disdain.

"You might think you can infer this from your longitudinal interviews," they would say, "but hard science doesn't have to make inferences. We're looking at *the real thing*. The brain simply doesn't undergo any significant change in capacity after later adolescence. Sorry." Of course, these hard scientists would grant that older people are often wiser or more capable than younger people, but this they attributed to the benefits of experience, a consequence of learning how to get more out of the same mental equipment rather than qualitative advances or upgrades to the equipment itself.

Forty years later? Whoops! It turns out everyone was making inferences, even the brain scientists who thought they were looking at "the thing itself." The hard scientists have better instruments now, and the brain doesn't look to them exactly the way it did forty years ago. Now they talk about neural plasticity and acknowledge the phenomenal capacities of the brain to keep adapting throughout life.

What if we were to draw the graph showing age and mental complexity now? On the basis of forty years of longitudinal research by us and our colleagues—as a result of thoroughly analyzing the transcripts of hundreds of people, interviewed and reinterviewed at several-year intervals—the graph would look like figure 2-2.

Two things are evident from this graph.

- With a large-enough sample size you can detect a mildly upward-sloping curve. That is, looking at a population as a whole, mental complexity tends to increase with age, throughout adulthood, at least until old age. When an evolution occurs from one level of complexity to another, adults take greater responsibility for their thinking and feeling, can retain more layers of information, and can think further into the future, to name only some of the well-researched consequences of mental development. So the story of mental complexity certainly does not end in our twenties.

- There is considerable variation within any age. For example, each of six people in their thirties (the darker dots) could be at a different place in their level of mental complexity, and some could be more complex than a person in her forties. People move through these evolutions at different speeds, and many of us, if not most of us, get stuck in our evolution and do not reach the most complex peaks.

FIGURE 2-2

Age and mental complexity: The revised view today

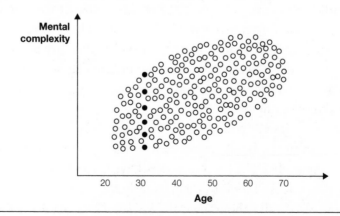

If we were to draw a quick picture of what we have learned about the individual trajectory of mental development in adulthood, it might look something like figure 2-3.

This picture suggests several elements.

- There are qualitatively different, distinct levels (the "plateaus"); the demarcations between levels of mental complexity are not arbitrary. Each level represents a different way of knowing the world.

- Development does not unfold continuously; there are periods of stability and periods of change. When a new plateau is reached, we tend to stay on that level for a considerable time (although elaborations and extensions within each system can occur).

- The intervals between transformations to new levels—the time on a plateau—get longer as time passes.

- The line gets thinner, representing the decreasing likelihood of reaching the higher plateaus.

What do these levels of mental complexity in adulthood look like? Can we say anything about what someone at a more complex level can see or do that he cannot do at a less complex level? Indeed, we can now say a great deal about these levels. They do not mark how smart

FIGURE 2-3

The trajectory of mental development in adulthood

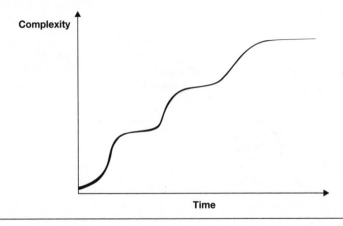

you are in the ordinary sense. Mental complexity is not about how much you know or how high your IQ is. It is not about developing increasingly abstruse apprehensions of the world, as if "most complex" meant finally being able to understand a physicist's blackboard filled with complex equations.

Then what does it mean? Read on.

Three Plateaus in Adult Mental Complexity

Let's begin with an overview of three qualitatively different plateaus in mental complexity we see among adults, as suggested in figure 2-4 and table 2-1. These three adult meaning systems—the socialized mind, the self-authoring mind, and the self-transforming mind—make sense of the world, and operate within it, in distinct ways. One way to see how this difference shows up at work is to focus on any significant aspect of organizational life and then consider how the same phenomenon—for example, the flow of information—differs through the lens of each perspective.

FIGURE 2-4

Three plateaus in adult mental development

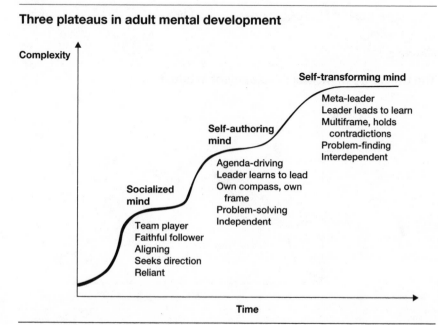

TABLE 2-1

The three adult plateaus

The socialized mind

- We are shaped by the definitions and expectations of our personal environment.
- Our self coheres by its alignment with, and loyalty to, that with which it identifies.
- This sense of self can express itself primarily in our relationships with people, with schools of thought (our ideas and beliefs), or both.

The self-authoring mind

- We are able to step back enough from the social environment to generate an internal seat of judgment, or personal authority, that evaluates and makes choices about external expectations.
- Our self coheres by its alignment with its own belief system, ideology, or personal code; by its ability to self-direct, take stands, set limits, and create and regulate its boundaries on behalf of its own voice.

The self-transforming mind

- We can step back from and reflect on the limits of our own ideology or personal authority; see that any one system or self-organization is in some way partial or incomplete; be friendlier toward contradiction and opposites; seek to hold on to multiple systems rather than project all except one onto the other.
- Our self coheres through its ability not to confuse internal consistency with wholeness or completeness, and through its alignment with the dialectic rather than either pole.

The way information does or does not flow through an organization—what people "send," to whom they send it, how they receive or attend to what flows to them—is a crucial feature of how any system works; nowhere is it more important than in a DDO, which stresses unprecedented forms of transparency. Experts on organizational culture, organizational behavior, or organizational change often address this subject with a sophisticated sense of how systems impact individual behavior, but with a naive sense of how powerful a factor is the level of mental complexity with which the individual views the culture. Let's look at how this factor operates.

The Socialized Mind and Information Flow

Having a socialized mind dramatically influences both the sending and receiving aspects of information flow at work. If this is the level of mental complexity with which I view the world, then what I think to send will be strongly influenced by what I believe others want to hear. You may be familiar with the classic groupthink studies, which show team members withholding crucial information from collective decision processes because (it is later learned in follow-up research), as one participant might put it, "although I believed the plan had almost no chance of succeeding, I saw that the leader wanted our support."

Some of these studies were originally done in Asian cultures, where withholding team members talked about the need to "save face" of the leaders and not subject them to shame, even at the price of setting the company on a losing path. The studies were often presented as if they were uncovering a particular cultural phenomenon. Similarly, Stanley Milgram's famous obedience-to-authority research was originally undertaken to fathom the mentality of "the good German" and to identify what about the German culture enabled otherwise decent, nonsadistic people to carry out orders to exterminate millions of Jews. But Milgram, in practice runs of his data-gathering method before he went overseas to Germany, was surprised to find "good Germans" all over Main Street USA. And although we think of sensitivity to shame as a particular feature of Asian culture, the research of Irving Janis and Paul 't Hart has made clear that groupthink is as robust a phenomenon in Texas and Toronto as it is in Tokyo and Taiwan.[2] In sum, groupthink and obedience to authority may owe their origins less to culture and more to complexity of mind.

The socialized mind strongly influences how information is received and attended to, as well as how it is sent. Because maintaining alignment with important others and valued "surrounds" is crucial to the coherence of one's being at this stage, the socialized mind is highly sensitive to, and influenced by, what it picks up. Because of this sensitivity, it often picks up information far beyond the explicit message. It may well include the results of highly invested attention to imagined subtexts and cues that may have more impact on the receiver than the sender intends. ("I could just tell he was impatient by his tone of voice." "When she leans in like that, you know she doesn't agree with what you're saying.") This kind of inference is often astonishing and dismaying to leaders and others, who cannot understand how subordinates and team members could possibly have interpreted a communication in an unintended way.

Keep in mind that levels of mental complexity are not the same thing as levels of intelligence in the IQ sense. People at the socialized level of mental complexity can differ widely among themselves with respect to IQ, and, like any level, it may include those with very high IQs. Recall Sergio, from Bridgewater, introduced in chapter 1.

He probably has a very high IQ, and it is also likely, at the time he appears in chapter 1, he is working on the transition out of the socialized mind. He tells us he "feels an acute need, almost at random, to please others," that he feels torn between a desire, on the one hand, to please founder Ray Dalio by staying at Bridgewater, and the pull, on the other hand, of leaving and going to medical school. "The thing I worry most about," he says, "is pleasing whoever is in front of me."

We all spend some portion of our adult lives in the socialized mind, and at any time, in any organization, a large percentage of people, in a DDO or otherwise, will organize their experience according to this psychologic. But notice that, in Sergio's case, the culture of a DDO may usefully trouble this mind-set and support his transition.

Even to please his boss, Sergio will pick up that Dalio will be most pleased by Sergio's speaking his mind, by his saying what is true for him, even if that truth is an inconvenient one for Dalio. When a culture acts in such a way to upend our current level of mental complexity, even as we are acting to preserve that level—in this case by seeking to align with (or get in sync with) the values and norms of authorities surrounding us—that culture is operating in a fashion that induces development.

You can see the effect on Sergio, who is having the opportunity, in the context of his work, not only to enact his socialized mind but also to identify how it works—and how it may no longer work very well. "This can get me in trouble," he says. He has not yet moved fully beyond the socialized mind, but clearly he is not so completely embedded in it as he once was. There was a time when he did not know he was a people pleaser, to use his term. This is what development always looks like. That which we were "subject to," or run by, gradually becomes "object," or something we can look *at* rather than only look *through.*

What if the life of a DDO is filled with such development-inducing opportunities, not only for those in the socialized mind but also for those at any point in their development?

The Self-Authoring Mind and Information Flow

Let's contrast the socialized mind with the self-authoring mind. If I view the world from this level of mental complexity, what I send is more likely to be a function of what I deem others need to or ought to hear to best further the agenda or mission of my design. Consciously or unconsciously, I have a direction, an agenda, a stance, a strategy, or an analysis of what is needed—a prior context from which my communication arises. My direction or plan may be an excellent one, or it may be riddled with blind spots. I may be masterful or inept at recruiting others to invest in my plan. These matters implicate other aspects of the self. But mental complexity strongly influences whether I orient my information toward getting myself behind the wheel so that I can drive (the self-authoring mind) or getting myself included in the car so that I can be driven (the socialized mind).

We see a similar mind-set operating when I, as someone with a self-authoring mind, receive information. I create a filter for what I allow to come through. The filter puts a high priority on some information—e.g., information I seek, or information I may not seek but that I can see is relevant to my plan, stance, or frame—and a lower priority on other information—e.g., information I haven't asked for that seems unimportant to my design.

It's easy to see how someone having a self-authoring mind could demonstrate an admirable capacity for focus, for distinguishing the important from the urgent, for making the best use of her limited time by having a means to cut through the unending and ever-mounting claims on her attention. This speaks to the way the self-authoring mind is an advance over the socialized mind. But the self-authoring mind may also be a recipe for disaster if her plan or stance is flawed, if it leaves out a crucial element of the equation not appreciated by the filter, or if the world changes so that a formerly effective filter becomes antiquated.

Consider Jackie from Next Jump, whom you met in chapter 1, and the way the world changed for her. "I have to be honest," Jackie told us. "When cultural contributions were first introduced to the company, I pretty much dismissed them. Why am I going to do them?" Her words convey more than a refreshing candor; they convey a long-lived internal authority that can consider a new companywide expectation and a reset of the definition of success, and just say, "Nope. Doesn't fit my filter. I'm tossing that in the wastebasket."

Imagine how differently someone with a socialized mind would be affected by a new norm that essentially says, "To be loved and respected around here, now you have to give as much attention to your contributions to culture as to revenue." If that person had a work profile like Jackie's, ignoring contributions to the culture, we would expect him to turn around on a dime and start attending to culture.

Not Jackie. The same self-direction, focus, and personal initiative that have no doubt contributed to her success as a marketing leader, as a champion of any project she can run on her own, also make it possible for her to independently evaluate the new information bumping up against her filter. Nothing about it forwards her self-authored agenda, so it doesn't register—until there are consequences. In Jackie's case, she was removed from the company's most prestigious leadership committee, which was a blow to her own self-authored definition of being successful.

But again, as with Sergio, we can do more than use these live examples to demonstrate how the differing minds show up in the real world. We can begin to see that a DDO is deliberately developmental precisely because it intersects continuously with its members' developmental position, whatever that position is, offering invitations for them to grow beyond the limits of their current mind-sets, if they are ready for the move.

Jackie could have responded to her setback by taking up contributions to culture in the same self-authoring way in which she was previously having nothing to do with it. "Okay," she could have said to herself, picking herself up and dusting herself off. "I'm Jackie. I get the A's. If the grading system has changed, and it remains my self-authored goal to be restored to my rightful place on the leadership committee, I will come up with a new plan to realign, not with what others want, but with what I want."

Initially, this is probably just what she did. But it's important to see that even if this were all she did, it would not be a defeat for her, or the company, or the purpose of a DDO. Not everyone is always ready to undergo the transformation it takes to climb to a new plateau. There also is a kind of human progress in making our way further along the horizontal line. There are many ways to be self-authoring, many agendas or filters that Jackie could create.

But notice that even if her initial move is a more lateral one, the particular one the DDO encourages brings her into experiences that may make it more likely for her to move beyond the self-authoring level. She may initially grit her teeth and spend more time trying to be helpful to others only to accomplish her self-authored goal. But doing so will give her the opportunity to do more than just accomplish her agenda; it may well lead her to a different definition of self, to different metrics for success and accomplishment and satisfaction— new ways of seeing that are genuinely more unselfish because they transcend the self-authoring level. A key indicator may be whether getting reelected to the leadership committee comes to pale in importance, for Jackie, to the satisfaction of being the new person she finds herself becoming.

The examples of Sergio and Jackie may make it tempting to consider that Next Jump's work to help people become less insecure or less arrogant (recall that these are the company's terms) amounts to powerful ways of helping people with socialized minds to become more self-authoring, and helping people with self-authoring minds to become more self-transforming, respectively. But the realities are not always so simple. Some people who lean arrogant do so with socialized minds. Their overcertainty and high confidence might be an expression of how well connected and well regarded they feel themselves to be. (If you're certain you have God on your side, for example, your faithful adherence can show up as "leaning arrogant.")

And some people with self-authoring minds can lean insecure. If, for example, your frame or personal philosophy puts a high premium on not being found wanting, or not being one who lets his heart cloud his good judgment, you may have an outlook of chronic caution or tempered enthusiasm that comes across as leaning insecure. An optimally effective DDO will offer a different set of developmental supports and provocations to arrogance or insecurity suited to differing levels of mental complexity.

The Self-Transforming Mind and Information Flow

In contrast to the self-authoring mind, the self-transforming mind also has a filter but is not fused with it. Someone with a self-transforming mind can stand back from his own filter and look at it and not only through it. And why would he do so? It's because he both values, and is wary of, any one stance, analysis, or agenda. He is mindful that, powerful though a given design might be, it almost inevitably omits something. A self-transforming mind is aware it lives in time and the world is in motion. It is aware that what might make sense today may not make as much sense tomorrow.

Therefore, when communicating, people with self-transforming minds are not only advancing their agenda and design but also making space for its modification or expansion. Like those with self-authoring minds, what those with self-transforming minds send may include inquiries and requests for information. But rather than inquire only within the frame of their design (seeking information that will advance their agenda), they also inquire about the design itself. They seek information that may lead them or their team to enhance, refine, or alter the original design or make it more inclusive. Unlike the socialized-minded person, for the self-transforming person, information sending isn't about being included in the car; and unlike the person with a self-authoring mind, it is not only about driving the car, but also about considering whether to remake the road map or reset the direction.

Similarly, the way the self-transforming mind receives information includes the advantage of having the self-authoring mind's filter, but the self-transforming mind is not a prisoner of the filter. People at this level of mental complexity can still focus, select, and drive when they feel they have a good map. But they place a higher priority on information that may also alert them to the limits of their current design or frame. They value their filter and its ability to separate the wheat from the chaff, but they know it can also screen out the "golden chaff": the unasked-for, the anomaly, the apparently inconsequential datum that may be what is needed to turn the design on its head and bring it to the next level of quality.

Those with self-transforming minds are more likely even to have the chance to consider such information, because people are more likely to send it to them. Why? It's because those with self-transforming minds not only attend to information once it gets to their door but also realize their behavior can have a big effect, upstream, on whether people even decide to approach the door. Others are not left guessing whether to send potentially "off-mission," but potentially important, communication. They send it because people with self-transforming minds have found ways to let them know such information will be welcomed.

Bridgewater's Ray Dalio, for example, places a high premium on what he calls "radical open-mindedness," by which he means something qualitatively beyond a mere willingness to listen to a competing view when and if it comes to call. "To be radically open-minded," he says, "you need to be so open to the possibility that you might be making a mistake and/or that you have a weakness that *you encourage others to tell you so.*"

The developmental journey of Decurion's Nora Dashwood, whom you met in chapter 1, is instructive in this regard. She is clearly and consciously at work on questions that come down to, "Can I be bigger than the self-authoring self that feels as if it has been so integral to my professional success and personal sense of well-being?" ("Can I lead others without withdrawing my goodwill when they don't see the world my way?" "Can I keep holding high standards for excellence in the business, while at the same time allowing others to step forward with their own ideas and solutions even when they run counter to my own instincts?")

Recall in chapter 1 that Dashwood talks about her growth as a leader, explaining that a low-ranking employee brought her up short when he told her that he felt "the air in the room turn cold" when things didn't go her way in meetings. Dashwood traced her take-charge tendency to her upbringing as the child of immigrants, who taught her, "You need to take care of yourself because no one else will . . . if you want all that life has to offer you, you need to count on yourself and take charge. That if you are not leading, you might as well be failing." But because of Decurion's practices, which pushed Dashwood "to be a [different kind of] leader, to be a mentor, to be with a community, and to count on other people," she has changed. "I am a better listener," she says. "I am more aware. I have a community that supports and challenges me . . . What I have learned at Decurion is that I can be a part of something that produces results much bigger than I can produce on my own. It was the hardest thing I've ever done and it has been the most meaningful growth and development I've ever experienced."

Her words express a developmental journey beyond the self-authoring mind, and they show how a deliberately developmental organization, through its community and its practices, slips its hand under its people, wherever they may be in their developmental journey, and supports their forward movement when they are ready.

Mental Complexity and Performance

The foregoing descriptions of the three plateaus of mental complexity, structured around a single important element of organizational life—information flow—begin to show you how a DDO is deliberately developmental. They show how an organization's *actions*—its communities and its practices—intersect with individuals, wherever they are in the developmental journey.

There is no denying that the descriptions suggest a value proposition for mental complexity. Theoretically, each successive level is formally "higher" than the preceding one, because people at the next level can perform all the mental functions of the prior level as well as additional ones. Each new level transcends and includes the prior level.

But the discussion so far has been about more than the formal theoretical properties and functions of the developmental levels. We have implied that the levels translate into real actions having real consequences for organizational behavior and work competence. The implication is that people having a higher level of mental complexity outperform those at a lower level in real life.

Is this only a hypothesis, albeit with plausible face validity, or has it been tested and systematically demonstrated? There are now a number of studies that correlate measures of mental complexity with independent assessments of work competence or performance. For now, let's peek into them to see the trends they suggest.

Leadership researcher Keith Eigel assessed the level of mental complexity of twenty-one CEOs of large, successful companies, each company an industry leader with average gross annual revenue of more than $5 billion.[3]

Using separate performance assessments, Eigel also evaluated the CEOs' effectiveness in terms of the ability to:

- Challenge existing processes

- Inspire a shared vision

- Manage conflict

- Solve problems

- Delegate

- Empower

- Build relationships

For comparison, Eigel did similar assessments in each of the same companies, interviewing promising middle managers nominated by their respective CEOs. Figure 2-5 summarizes his findings.

Several results stand out. First is the clearly discernible upward slope, signifying that increased mental complexity and work competence, assessed on a number of dimensions, are correlated. Thus, not only is it possible to reach higher planes of mental complexity, but also such growth correlates with effectiveness, for CEOs as well as middle managers. This finding has been replicated in a variety of fine-grained studies of small numbers of leaders, assessed on

FIGURE 2-5

Individual mental capacity and business effectiveness: Eigel's results

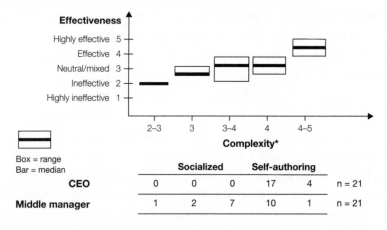

	Socialized		Self-authoring		
CEO	0	0	0	17	4	n = 21
Middle manager	1	2	7	10	1	n = 21

Box = range
Bar = median

*3 = socialized mind; 4 = self-authoring mind; 5 = self-transforming mind
Source: K. Eigel, "Leader Effectiveness" (PhD dissertation, University of Georgia, 1998).

particular competencies. Taken together, the cumulative data supports the proposition that for those at a higher level of mental complexity, a complex world is more manageable.[4]

Shifts in the Demands on Followers and Leaders

We can take a more sweeping view of the same issue by considering the new demands on leaders and their subordinates in the volatile, uncertain, complex, and ambiguous world in which we live. Take another look at figure 2-4, the chart of the plateaus in adult mental complexity.

Now let's consider what was once asked of people at work, generally, in any organization, compared with what is now asked. Formerly, it was usually enough if people were good team players, pulled their weight, were loyal to the organization, and could be counted on to follow conscientiously the directions and signals of their boss. In other words, the socialized mind would be perfectly adequate to handle the nature of yesterday's demands on employees.

But things have changed. In 1995, psychotherapist Nathaniel Branden writes as follows.

> In the past two or three decades, extraordinary develop-
> ments have occurred in the American and global economies.
> The United States has shifted from a manufacturing society
> to an information society. We have witnessed the transition
> from physical labor to mind work as the dominant employee
> activity. We now live in a global economy characterized by
> rapid change, accelerating scientific and technological break-
> throughs, and an unprecedented level of competitiveness.
> These developments create demand for higher levels of edu-
> cation and training than were required of previous genera-
> tions. Everyone acquainted with business culture knows this.
> What is not understood is that these developments also create
> new demands on our psychological resources. Specifically,
> these developments ask for a greater capacity for innovation,
> self-management, personal responsibility, and self-direction.
> This is not just asked at the top, it is asked at every level of

a business enterprise, from senior management to first-line supervisors and even to entry-level personnel . . . Today, organizations need not only an unprecedentedly higher level of knowledge and skill among all those who participate but also a higher level of independence, self-reliance, self-trust, and the capacity to exercise initiative.[5]

What is Branden—and many others who write about what we now look for from our workforce—saying, as it relates to level of mental complexity? He is saying that it used to be sufficient for workers to be at the level of the socialized mind, but now we need workers who are at the level of the self-authoring mind. In effect, we now call on workers to understand themselves and their world at a qualitatively higher level of mental complexity.

And what is the picture if we look not at lower-level employees but at bosses and leaders? Organizational theorist Chris Argyris raises similar issues about the growing insufficiency of traditional conceptions of managerial and leadership effectiveness that still dominate our thinking. There may have been a day, Argyris suggests, when it was enough for leaders to develop worthy goals and sensible norms, cultivate alignment, and work "to keep organizational performance within the range specified"—all the while exercising the strength of character to advocate for one's position and hold one's ground in the face of opposition.[6]

Skillful as such managers may be, however, their abilities no longer suffice. Needed now are leaders who can not only run but also reconstitute their organizations—their norms, missions, and cultures—in an increasingly fast-changing environment. For example, a company that chooses to transform itself from a low-cost, standardized-product organization to a mass customizer or a provider of organization-wide solutions will need to develop a new set of individual and team capabilities.

Argyris and Donald Schön describe the challenges of such a shift.

[It] requires that members of the corporation adopt new approaches to marketing, managing, and advertising; that they become accustomed to a much shorter product life cycle and to a more rapid cycle of changes in their pattern of activities; that they, in fact, change the very image of the business they are in. And these requirements for change come into conflict with another sort of corporate norm, one that requires predictability in the management of corporate affairs . . . A process of change initiated with an eye to effectiveness under existing norms turns out to yield a conflict in the norms themselves.[7]

For more than a generation, Argyris (and those who have been influenced by him) has been calling for, in our terminology, a new capacity of mind. This new mind must have the ability to author a view of how the organization should run and have the courage to hold steadfastly to that view. But more, the new mind also must be able to step outside its own ideology or framework, observe the framework's limitations or defects, and author a more comprehensive view—a view it will hold with sufficient tentativeness that it may discover its limitations as well. In other words, the kind of learner Argyris rightly looks for in a leader may need to be a person who is making meaning with a self-transforming mind.

Thus, organizations are asking workers who once performed their work successfully with socialized minds—good soldiers—to shift to self-authoring minds. And organizations are asking leaders who once led successfully with self-authoring minds—sure and certain captains—to develop self-transforming minds. In short, organizations are asking for a quantum shift in individual mental complexity across the board.

Meeting the Demand

How big is the gap between what we now expect of people's mental capacities and what their minds are actually like? Are we expecting something that is a big reach? After all, if the world has become more complex in the past half-century, then perhaps the world also has become a better incubator of mental complexity, and the supply of mental complexity has kept up with the demand.

Two sophisticated, reliable, widely used measures exist for assessing mental complexity along the lines we talk about here. (This is something quite different, obviously, from IQ testing, which has only a modest correlation with mental complexity; you can have an above-average IQ—say, 125—and operate at any of the three plateaus.) These measures are the Washington University Sentence Completion Test (SCT) and the Subject-Object Interview (SOI) we introduced earlier.

Two large meta-analyses of studies using one or the other of these measures have been performed, with several hundred participants in each study. Figure 2-6 summarizes the results.

Two observations stand out from the data in figure 2-6:

- Both studies, each done with different samples, arrive at the same finding: that in a majority of respondents, mental complexity is not as far along as the self-authoring mind (in fact, the separate studies show nearly the exact same percentage— 58 or 59 percent—is not at this level). Because both studies are skewed toward middle-class, college-educated professionals, the actual percentage in the general population may be higher.

- The percentages of people beyond the plateau of the self-authoring mind are quite small.

FIGURE 2-6

Results from two large-scale studies of the distribution of levels of mental complexity among adults

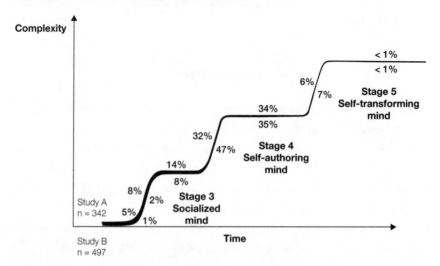

Sources: Study A: R. Kegan, *In Over Our Heads* (Cambridge, MA: Harvard University Press, 1994). Study B: W. Torbert, *Managing the Corporate Dream* (Homewood, IL: Dow-Jones, 1987).

The data suggests that the gap is large between what we now expect of people's mental complexity and what our minds are actually like. We expect most workers to be self-authoring, but most are not. We expect most leaders to be more complex than self-authoring, but few are.

These same macro trends are confirmed at the micro level in the Eigel study (have another look at figure 2-5). Note that only about half of the "promising middle managers" are self-authoring (and those who are, do better than those who are not), and only four of the twenty-one CEOs from industry-leading companies are beyond self-authoring (and those who are, do better than those who are not).

What We Mean by Development in a DDO

Where are we in defining the development that occurs in a deliberately developmental organization?

1. Development is a specific, describable, and detectable phenomenon (the growth of our mind-sets, or meaning-making logics; qualitative advances in our abilities to see more deeply and accurately into ourselves and our worlds; the process of successively being able to look *at* premises and assumptions we formerly looked *through*).

2. Development has a robust scientific foundation (forty years of research, by investigators across the world, with a wide diversity of samples and reliable means of measurement).

3. Development has a business value (organizations need more employees in possession of the more complex mind-sets, and this need will intensify in the years ahead).

This specific, theoretically robust, reliably measurable, and business-valuable phenomenon is the underground river running through a DDO. Chapter 4 takes a more thorough look at the practices of all three DDOs, including the way they support development as we define it here. But even the glimpses in chapter 1, seen now through the lens of developmental theory, should help you begin to see a kind of method to the madness in a DDO.

At first glance, it may seem strange, even unfriendly, to, for example, continuously provide people with critical feedback, or to move them out of a work role as soon as they have mastered it. But this chapter raises the possibility that these DDOs in the wild are accomplishing their ends because, by trial and error over years, they have hit upon practices that actually put them in sync with the contemporary science of adult development.

As it happens, Decurion's leaders were deeply familiar with this science and our work; Bridgewater's originally were not at all familiar with it; and Next Jump, a voracious digester of management science, may have had a passing exposure. What is common to all of them is not their explicit theoretical grasp of the science, but rather their ingenious and intuitive practical grasp of what it might mean to craft an organizational culture more likely to accelerate the development of personal mind-sets than any previously seen.

As you will see in chapter 7, when we turn to the subject of fledgling DDOs (organizations we are helping find their own path to DDO-hood, in light of the science elaborated in this book), it is our hope that keeping the theory in mind can be a means for you to test and strengthen the pervasiveness and diversity of your culture's support for development.

Incubators of Development

But for now, we can just as easily use the theory to deconstruct the hard-won wisdom reflected in the three exemplar DDOs ("Sure, sure, it works in practice; but does it work in theory?" Yes, indeed it does.)

Consider, for a moment, not only the pervasiveness but also the nature of feedback in the three DDOs. Ordinary organizations seldom make feedback a continuous experience (and in some sectors it can be as infrequent as an annual review), but even in organizations where feedback is frequent, the feedback strongly tends to be oriented to tracking and correcting behavior. In contrast, feedback in a DDO is considered incomplete or superficial unless it penetrates ("probes," in Bridgewater language) beneath behavior to the assumptions and mind-sets that underlie it. Admitting people's interior life into the realm of what can be improved, acted on, and managed is what makes a DDO's culture truly developmental—namely, the development of mental complexity.

Notice how evergreen or developmentally universal this kind of feedback is, whether we're talking about someone at the limits of the socialized mind presented with the opportunity to evaluate, rather than be defined by, the feedback; or someone at the limits of the self-authoring mind having the opportunity now to use the feedback to upend the sufficiency of his personal theory, rather than taking it as the occasion to further fortify his personal theory. In a DDO the experience of feedback, although meaning different things to people at different stages of adult development, is a continuously rich curriculum. A good curriculum is something with which the learner interacts daily, not once a year in an annual review.

Let's look at additional ways the DDO culture is, in effect, a multisurface, multistage incubator of development. Consider Bridgewater's use of the metaphor of the machine. At first, this may raise an off-putting specter of robotic dehumanization; but when you look into what the organization intends by the metaphor, it is actually a developmentally apt *plurasignative* (a term from semiotics—the science of signs and symbols—for those words that bundle multiple meanings).

One such meaning—one way the metaphor of the machine works on an individual's reality-making—is that any outcome or result (an external event or internal conclusion) gets now seen as the product of a bigger system, which produced the result. Every effect has a cause. Sergio, the self-identified people pleaser, ends up with a suboptimal set of slides for a presentation. Bridgewater's culture, rather than engage this shortcoming only at the level of improving the slide deck (the effect), pulls Sergio into a bigger field of consideration (the cause): What was his visualization of the process by which he was going to produce the slide deck? What was his bigger purpose, in the first place, of which the slide deck is only a part? How does his people-pleasing give him a bigger inner context for understanding how he ends up defending the merits of slides he doesn't even agree with?

The message behind the Bridgewater idea of the machine is that "things don't just happen" (a bigger system produced them); and "things don't just happen *to* you" (you have some responsibility, upstream, for this downstream outcome). This is exactly the message of the self-authoring mind: your thoughts and feelings, for example, don't just happen to you, and other people can't "make" you feel a certain way; rather, you create your thoughts and feelings, including the thoughts and feelings you "make" in response to the things other people do. The "making" of our thoughts and feelings is a mystery to us when we are in the socialized mind, precisely because we do not yet see ourselves as the author of them.

The gradual move from the socialized to the self-authoring mind is the most well-traveled passage in the journey of adult development. Is it any wonder the metaphor of the machine is one of the most pervasive in Bridgewater's conceptual toolkit?

But the move from the socialized to the self-authoring mind is not the only passage. For example, a place like Bridgewater—which puts a premium on relentlessly pursuing the question, "How might I be wrong?"—understandably has as much interest in disturbing the self-reinforcing loops of the self-authoring mind. Can the machine idea be as helpful to this later passage? Absolutely. Whereas the machine metaphor forces the socialized mind to *look at* the result or outcome (the effect) and step back to the level of the bigger system that produced it (the cause), the same idea can lead the self-authoring mind to *look at* (take as object) not only the result but also the machine itself. The machine idea can raise the question of your responsibility, not only for systematically producing the result, but also for producing the machine.

If you are not yet ready to move beyond the self-authoring mind, then perhaps your progress here will be of a more lateral sort (you will stay on the self-authoring plateau but use the opportunity to correct some flaw within the system); this is still a form of progress or development. But if you are ready to climb the next slope, you may use this opportunity to detect limits in the (meta-systemic) nature of your machine creating more generally. You may discover not only a further *implication* of your underlying principle or design—an implication you had been blind to—but also limits to the principle itself (an improvement beyond the system). Ray Dalio is very clear, in the company's principles, that his concept of the machine is ultimately evolutionary, and not only mechanistic. The machine can evolve.

Moving to the Next Plateau

When Decurion says, "The crew runs the business," it is saying to the popcorn attendant, for example, "Don't think of yourself as just making popcorn; you're going to rotate through many roles in the theater." More importantly (because more interiorly), it is saying, "Don't think of yourself as just a popcorn maker; you are a businessperson, part of a group of businesspeople running this theater." If you're working popcorn at a Decurion theater, the tools and materials to make popcorn aren't the only things available to you; you also see all the cost and revenue numbers, all the targets and actuals for your shift. "What do I need with all that?" you might ask.

What is going on here, developmentally? You might well be an adolescent just moving into the socialized mind. You need an educative environment that draws you out of a self-construction oriented mainly to your own concrete needs and short-term ends (completing my shift hassle-free, staying out of trouble, getting paid). Your initial motivation in taking part in any beyond-the-popcorn, bigger-goal activities (such as thinking more generally about the theater operation) might simply be related to that same self-construction ("Doing this other weird stuff is how they roll here; the no-hassle choice is to go along").

But in the same ironic way that Sergio, at a whole different developmental juncture, may initially tell his boss his inconvenient truth more to please his boss than to transcend his people pleasing, the very activity of the concession worker now participating in team activities—having his thoughts and feelings held by others, being let in to other people's thoughts and feelings, coming to be part of something bigger than his own short-term goals and concrete needs—may begin to create new satisfactions, new ways of prizing the self and valuing others, that draws him more fully *into* the socialized mind (the very position that Sergio is leaving). The research shows that these activities and support are well matched to helping adolescents and young adults move into the socialized mind.

Or perhaps our hypothetical popcorn maker is further along in his development. Do the same demands—to lift your head beyond your role, to see yourself as part of a group collectively responsible for a whole operation—have a development-inducing value for someone further along in the developmental journey? We imagine you can answer this one for yourself by now. The same demand that can pull you more fully into the socialized mind (for one set of reasons) can also begin to pull you out of it (for a different set of reasons). To be asked to take your role as an object, to be more identified with the bigger system, to see how all the roles and relationships come under the governance of that bigger system—all this may draw you toward self-authoring.

Or consider Next Jump's boot camp, where you work for a stretch in customer service. The goal is not only to get you closer to the heart of the business or to make sure you put in your dues or share the load. You need to take on what the company calls a "plus-1 project." You need to look at an accepted process and not only fit yourself into it but also stand outside it, critique it, and come up with a proposed improvement. Can you see how this project could be a part of valuable curricula for people at different places in the developmental journey?

Bridgewater puts a premium on getting in sync. Can you see how the actual work of getting in sync, the risks of *not* being in sync, the complications of ensuring one even knows whether one is or isn't in sync, will all differ at each of the stages in development?

Right about now you could be thinking something like this: "Now that you have me thinking about development and developmental differences, I see how so many features of a DDO seem well suited to support the developmental journey. But I haven't thought in these terms before. Maybe if I just think about ordinary companies, or my own place of work, through the same developmental lens, I will find that these places are also filled with developmental provocations and invitations."

That's a good idea—and you should give it a try. We think it will help you see the differences between DDOs and ordinary organizations. Ordinary organizations do not continuously give you critical feedback; they do not constantly ask you to lift your head from your local neighborhood and take a bigger perspective; they do not devote time to teach you to beware of the mere appearance of being in sync when really you are not (and that's why there is so much groupthink in ordinary organizations, as discussed at the start of this chapter).

Running through these glimpses into DDOs is a common thread that distinguishes them from ordinary organizations: DDOs continuously stir things up, troubling the waters; ordinary organizations continuously try to calm things down, instituting repeatable routines. Ordinary organizations don't move you into a new role as soon as you've mastered the old one; instead, they commend you for having mastered it and call you reliable and dependable, appreciating the way you can be counted on now to keep performing the role indefinitely.

An ordinary organization may not even know it is doing it, but, at bottom, it is trying to minimize a certain kind of disturbance. It wants threats to certainty, predictability, routine, control, and connection to be as few as possible so that the work can get done without unnecessary emotional noise and distraction. A DDO, in contrast, strange though it may sound, values disturbances and is designed to preserve them at an optimal level—not overwhelmingly high, but never down to zero.

Does this mean a DDO is a sadistic home for lovers of emotional drama and alarm? After all, who in her right mind would purposely create such a setting, not to mention prefer it? The answer is that such a design is optimal for exactly one thing: developmental transformation. And it is favored by those who regard as precious the opportunity to learn and grow. Recall Nora Dashwood's words: "It was the hardest thing I have ever done. And it has been the most meaningful growth and development I've ever experienced."

A Scientific Approach

This chapter has introduced you to a science to help you understand what we mean by development when we talk about the deliberately developmental organization. We've tried to show you that—whether or not the DDO exemplars know it—they may be pursuing the first genuinely scientific approach to organizational design since Frederick Taylor a century ago.[8]

Taylor's watchword was, of course, *efficiency*.[9] Ours is *development*. Later in this book, we address directly how efficient development may be. For now, we point out that for all the effort in an ordinary organization to keep distracting alarm to a minimum, the single most important feature of ordinary organizational life, from the point of view of a DDO, is that, in the ordinary organization, everyone is doing a second job that no one is paying her for—looking good, staying safe, avoiding vulnerability. How efficient can that be?

Having spent this chapter bringing you into the adult developmental science underneath a DDO's design, we turn next to an exploration of its visible features. What does a culture look like if it so values developing the capabilities of all its people that it seeks to fashion a space where everyone can bring their full, imperfect selves to work every day?

3

A Conceptual Tour of the DDO

Edge, Home, and Groove

We've found it useful to think of the conceptual structure of a DDO in terms of depth, breadth, and height—the depth of its developmental communities (which we call *home*); the breadth of its developmental practices (which we call its *groove*); and the height of its developmental aspirations (which we call its *edge*). By considering all three dimensions at once (and the way each intersects with the other two) the DDO comes into view as a single, dynamic system (see figure 3-1). As you take the conceptual tour in this chapter, you'll see that you've already met concrete instances of each of these dimensions, and you'll meet more examples in the chapters ahead. For now, we acquaint you with what seem to us the more general, conceptual ideas behind each dimension.

This chapter is a substantially revised version of an earlier working paper by Robert Kegan, Lisa Laskow Lahey, Andy Fleming, Matthew L. Miller, and Inna M. Leiter, "What Is a DDO?" www.waytogrowinc.com, 2014.

FIGURE 3-1

The three dimensions of a DDO

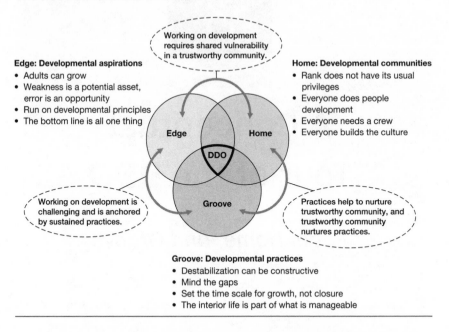

Working on development requires shared vulnerability in a trustworthy community.

Edge: Developmental aspirations
- Adults can grow
- Weakness is a potential asset, error is an opportunity
- Run on developmental principles
- The bottom line is all one thing

Home: Developmental communities
- Rank does not have its usual privileges
- Everyone does people development
- Everyone needs a crew
- Everyone builds the culture

Edge

Home

DDO

Working on development is challenging and is anchored by sustained practices.

Groove

Practices help to nurture trustworthy community, and trustworthy community nurtures practices.

Groove: Developmental practices
- Destabilization can be constructive
- Mind the gaps
- Set the time scale for growth, not closure
- The interior life is part of what is manageable

A deliberately developmental approach to more fully realizing organizational potential is not a matter of only "being better to our people"—providing more generous employee benefits, for example, or supporting so-called work-life balance. It is not about doing something familiar a great deal harder, a great deal longer, or a great deal more. Similarly, an interest in environmental sustainability, contributions to the local community, worker ownership, and other contemporary forms of conscious capitalism are inspiring and commendable, but they do not ensure that a company is doing anything different to develop its people.

A DDO is thus something different from an accelerated version of business as usual and from other admirable emerging departures (many complementary to the DDO). A DDO represents, instead, a rethinking of the very place of people development in organizational life.

What if a company did everything within its power to create the conditions for individuals to overcome their own internal barriers to change, to take stock of and transcend their own blind spots, and to see errors and weaknesses as prime opportunities for personal growth? What would it look like to "do work" in a way that enabled organizations and their employees to be partners in each other's flourishing?

Edge, home, and groove mutually reinforce one another, and together foster a deliberately developmental culture. These dimensions are like the three legs of a stool. Take one of the defining elements of the culture away, and the organization can't sustain being *deliberately developmental*. Imagine trying to maintain a focus on employees taking risks to overcome their personal limitations (edge) *without* the benefit of trustworthy communities (home) and regular practices and routines (groove) to ground the work. Or think of how many organizations have safe and trustworthy communities and catalogs of practices for hiring, onboarding, training, mentoring, and performance management but still lack the fundamental aspiration of keeping employees continually growing at their *developmental* edge. As you next explore the texture of each of the three dimensions of a DDO, we hope you will think of edge, home, and groove as animating qualities that are always interacting, each strengthening and reinforcing the others.

Edge: Developmental Aspiration Oriented to the Growing Edge

The three dimensions comprise twelve features, what we call *discontinuous departures*: departures from familiar, business-as-usual principles, practices, and structures. By "discontinuous" we mean that they are not slight tweaks, adjustments, or reforms to standard practice; rather, they're qualitative departures. Let's look at how these design features combine to create a *new continuity*: a single continuous and immersive focus on people development for every member of the organization.

1. Adults Can Grow

Adults, not just children, can and need to keep growing. This principle can be stated in ten simple words, but it represents a discontinuous departure from the fundamental operation of nearly all organizations in every sector we've explored (including, ironically, education). An organization can sign on to the principle in spirit, value it as nice to have, and even make investments to promote more of it—but this is very different from asking, "From the ground up, have we designed our organization so that it supports the growth of its members—something they, as well as the organization, need in order to thrive?"

Think about your own organization. Is your company designed to support its employees' development as people (and not only their careers)? If we walked up to a random member—a leader, a manager, a support staff member—would she say yes to any of the following questions?

- Does your organization help you identify a personal challenge—meaningful to you and valuable for the company—that you can work on in order to grow?

- Are there others who are aware of this growing edge and who care that you transcend it?

- Are you given support to overcome your limitations? Can you name or describe this support?

- Do you experience yourself actively working on transcending this growing edge daily or at least weekly?

- When you do become a more capable version of yourself, is it recognized, is it celebrated, and—when you're ready—are you given the opportunity to keep growing?

There are organizations that are great at what they do, that are relentless at it. But it turns out there are very few that are great and relentless at people development. Organizations (and management science), for example, talk about "continuous improvement." But it is one thing to be relentless about continuously improving the processes by which work gets done; it is quite another to be relentless about continuously improving the people who do the work.

Hedge fund managers, movie theater operators, and software engineers would probably not be most people's first idea of who might be interested in self-reflection and working on one's weaknesses. But at Bridgewater, Decurion, and Next Jump, respectively, people told us a version of the same thing: "Every day I get up and

I am absolutely clear what I am working on—myself." These are not psychotherapists or priests. They are not New Age professionals working at the Esalen Institute. They are investors, theater managers, techies—and very good ones, by the way, constantly sought after by the leading, conventional competitors in their sector.

As discussed in chapter 2, the idea that adults can grow is hard-wired into the DNA of a DDO. Of course, each of these companies tries to hire the most talented people it can, but the moment it does, it seeks to place them in an environment where every job is a kind of towrope that will pull them—if they will hold on tightly—into the challenge of developing themselves. "I heard all this stuff about personal development," a senior executive at Decurion told us, "and I was very impressed. I just didn't realize they meant *me*, too!" "I knew Bridgewater hired me because of my track record," a well-known investment banker said. "I had developed a pretty good playbook. I assumed I could just spray paint my playbook with the Bridgewater colors and all would be well. Man, was I wrong!"

Recall the Next Jump formula:

Better Me + Better You = Better Us

Next Jump wants the company to grow (Better Us), but its culture continuously says, "The way we're going to be a better company is by your working on yourself, and helping others work on themselves." But the culture does not just say it; it walks its talk. As mentioned earlier, every Next Jumper's compensation is tied 50/50 to performance in revenue (what you contribute to the business) and culture (what you contribute to Better Me and Better You). At Next Jump you can be a revenue hero and still be penalized in compensation if you're not working on personal growth. The highest bonus and salary increases go to those who improve the culture.

Bridgewater's mantra has to do with a relentless pursuit of the truth. This can sound abstract and philosophical—or, worse, dogmatic and cultish—if it suggests that someone, or something, is in secure possession of The Truth. It is neither. Bridgewater's inquiry, "Is this true?" is related to the psychology of people's meaning-making logic discussed in chapter 2. When you're under the influence of a given logic, it may look (and feel and be) *true* that risking the boss's disapproval or screwing up in public is a terrible fate. But exploring the question, "Is this true?" can amount to the very process by which people grow beyond the socialized or self-authoring mind.

Ray Dalio, founder of Bridgewater, identifies the "master dynamic" in human beings as the quest to evolve. Christopher Forman, head of Decurion, talks about human "flourishing." Charlie Kim, founder of Next Jump, talks about becoming a better version of ourselves. Personal evolution, human flourishing, becoming a better person—these are at the center of the culture of each organization.

This is what we mean by a DDO's (and its workers') edge. How central is the developmental aspiration? The three companies had never heard of each other, and yet their cultures have strong underlying similarities. It is no accident that at the root of these similarities we find a fascination with, and devotion to, the possibility of ongoing personal growth.

2. Weakness Is a Potential Asset; Error Is an Opportunity

Anthropologists say they study other cultures, in part, to better understand their own. If you spend a lot of time in DDOs, you cannot help learning, not only about this novel setting, but also about aspects of normal organizational life that often are hiding in plain sight.

As we've said, our key premise is that, in a normal organization, nearly everyone is doing a second job for which no one is paying them. To an extent we're only beginning to appreciate, the prevailing stance of most people at work (even highly accomplished people working in highly respected organizations) is to act so as to preserve or enhance their personal standing, to make sure their stock is not falling and hopefully even is rising.

To manage others' perceptions of us (at the expense of managing the responsibilities and opportunities of our work), we constantly seek to cover up possible weaknesses and promote our greatest assets. If the vulnerable, less-than-perfect, or even less-than-adequate self has any chosen expression in our work life, it is in rare moments, behind closed doors, with official or unofficial trusted advisers who swear to maintain our privacy and confidentiality (see "Life in a DDO: The Value of Weaknesses and Errors"). Any *unchosen* expression of our

Life in a DDO: The Value of Weaknesses and Errors

Near the end of a companywide e-mail whose subject line read, "I constantly fail," Bridgewater leader Ray Dalio challenged the members of his organization to sit with this question: "Do you worry more about how good you are or about how fast you are learning?" At Bridgewater, learning from one's mistakes is a job requirement. The company's culture supports treating errors as opportunities for growth through a variety of tools and practices.

First, every employee is required to record problems and failures in a companywide "issues log," one that requires detailing one's own and others' contributions to mistakes. The logging of errors and problems is applauded and rewarded, but failure to record a mistake in the issues log is viewed as a serious breach of duty. The data collected in the issues log is treated as a resource for collective diagnosis of root causes—both individual and organizational—of failure.

Another reflective practice involves recording one's experience of psychological pain at work. The Pain Button app, mentioned earlier, allows employees to record and share experiences of negative emotions at work—especially times when one's ego defenses are activated by interactions with others. Open sharing of these experiences then triggers follow-up conversations among the parties as they explore the truth of the situation and identify actions individuals might take to address underlying causes. This practice is intended to help individuals work through and actively manage forms of emotional self-protection that can otherwise be barriers to personal growth.

In these and other supportive processes, Bridgewater destigmatizes (and even celebrates) making mistakes. More than that, it treats the ongoing, often painful experience of one's imperfections as valuable data for learning rather than unproductive blame.

vulnerability—demonstrations of our incompetence or inadequacy in a given instance—is a good definition of most people's classic work nightmare, the thing we most dread or least want to happen.

In contrast, what we see at DDOs is a pervasive (and often effective) effort to counter this tendency to hide evidence of weakness. A DDO enables people to uncover and value their growing edge, and experience themselves as still valuable even as they are screwing up—and they can potentially be even more valuable if they can overcome the limitations they are exposing. People's limitations are seen as their growing edge—a company resource, an asset—that should be continuously and publicly engaged. Paradoxically, especially to those of us working outside DDOs, the identification of weakness or lack of experience provides the key to growth, both for the individual and the organization. Recall Bridgewater's formula (Pain + Reflection = Progress). At Decurion, managers try to identify situations that will promote development ("pulls"), where members will find themselves in over their heads, just enough to stimulate them to grow.

At Next Jump, people bring challenging situations into a weekly meeting called the "situational workshop." What goes under the microscope is not the situation but rather the person embroiled in the situation. A typical workshop question might be, "What are you learning about yourself in having this problem—or yet another instance of this problem that we are now coming to see is a pattern or theme?" The conversation is not carried out in a "gotcha" spirit but in the spirit of bringing water, sunlight, and nutrients to a growing plant, which, like any growing thing, needs a little attention at regular intervals.

A DDO is all about the difference between what social psychologist Carol Dweck calls the "fixed" mind-set and the "growth" mind-set. No matter how aligned a person feels intellectually with the spirit of a DDO, most successful people have some attachment to the fixed mind-set (including every author of this book)—the idea that our success is a function of some innate quality or talent we possess, rather than a function of one's determined effort in the face of expected stumbles.[1] Ambitious people with this mind-set may indeed want to work to get the most out of this fixed quality; they see their "development," then, as the fuller expression of their God-given abilities, and they expect the culture of a DDO to spur them to step up in this way. They are in for a surprise. No real growth occurs without first experiencing some limitation at one's core. Until you begin to question even your fixed, taken-for-granted talents, you have not fully derived the benefits of being in a DDO.

Obviously, regularly being this vulnerable is not always comfortable. One of the most common experiences we have had in talking with people about the DDO is that the ideas bring up anxieties, which in turn can interfere with our listeners' thinking about these ideas. ("What is this? A revival of Maoist self-criticism?") They get triggered, they stop listening, and they start doing what all of us do when we're triggered: they take care of themselves by fighting or fleeing.

People at Decurion, Bridgewater, and Next Jump say a similar thing about life in this non-normal organization: "It's not always fun; it can even be very painful to work here—and it's the most exhilarating place I have ever worked, and I would never consider working anywhere else!" People also acknowledge, in different DDOs, that the environment is not for everyone, and it's not unusual (or alarming) to have higher-than-usual turnover during the first twelve to eighteen months.

3. Run on Developmental Principles

It may seem strange to say, but most organizations—even well-functioning, admired organizations—are not actually run on a set of principles, known throughout the organization and visible to even a casual observer, that drive the daily practice of everyone's work. Yes, most organizations have mission statements. They have purposes. They have goals. They have procedures. They have employee manuals. They may also have mottos or mantras that reflect principles—"the client comes first"; "something only we can do"; "progress is our most important product." But without a pervasive ecology—structures, practices, tools, and shared language that allow the organization to embody and orient to these values—they become slogans rather than drivers of the culture.

It is rare enough for an organization to be run by a set of *any* principles, but a DDO is run by a *particular* set of principles—namely, developmental ones. Researcher Karl Weick's "high-reliability organizations" (such as combat units, air traffic controllers, and surgical teams) can be said to be tight cultures run by a set of principles related to survival—one's own or that of others.[2] Understandably, when error can lead to death, that prospect guides the creation of organizational structures that support continuously shared practices that promote survival. In contrast, a DDO's principles are rooted, not in the possibility of mortal danger but in the possibility of new life, of emergence, new capability, and evolution at the individual and collective level—in short, guided by the possibility of development.

In a DDO, the North Star of the organization is a set of deeply held principles that animate daily decisions. These principles, although a unique reflection of the organization, share a fundamental belief in the power of individual growth for members.

Next Jump, Decurion, and Bridgewater can produce written documents stating their principles, but by itself this is not a discontinuous departure from life in other kinds of organizations. Instead, what is distinctive is that shared principles actively shape conduct and decisions from the smallest to the most strategic.

Decurion describes its purpose as "provid[ing] places for people to flourish." The series of axioms is one visible expression of Decurion's principles: that work is meaningful; that people are not only means but also ends in themselves; that individuals and communities naturally develop; and that pursuing human development and pursuing profitability are one thing. When we see a crew member in one of Decurion's ArcLight cinemas beginning his work day aligning his tasks with his deeper purposes as a person, we are seeing Decurion's principles in action.

Bridgewater's principles are described in an evolving document that is continually referred to and interpreted by members.[3] These principles commit the company to a continuing search for what is true, even when the truth can be personally difficult to accept, and for evolution and improvement as fundamental forces for good in people's lives and in the world. In the same spirit, the principles call for a culture in which it is "OK to make mistakes but unacceptable not to identify, analyze, and learn from them." Earlier we saw a Bridgewater manager debriefing a disappointing outcome—not only to clarify new agreements about handling such situations in the future but also to explore openly with a key player how his actions illuminated a self-protective distortion in his thinking, one that is likely to lead him to repeat the error unless corrected. This experience embodies the Bridgewater principles. It is a discontinuous departure that, quite simply, principles shape the way work is done, by everyone, every day.

By contrast, consider the role of the mission in most organizations. Great companies seek to align common efforts to advance a mission and live out shared values. Profitability and long-term growth depend on it.

But if you ask people in these typical organizations, "By what set of shared principles do you carry out your mission?" the answer might be hard to come by or focused on technical "best practices" for the industry. Indeed, in cultures that focus least on development, principles identified might even be principles in the negative: "Don't let them see you sweat," "Do anything to avoid a bad quarterly result," or worse.

DDOs run on affirmative principles—principles its members choose to be guided by and that they're asked to apply and reflect on from the moment they consider working for the organization. In a strongly woven developmental culture, principles are discussed, debated, applied, revised, and posted; in short, they're ever-present and play an active role in daily life.

Think about your own organization or others you know. Are there any definable principles that regulate how work is carried out? Note that "the maximization of profit" is not in itself a principle. It is a goal or an outcome (and an understandable one). How we should regulate our conduct, what ongoing structures and practices we should build, preserve, and refresh so that we can maximize profit—these are principles. Do they exist in your organization?

Interestingly, it's taken for granted that we will live and work in organizations that are not continuously guided by their principles, and that is what leads some people, when they get a good look at a DDO, to think they're looking at a cult. DDOs are not cults. Their principles are not about mind control. As organizations, they expand, rather than contract, individual freedom and possibilities for growth. They encourage—even obligate—dissent if you disagree, rather than suppress it. We're so unaccustomed to seeing routines and practices that are clearly guided by principles that we're more inclined to question the wholesomeness of a DDO than to question the default modes of normal organizational life.

4. The Bottom Line Is All One Thing

We have seen the leaders of all three DDOs asked an identical question: "What do you do when you have to choose between the profit motive and the development motive?" And we've seen them give identical answers: "You are presuming a tension we don't experience. We don't think about it like that."

A for-profit DDO is as interested in profit as any other for-profit organization, but in a different way (see "Life in a DDO: Not One or the Other but Both"). It does not subordinate profitability to some supposedly more exalted goal such as human development. It does not consider profitability a merely necessary means to the more-valued end of sustaining a place for people to grow. It is not a question of one motive having priority over the other, nor even of their being equally important, like a "double bottom line."

In a DDO, the goals of profitability and fostering development are not a both/and, and they are not an either/or. Rather, a DDO looks at the way bold institutional aspirations, on the one hand (such as high profitability or breaking the mold in one's sector), and further-developed human capabilities, on the other, are part of a single whole. Each depends on the other. There is as much interest in how the profit motive is a spur to development as there is in how development is a spur to profit. We see that in Next Jump's evaluating every employee 50/50 on contributions to revenue and to the developmental culture. And at Decurion, as Forman told us, "For us, pursuing profitability and human development emerges as one thing. We do not see a trade-off, and the moment we consider sacrificing one for the other, we recognize that we have lost both."

This is how you maintain a focus on the developmental aspiration. This is how you keep the edge from becoming dull.

Life in a DDO: Not One or the Other but Both

In an ordinary company, the sun rises and sets on the achievement of periodic targets. "Did we make our numbers this quarter?" "Does our year-on-year growth match our projections?" "Have we reduced [cost, time to market, employee turnover, production stop-outs] by X percent?"

DDOs do not ignore the numbers, and they do not eschew targets. When we were last at Decurion, people in the theater business made continuous reference to specific strategies for increasing net profit. Next Jump has a relentless focus on traffic and conversion into e-commerce sales. Bridgewater obviously wants the returns on its funds to outperform the market.

But in a DDO, outcome achievement is not the ultimate measure of success. "Given all the extraneous factors that go into whether a project or business succeeds in the traditional sense," Decurion president Christopher Forman says, "there is no way we can be said to control or cause the outcome. The only thing we can come close to controlling is our own actions." Forman acknowledges that most people see success as a matter of achieving a certain outcome. "But we think there is a deeper level of success associated with how one conducts oneself in the face of the challenges life presents. Does one act in accordance with one's own highest values?" Referring to Victor Frankl, author of *Man's Search for Meaning*, Forman asks, "Did we create or do something significant? Did we care for another person? Did we face difficult circumstances with courage?"

Bridgewater's Ray Dalio makes the identical point in his own idiom when he distinguishes between a poor outcome and a mistake. "If we relentlessly pursued the truth," he says, "especially those truths about ourselves and the world that are most uncomfortable and least convenient—if we did our best to uncover what is—and the outcome is still not to our liking, we didn't necessarily make a mistake. We are not living in a world of certainties and 100 percent probabilities. We stayed true to our process. If we ignore what is, we have, without any doubt, made a mistake—whether we

(continued)

(continued)

got the money or not." You can hear how process integrity trumps outcome achievement if you listen, as we did, to Dalio talking to his people about his feelings after the fund results came in on a particularly sensational year: "I worry about us more after a year like this, because we can delude ourselves by confusing big returns with doing a good job relentlessly pursuing our process."

Next Jump executives state that revenue is the fuel that funds their culture, and not only the other way around. "The pursuit of revenue also serves as the ultimate stressor," says CEO Charlie Kim, "the practice ground for growth."

Process integrity trumps outcome achievement, but the latter is still a high-ranking card in the deck. Forman, Dalio, and Kim care about their numbers. You can't have a place where people can flourish or evolve or become a Better Me if there isn't a flow of revenue to pay people's salaries and the electric bill. But these decision makers are asking a new question: "Which will be the master?" In a DDO the sun rises and sets on a different kind of day.

The Groove: Developmental Practices and Tools

DDOs live out their developmental principles through an immersive and seamless set of practices, which we call its groove. These practices include how meetings are structured, how employee performance is monitored and discussed, and how people talk to one another about their work and the challenges they face personally and in advancing the interests of the company.

These practices represent another set of discontinuous departures from the routines, language, and structures of most organizations. And these practices are natural extensions of, and deeply aligned with, growth-based principles. They are the practical means by which people, at every level, engage their growing edge. We see four underlying dimensions to the groove in the DDOs we studied.

5. Destabilization Can Be Constructive

Because DDOs regard members' inadequacies or incompetencies as resources, they actively promote these experiences. At all three companies, if you can perform all your responsibilities to a high level, you're no longer in the right job. (And if you prefer to stay in this job, having mastered it, you're seen as someone who prefers to coast, and not at the right company.) At Decurion, people regularly say, "As soon as something is working perfectly, it's time to blow it up and move to the next level."

Elise, who has held several positions at Next Jump, told us she felt overwhelmed when she was first made the assistant to the CEO. Then she gained a lot of satisfaction when she grew into the role well enough to be promoted to a new role in public relations—only to find herself overwhelmed again. When we talked to her, she was new enough in this position—and self-aware and open enough—to concede she was experiencing a lot of mixed feelings: "Of course, it's exciting to have this bigger job, but, if I'm honest, there is a big part of me that's feeling, 'It took me this long to master the old job, and now I have got to wrestle with all those feelings of inadequacy and uncertainty all over again? Who wants to do that?'"

At Bridgewater a lot of attention is paid, as in any organization, to finding the right fit between people and their current roles (finding the "click," they call it), but "good fit" doesn't mean, as it likely does in most organizations, "She can do the job as described." It's more likely to mean, "She will run into plenty of useful trouble; she will know how to use her trouble to learn and grow from it; she will draw on the resources of a remarkably supportive community to help her."

Talk about a discontinuous departure! This is nearly the opposite of business as usual in most organizations, where the conservative side of human nature tends to conspire with the conservative side of human organizations: the employee seeks to reduce the complexity of the work by establishing and mastering its routines; and the organization "supports" employees by finding ways to keep them happy in those routines for as long as possible.

DDOs practice "constructive destabilization." Both words are crucial (see "Life in a DDO: Learning from Destabilization"). If you

Life in a DDO: Learning from Destabilization

At Decurion, members expect to be regularly, but manageably, in over their heads. Using a complementary set of practices, the organization continually matches individuals and groups to developmental opportunities.

In ArcLight cinemas, for example, managers use data about individual growth ("energy maps") to identify each week's ideal job assignments for individuals—assignments meant to maximize both the growth of each crew member (creating a developmental pull for the employee) and the business needs of the operation. As one theater manager explained, "We talk about not just where to place people, but most importantly—why." This practice is supported by Decurion's commitment not to build person-dependent systems. In other words, no job relies on or is completely identified with one person. This allows for movement among roles to create conditions for learning.

Decurion leaders also are suspicious when people profess their expertise, which can lead to overidentification of a person with a narrow role. Job rotation gives the company a powerful way to create development pulls for individual growth. At Decurion, just when someone is comfortable with a work process, he can expect to move on to a new challenge.

were to talk about company culture to people in these three companies and then create a Wordle "word cloud" display of the speech, three large words would be *trust, pain,* and *care.* Feeling regularly destabilized is more the rule than the exception in the junior as well as senior ranks, but not shamefully (at least not for long), not depressively, and not masochistically. Why not? We think it has everything to do with people's experience of the intent of a culture. The process of getting to the root cause of one's actions at Bridgewater may be relentless, but, practiced properly, there is nothing hostile or aggressive about it. To be sure, one principle held by the organization frames the experience of pain as normal and expected, creating opportunity for growth: Pain + Reflection = Progress.

People in all three organizations talk about times of being in pain but in the same breath talk about feeling deep and genuine care, and a valuable sense of community in the same experiences that cause them the pain. As important, perhaps, is their sense of what the pain leads to—their own fuller self-realization. They talk about the difference between destructive pain and "labor pains," with the latter—however excruciating—leading to new life. Remember Brené Brown's words in chapter 1, here paraphrased: vulnerability can be about feelings of shame and unworthiness and disconnection, but it can also be the beginning of joy and creativity. The key variable is whether our vulnerability is well held, whether we continue to feel respected, worthy, and included, even at our worst. (This feeling is at the heart of what we mean by home, which we will come to a bit later.)

6. Mind the Gaps

In a typical organization, as we have said, individuals expend enormous energy protecting themselves. People hide parts of themselves, avoid conflict, unwittingly sabotage change efforts, and subtly enforce a separation between "the me at work" and the "real me."

In a never-ending quest to keep ourselves safe in the workplace, we allow gaps to form between ourselves and others, between plans and actions, and even between parts of ourselves. Rather than remain aligned around a shared vision for the execution of an important project, for example, we may allow each participant to go his own way. We may quietly hope to deliver a halfhearted effort and not be called on it, and in a private chat we may say one thing about how a colleague is managing the effort, and something very different in a larger meeting. Gaps in organizations, in this sense, are most often defined by the conversations we're not having, the things we're not discussing, the synchronicities we're not achieving, and the work that, because of some self-protective fear, we're avoiding. Gaps may arise between:

- What we do and what we say

- What we feel and what we say

- What we say at the water cooler and what we say in the meeting

- How we assess someone's performance at the time and how we later provide feedback

- What we know about the organization's principles and how we apply them

- What we know to be the organization's deepest purposes and how we actually operate at every level (Decurion's Bryan Ungard: "We want to see our deepest purpose—'flourishing,' we call it—reflected in every aspect of our day-to-day operations, whether we are talking about something as simple as tearing theater tickets, or as complex as formulating a long-range business strategy.")

In a DDO, a constant effort to close these gaps is an essential part of day-to-day practice, knitting people together in their work even as the fabric is acknowledged to need continuous work. In a way that's qualitatively different from typical forms of managerial coordination and project management, members of a DDO engage in continuous efforts—in nearly every setting and form of communication—to achieve interpersonal and cognitive immediacy (rather than hide themselves or their thinking to stay safe).

DDOs take a more fundamental approach to keeping collective work on track than merely setting goals and monitoring progress toward them, even if the DDO approach may cause individuals discomfort. One example is Decurion's fishbowl exercise, as mentioned in chapter 1. Recall, too, that Bridgewater places a high value on getting in sync, its way of being continuously aware of the emergence of gaps and the need for tools and practices to close them. Next Jumpers, for their part, meet every day with a "talking partner" to conduct an "unloading" exercise, which they see as a Western version of a contemplative practice. The result is a closing of gaps not only between colleagues but also within oneself. Decurion's practice of a deep form of checking in at the start of each meeting ensures that no one has to preserve a gap between the "work me" and the "real me" (see "Life in a DDO: Checking In").

DDO leaders understand that we make the greatest progress on the toughest business issues if we can overcome ways of thinking

Life in a DDO: Checking In

In a DDO like Decurion, every day provides multiple opportunities for workers to connect their larger lives to their day-to-day work, and vice versa. In the ArcLight cinemas, the check-ins at each meeting let people focus on reconnecting with one another and voluntarily sharing anything they choose. Check-ins are a critical way of closing gaps, reducing disconnection, and preventing people from operating on autopilot or forgetting that at Decurion people are ends rather than means.

As one Decurion leader told us, "Full humanity is not just welcome but required here. This is a space to allow individuals to become fully present." Similarly, check-outs help maintain authentic connections among members. As another leader explained, "When conversations become difficult, we check in with each other's humanity."

These check-ins and check-outs are part of a range of practices workers use for engaging authentically with one another. In the end, ArcLight members experience over time that even "hot" conversations with high stakes for individuals and the company take place in a context that combines support with authenticity.

and acting that serve only to protect us from conflict and embarrassment. Leaders create the conditions, conversational routines, and leadership support for their members to gain immediate access to the core business issues, and to work through the understandable pain that can arise from breaking silences, confronting one's weaknesses directly, or openly experiencing interpersonal disagreement.

In another paradox, the genuine business issues become more discussable only after the organization develops ways of fluently working through the nonbusiness issues that keep individuals from doing their best work. Gaps are part of natural human defensive routines, and so DDOs seek to create the conditions for safely working through these gaps in ways that prioritize speaking the truth about what is going on in a setting of trust—one that assumes the continued growth and good intentions of all involved.

To gain immediate and unmediated access to resolving the business issues at stake, DDOs create special discussion formats that allow members to be authentic in talking about the personal dimensions of business issues, helping people discuss aspects of working life that are not, in other organizations, discussable. These forums—whether a group probing of one's reasoning at Bridgewater, a fishbowl conversation at Decurion, or a situational workshop at Next Jump—are shared crucibles for individual and group development. In these settings, there is no penalty for participating honestly and openly, only for failing to participate authentically. Participants celebrate the identification of gaps to be closed and of new ways of working together. (You will learn more about each company's specific practices in chapter 4.)

In this way, DDOs create a community of continual practice that, over time, earns the trust of its members. For workers, the continual practice of risking vulnerability becomes less risky and is seen as worthwhile as they witness over time that despite the exposure of conflict, revelation to one's colleagues of a growing edge, or discussion of some other formerly undiscussable matter, everyone will be OK in the end. In other words, members come to trust the organization as an ongoing engine for growth.

In the end, one of a DDO's most surprising and hopeful accomplishments may be converting its members' default "unimaginably bad" result of being vulnerable ("If I risk showing my weaknesses, it will be horrible") into a sense of trust in a longer-term developmental process ("If I risk showing my weaknesses, I'll probably learn something, and I will be okay in the end"). The result is the regular, often continuous closing of the single biggest gap that exists in normal organizational life: the gap between who we are at work and who we really are.

In all three organizations, people talk about the sheer relief of not living a divided life, of bringing their full humanity to work. When people outside a DDO try to calculate the cost they imagine they would pay working in a DDO ("always being on edge," "people seeing my weaknesses"), they are not recognizing the costs we pay without thinking, every day, by not fully being ourselves at work.

7. Set the Time Scale for Growth, Not Closure

When people first see or hear about a DDO, a common first reaction is, "I can't believe the time they devote to the people processes," usually in a tone that suggests something like, "This is crazy! How can you do this and get anything else done?" But Decurion, Bridgewater, and Next Jump are not only successful incubators of adult development; they are very successful companies by conventional business benchmarks. (Chapter 5 is devoted to exploring the strictly business value of a DDO.) Clearly they get things done, and very well. Nevertheless, these first impressions point to something important: it is true that DDOs have a discontinuously different concept of the value of time.

You can understand the difference through the Bridgewater distinction between first- and second-order consequences. The culture warns that we tend to conflate these. We may not like to exercise, for example, because the first-order consequence is discomfort or lost time; but the second-order consequence is better health and more energy. If our fundamental goal is greater vitality (rather than minimizing discomfort), regular exercise is a good choice, even granting it can be uncomfortable and takes time.

Conventional organizations may analyze problems and may take pride in their efficiency, their ability to get to a new plan and agreement in short order. DDOs might suggest these organizations total the "efficient" meetings they hold and consider whether the reason they have so many is that they did not, in the first place, identify the personal and group limitations that create recurring versions of the same problem. Efficiency and effectiveness are two different things. In a DDO, what looks inefficient may be highly effective. By addressing the personal and group root causes (in Bridgewater's terms), DDOs invest time learning and growing now for everyone in order to create the conditions for even greater success in the future.

The simplest way to consider how DDOs can spend so much time on things ordinary organizations don't have time for is this: if, in the ordinary organization, we are all doing a second job for which no one is paying us (covering our weaknesses, managing others' good impressions), imagine the time that's freed up if half of us spend half as much time doing the second job. Now imagine the time that is freed up if *all* of us quit the second job entirely.

8. The Interior Life Is Part of What Is Manageable

In the ordinary organization, the things that are valued are those that are tangible and outwardly visible. It's no surprise, then, that leaders direct their attention to those things. Understandably, *operations* refers exclusively to external behaviors and visible processes on behalf of collective and individual key performance indicators, deliverables, and goals, serving external strategies. In contrast, for a DDO, interior operations—internal behaviors, patterns of thinking, and psychological strategies (especially those for managing difficult emotions)—are no less real for being intangible or invisible.

Admitting the interior to the world of what is manageable does not mean that leadership aspires to a form of intrusive mind control or psychotherapy. Rather, it means that the culture as a whole, and each individual within it, places inner experience in-bounds rather than out-of-bounds in the life of work: planning, strategizing, operations, execution, performance enhancement, process improvement—all these business functions are carried out by people who come to them with their whole selves. DDOs explicitly uncover and overturn the customary pretense that work is public (i.e., external), the personal is private (i.e., internal), and so the personal should not be part of work.

As we say in chapter 1, everyone who has ever worked anywhere knows that work is intensely personal. We all bring our whole selves to work every day. In ordinary organizations, this is regarded as an inconvenient truth to be ignored, and executives try to "manage around" the inevitable manifestations of the internal person. But the expression of our humanity comes out in all the nonwork preserves we savor "to keep us sane"—water-cooler conversation, lunch breaks, stolen moments on the phone or texting friends, schmoozing in the doorway or with the person at the next desk. It's different in a DDO, where routine practices openly encourage, and seek to make regular room for, the personal and the interior, on behalf of explicitly welcoming the whole person into work every day.

Bridgewater's notion of getting in sync, for example, speaks to the need not only to have all the stakeholders sign off on a given plan of action, but also for each to understand how the plan aligns with, and implicates, interior passions and proclivities (including proclivities that could derail the initiative). Second, no debrief of less-than-satisfactory outcomes is complete if it deals only with what went wrong externally, and what, externally, should be done next time. Instead, a Bridgewater debrief gets to the interior world: What can you learn from the choices you made about the way you work psychologically?

Third, given Bridgewater's central focus on overcoming our tendencies to distort reality (which is what pursuing "what is true?" amounts to in practice), one of its universal practices is to help people better understand their own version of those automatic, reflexive patterns of self-protection that can lead any of us to develop blind spots. In Bridgewater parlance, "probing" to "touch the nerve" is not undertaken to make someone uncomfortable. Rather, it's done to show an early-career hire, for example, how his interior strategies to protect himself from being displeasing to his boss (or to show a senior hire how her interior efforts to preserve her prior professional stature) can systematically lead us to distort reality.

You've read that every person at Next Jump, from the newest hire from Georgia Tech to the CEO, can easily self-identify as tilting in the direction of arrogance or insecurity. In most cases, a talking partner pair consists of one of each. Each person takes a turn, and a turn begins with venting, which seeks to answer the question, "What is going on inside that may have an effect on what will happen outside?"

Done in pairs, the talking partner practice is identical in spirit to the Decurion teamwide check-in at the beginning of meetings. When the talking partners vent, no topic or feeling is out-of-bounds, whether or not it has anything directly to do with work. From venting, the talk turns to the day ahead. "What will be most challenging, rewarding, significant, or meaningful?" And especially, "What opportunities will there be to practice my backhand (practice overcoming my difficulty)?" For example, if I lean insecure, I may have difficulty speaking up; if I lean arrogant, my backhand may be that I'm not open to contrary views. What Next Jump calls practicing one's backhand is a form of managing the interior.

A DDO's groove, its set of practices, permits individuals to work on their growing edge. But none of this can happen in the absence of a special kind of community, a topic we turn to next.

Home: Developmental Communities to Provoke and Hold Vulnerability

One of the most striking lessons from a DDO is the central role played by the community—what we call its home—in individual development. The three DDOs we observed understand that growth can happen only through membership in workplace communities where people are deeply valued as individual human beings, constantly held accountable, and engaged in real and sustained dialogue. DDOs evidence several discontinuous departures from typical organizations in the way they nurture strong forms of community and the way these communities serve as vehicles for enacting and negotiating the developmental edge and groove of the organization.

9. Rank Does Not Have Its Usual Privileges

In most organizations, the higher you climb, the more you are deferred to, and the less you are criticized to your face. Fewer people have the right to take you on, and more layers of interference or insulation divide you from those in the lower ranks. Rank hath its privileges.

Bridgewater, Decurion, and Next Jump are not flat organizations. They do have hierarchies. People report to other people. But—and this is the discontinuous departure—higher rank gives you no free pass on the merits of your ideas, freedom from the disagreement or friendly advice of those in lower ranks, or immunity from the requirement to keep growing and changing to serve your needs and those of the business (see "Life in a DDO: Rank Doesn't Give You a Pass").

If you would find it impertinent or offensive for people many years and ranks your junior to tell you to your face, in front of colleagues, that they do not agree with the way you're carrying out a particular responsibility, or to suggest, as you embark on an activity, that you might do well to watch out for your tendency to dominate or get

Life in a DDO: Rank Doesn't Give You a Pass

I had a uniquely Bridgewater moment when I had been here about a month. I was talking to somebody in the organization—he was probably about twenty-five years old—and I was interviewing him about some subject, and when I finished interviewing him, he said, "Can I ask you something?"

I said, "Sure," and he said, "I heard you say something in a meeting a couple weeks ago that didn't make any sense to me. It seemed illogical. Can I ask you why you said that?"

And my initial reaction was, "Wh—what? You, kid, are asking me that question?" And then I realized, I'm at Bridgewater. That is something that would not happen anywhere else. I mean, I was the deputy attorney general of the United States, I was the general counsel of a huge, huge company. No twenty-five-year-old is gonna ask me a question about my logic. That's what makes this place so great. Because my logic is often flawed. But no one's gonna tell you that, at the other places I've worked. Here they're gonna tell you that. It's not an act of courage—right?—it's an obligation. We hire him, he promises to ask those questions . . .

We have a term here called "probing"—that's what we mean by questioning each other; and I have been probed, in this strange field trip of a life that I've had, in a lot of different places. I've testified in court, I have briefed the president of the United States repeatedly, I've argued in front of the United States Supreme Court, and I've been probed at Bridgewater, and Bridgewater is by far the hardest . . . If you say something stupid to the president of the United States, he may backhand you and say, "That's a dumb answer," but he doesn't want to know [as people do at Bridgewater], "Why did you say that? And what does that tell me about the way in which you're approaching your work, and what does it tell me about you?" He's never gonna ask that . . . and then the vector of questionings, right? The angle from which questions will come. The Supreme Court is limited to the case, right? They're not gonna ask you about something else. At Bridgewater, we're gonna ask you about anything we

(continued)

(continued)

want to ask you about. You know, "Why did you think this way?" "Okay, why have you been that way in other cases? What are other cases you've been involved in?"

So you combine the intelligence, the depth, and the almost 360 vector of questioning. There is no more demanding, probing, questioning environment in the world than Bridgewater. And I don't say that to be critical, although sometimes I felt my head spinning when people were questioning me.

—James Comey, former Bridgewater employee,
  currently director of the FBI

too involved in the details, then you might find yourself regularly offended in a DDO. In these organizations, a meritocracy of ideas is the ideal. Titles are viewed as unimportant, and professions of expertise are seen as mild power plays that get in the way of truly sharing ideas (creating yet another potential gap among members of the community, one that may ultimately get in the way of good business results by stifling opportunities for learning).

Ordinary organizations tend to protect their senior members from ongoing challenge. They take each other to task only rarely, for extreme violations that put the organization at risk, as if senior leaders are completely grown, finished products, and the only necessary accountability is to punish wrongdoing. DDOs recognize that leadership's tendency to use its power to design and sustain structures that protect itself from challenge sets a limit on the organization's ability to exceed itself.

10. *Everyone Does People Development*

In most forward-thinking organizations, human resources (HR) has a mandate that goes beyond technical attention to employment particulars to include support for the ongoing development of the organization's employees. The human-capital, talent-development, or people-development function in such organizations becomes the go-to place for learning more about how you tick, how that shows up as a set of work strengths and limitations, and where you might access resources—learning programs, coaching, mentors—that could help you overcome your limitations.

The discontinuous departure in a DDO is that people development is everyone's responsibility. In most organizations when something is everyone's responsibility, it means that no one is doing it, and it isn't getting done; but in a DDO, it is everyone's responsibility, and it's getting done every day.

This seamlessness between the support for the development of people and the business of the business (for Bridgewater, the managing of hedge funds; for Decurion, the management of movie theaters, senior living facilities, and real estate properties; for Next Jump, the management of a growing set of e-commerce relationships) is captured in the Decurion phrase "nothing extra." People development is not a separate activity, nor an additive to the business engine. It is an essential and integrated component of the business engine (see "Life in a DDO: Development Is Everyone's Job").

The shared responsibility for development was captured in our first visit to Bridgewater in the first five minutes of a meeting with several investment strategists. Our team had been interviewing management committee members, who talked easily and knowledgeably about the culture. The meeting with investment team members was billed as an opportunity to hear about the technical work that goes into creating and managing a hedge fund.

We were going to meet with several men who had spent their lives in banking, and we expected to hear about banking. In our two-minute introduction we said something like, "It will be good to hear what you do, and then at some point we will also want to talk with you about how you experience the culture, the effect it has had on you personally." In the first few minutes of their speaking, it became clear that this distinction was meaningless. It was simply not possible for them to talk with us about their core business activities independent of the culture.

Life in a DDO: Development Is Everyone's Job

At each of our DDO sites, professional development is not something one does away from the office. The senior leaders are themselves the teachers in work-integrated learning that uses, as content, individual and group challenges in the life of the business.

At Next Jump, the company's leaders are the chief coaches. The work at Personal Leadership Boot Camp is led not by a separate training team but by the company's cofounders. Boot camp gives new employees insight into the limitations that may hold them back and identifies the areas they most need to practice to develop their weaknesses.

In regular situational workshops, Next Jumpers present live workplace dilemmas of decision making to a workshop leader, who in turn poses questions and helps expand the range of options for diagnosis and action. Workshop leaders are actively developed by the company. All the senior managers are workshop leaders, but anyone in the company can earn the honor of being a sounding board and coach for colleagues.

At Decurion, companywide seminars on self-management are facilitated by senior leaders. Through these seminars, members explore their individual capabilities, areas for growth, and defensive routines that shape behavior. Discussions and exercises draw on the actual work dilemmas and projects that members are living, treating them as the most valuable resources available for learning (using "the operations as curriculum," in Decurion's phrase). For company executives, serving as seminar facilitators is an essential responsibility. One Decurion leader explained that his colleagues thought he wasn't yet experienced enough at the practice of self-reflection, and so, in a move typical of this DDO, he was asked to take over leadership of the seminar.

At Bridgewater, too, senior leaders are the chief people developers. Time and again, employees describe senior leaders spending many hours in candid dialogue, coaching junior employees. Members of the management committee lead companywide learning experiences on applying the principles and values of Bridgewater. Executives are also curators of an evolving curriculum of video-based and text stories of individual learning (called "tidbits"), which are shared and discussed as case studies across the company. At any time, routine business discussions can shift into a classroom-like form of dialogue. It is common to pause for a "step-back moment" in the middle of a meeting to take stock of errors, diagnose their root causes in an individual's behavior and thinking, and identify things people can do to learn from those errors—potentially casting a developmental spotlight on any meeting. Finally, every manager is expected to coach her direct reports, but everyone in the organization is also part of the coaching team. Daily reflections are sent by employees to their supervisors, and these reflections are also available to everyone in the company, making it possible for everyone to appreciate the developmental challenges and emerging insights of individual colleagues.

They did talk to us about investing—for example, how they had been working on a study having to do with an aspect of how banks extend credit. But simultaneously, they told us how the critique they received of their first draft of the study led to uncovering some of their own personal limitations. They spoke of experiences of senior leaders probing their thinking process that were painful and productive at the same time, and that ultimately transformed not only their analysis, but themselves. Although we had sought to discuss the business of investing, we discovered that the role of personal growth was an essential part of even the most technical aspects of finance. We did not expect an investor to tell us, "I get up every morning and I know what I am working on—myself."

The business of the business—at all the DDOs—is as much one's own development as running hedge funds, movie theaters, or e-commerce. A Better Me and a Better You, in Next Jump parlance, leads to a Better Us.

11. Everyone Needs a Crew

If people must be willing to be vulnerable in order to grow, they also need a community that will support them in—and through—their vulnerability. In a DDO everyone (from entry level to CEO) has a "crew": an ongoing group that can be counted on to be an instrument of your vulnerability—calling you on your own blind spots and reactivity—and also to support your growth as a result of your vulnerability.

Consider how this arrangement dramatically departs from business as usual in even the most supportive and productive of work teams. A good team in a conventional company not only produces high-quality work in a timely way (which, of course, a good DDO team also must do) but also offers moral support; you feel you can trust and talk with your team members about personal things that relate to work, and life beyond work. But notice that this personal dimension is about supporting people to *cope* with the bumps and stresses of the job and perhaps the way private life stresses may interfere with the job.

Coping is essentially about maintaining yourself in the face of potentially destabilizing forces. But development requires a willingness to surrender a familiar equilibrium for what will eventually be a new, more adaptive one. In the meantime, the path can be rocky. In the DDOs, people regularly talked to us about times when they feel "ill equipped," "out on a rope without a net," "beyond my competencies," "repeatedly ineffective with no guarantees I would get it." (Keep in mind that these people included leaders who were extremely capable, with work histories in other companies marked by extraordinary success.) But a team that tries to support you by reducing destabilization, to help you restore the old equilibrium—business as usual in the best of teams—would, in a DDO, be seen as doing you no service at all. This is yet another discontinuous departure from established practice.

When we talk with others outside a DDO about the idea of the DDO, a common response is, "You would have to have an incredibly trustworthy environment for any of this to work." And this is true. People often realize, in looking at their own reaction to the thought of working in a DDO, that they're already assuming that no workplace could be sufficiently trustworthy, and that explains their negative or skeptical reaction: "If I could really believe my vulnerability would not be used against me, of course, I would love to work in a place like this." You have heard Bridgewater's formula, Pain + Reflection = Progress, but a more accurate rendering of that formula is probably something more like, Pain + Reflection (in a highly trustworthy environment) = Progress.

12. *Everyone Builds the Culture*

Like all companies, each DDO has its own distinctive culture—among other things, a set of routines and practices for getting work done, a unique language, and shared deep assumptions about how the world works, how problems can get solved, and what is valued.[4] In many companies, employees receive recognition for living the values of the culture through their attitudes and standards, ways of behaving, and interactions with others. In a DDO, individual alignment with the best of the organization's culture is also essential—but it is not sufficient.

Moreover, all employees in a DDO are expected to contribute to the shaping of the culture, to step forward at any time to improve how the organization does its work. From the entry-level analyst to the CEO, everyone is expected both to embody the culture and to strengthen it by participating continuously and collectively in the redesign of structures and routines. Bridgewater CEO Greg Jensen says, "We have a set of principles, but we do not want people to merely follow them. We want people to engage them, wrestle with them. Follow them if they make sense. But most importantly, if they do not make sense, we want people to fight like hell to get them changed, show us why they don't make sense."

DDOs seem to have an especially intense focus on the shared design of work processes. If something isn't working optimally, it's not someone else's problem; it's everyone's responsibility. If a new line of business is being launched, a community of individuals will spend comparably lavish amounts of time on designing the right process for doing and managing the work.

Each DDO also has a broadly shared language for describing process design. Throughout Bridgewater, people talk about understanding and revising a given machine, by which they mean the design of any process or system for producing outcomes (including an individual's habitual ways of thinking). Similarly, Decurion members operate with the assumption that structure drives behavior, and so they often focus on subtle aspects of organizational design (including how offices are arranged, how often conversations happen, which task structures will require certain people to collaborate, and more). Next Jump tries to crack the code of self-improvement practice. These leaders believe it is not that practice makes perfect but that perfect practice makes perfect, and they're continuously working to perfect their forms of practicing.

Why do the companies insist on getting the processes and routines right and involving everyone as designers? In a DDO, the way the work is done is the way the developmental principles of the organization are given life. If people are to develop, then they require the right processes, both for doing excellent work and for their own growth. In the same way, if the company is to be successful, then all employees must be naturally developing by doing the work.

Enacting these developmental principles in the culture requires constant attention to how people interact routinely. Unlike quality-improvement approaches such as Lean Six Sigma, a DDO's focus on improving processes is as likely to be about improving the quality of work done on members' interiors (the development of individual psychological selves) and communities (how people relate to one another in collective responsibility) as it is on the external (such as measures of production-process errors and anomalies).

In DDOs, every employee, from entry-level crew members welcoming guests in a theater location to senior leaders in the management committee, reflects on, talks about, and redesigns processes together with others. As a result, two common forms of drag on performance, seen in some other organizations, are minimized. First, no one in a DDO is given cover to passively go through decontextualized motions, and no one is permitted to be merely an actor in processes of someone else's design. As Decurion members say, "Everyone is a participant," and, "Everyone is teaching and learning."

Second, all business outcomes, and even small day-to-day actions, are constantly and productively reframed from being seen as single, one-off events to being regarded as the results of business processes that can be understood and revised. Whether immediate or companywide, outcomes can be improved by collectively inspecting and remaking the people-centered processes that lead to the outcomes.

People in all levels of the three companies have told us stories about the excitement and challenges of constantly working to redesign the conditions of your own work (something that's considered above your pay grade in many other organizations). First, frontline employees are not subject to someone else's operational rule book when they, for example, negotiate a rental agreement or clean a theater. Rather, they're expected to help write and revise the rule book whenever they see something that could be improved. In turn, managers are not implementers and enforcers of standard operating procedures; instead they're shapers of the conditions and structures that will allow crew members on the front lines to continually participate in improving the way they work. Finally, executives do not merely develop strategy and then oversee its execution by others; instead they're trustees for the principles that guide process design. They are coaches and mentors in the complex, ongoing process of organizational adaptation of which everyone in the DDO is a part.

Because "the company" is, at any given moment, the emergent result of the existing processes of people working together in communities, everyone is expected to contribute to the observation, diagnosis, and revision of the processes at the heart of the work. Moreover, failures of organizational design not only may limit business results directly but also waste opportunities for the development of members, the longer-term engine of business success.

More Than the Sum of Its Parts

It may be possible to adequately describe the deconstructed elements of a DDO while still missing the soul of the whole. More than a hundred people from the three organizations read earlier versions of our descriptions of their settings. It was gratifying to hear the same major chord from all three places ("Like looking in a mirror," "You may understand us better than we understand ourselves," "I had my parents read it so they could finally understand where I work").

Equally gratifying, and genuinely instructive, we heard the same minor chord—what people felt a reader might not grasp. The issues they pinpointed may seem like a miscellaneous mix—how hard it is to work on your weaknesses, how vital the community is, how crucial the bedrock reliability of goodwill and best intentions is—but we see them as parts of single whole. That whole reminds us we cannot end this chapter without a word about the heightened significance of leadership, and the indispensable tonics that prevent a DDO from becoming toxic or going off the rails.

It Is Hard

"It's not like you're sugarcoating it," one employee told us. "You talk about how painful it can be, about being thrown back on your heels, about being destabilized. But you are developmentalists, and you're excited about the human *results*, about what it all *leads to*. The reader could tune out, or tune down, the hard part, and over-listen to the rewards. It's true it's the most transformational work experience I have ever had in my life, but people need to know there are lots of scratches and bruises along the way."

In the current literature there is a lot of enthusiasm for strength-based approaches to professional development, assessment, and feedback: "Focus on what people do well, and quit torturing them with their weaknesses. People don't change much anyway. Leverage their strengths, and forget about the weaknesses." A DDO does not ignore people's strengths, and it is not above guardrailing around weaknesses that have no likelihood of improving. But a DDO is about as far as you can get from a strength-based work setting. Call them "weaknesses," "challenges," "developmental opportunities," "growing edge," or "backhand," DDOs run against the grain of current fashion as well as the ego's devotion to looking good; leaders in a DDO have a deep conviction that our weaknesses are pure gold if we will only dig into them. And there is no getting around the fact that this digging can be very uncomfortable.

The Community Is Vital

Many people will never want to work in a DDO, but what makes the discomfort palatable for those who do is not a matter of individual fortitude. DDO employees get a lot of help from a culture that, underneath all its provocation, is extraordinarily supportive. Many fine organizations that are clearly not DDOs, and that may have no interest in becoming one, nonetheless are able to create cultures fostering an unusual quality of family fellowship, "we-feeling," or human solidarity. Although such organizations are a minority, they show there are many ways to unleash a meaningful sense of human connectedness at work.

But if Decurion, Bridgewater, and Next Jump are truly examples, then a DDO may create a special kind of human community, one that arises especially from the gifts of vulnerability and the growth that can flower in it. As you experience yourself as incomplete or inadequate—but still included and accepted—and experience the capable people around you as incomplete and inadequate—but no less admirable—these experiences seem to unleash compassion and appreciation that all of us might hope for in our relationships, and that characterize the underlying feeling in a DDO.

As psychologists, we have sometimes seen this unusual kind of connection in the temporary communities that can be fostered in a multiday personal learning program or in a facilitated support group over several months. From such groups we can glimpse possibilities of new forms of community as we take up the interior work of our own growth; but, of course, such groups and programs are not built to simultaneously take up the work of the world, nor to last permanently. Imagine a group or a program that was.

In sum, companies like Decurion, Bridgewater, and Next Jump systematically work at creating the conditions to drive human flourishing and business flourishing as part of one interdependent and mutually reinforcing set of goals. Guided by growth-focused principles (their edge), they implement a closely aligned and complementary set of practices (their groove), in the context of a community (their home) devoted not only to the learning of their people but also to their further unfolding. Creating conditions where the twelve discontinuous departures described here can take hold requires commitment to nurturing a different kind of culture—one that sees individual growth not only as a means but also as an end; error and inadequacy, as opportunities to transcend current limitations; and powerful communities at work, as homes for the rewarding disturbances that develop personal and organizational potential.

Earlier we said that the three central dimensions of a DDO were like a three-legged stool; each is essential to provide support. You want to cultivate the quality of edge? Then you'll need to nurture trust and safety in a supportive community, and you'll require a systemic orientation to practices that make a regular habit of uncovering and overcoming personal limitations.

The interdependence of the three dimensions of edge, home, and groove in a mature DDO raises a natural question. "I get that sustaining a DDO involves creating a special set of conditions," you might ask, "but if we are just getting started, which comes *first*: the practices, the sense of community, or the developmental aspirations?" We'll take on answering that question in the chapters ahead, but for now, we hope you are more attuned to the ways that the three dimensions—and the twelve features that make them tangible—work together to create powerful containers enabling challenging and meaningful work to take place.

Leadership Is Crucial

As we have described the deliberately developmental organization to audiences all over the world, we see some people tear up as we clearly touch deep longings and unanswered hopes for what work life can feel like and be. But we also see that these same descriptions give some people the creeps. They worry that such a powerful community could run amok, that "helping people grow" could become a form of social control and intrusion, that "gold-mining weaknesses" could devolve into staged rituals of self-criticism.

For personal and professional reasons, the five authors of this book, as a group, have developed heightened sensitivities to anything moving toward cultlike mind control, and we can tell you, not one of us has ever felt a ripple of such concern in these organizations. But we still greatly respect the worry, and we can imagine, along with anyone feeling such alarm, a dark, distorted version of what we call a DDO.

What are the indispensable tonics that can protect a culture from taking such a disturbing turn? Two things stand out for us: first, the day-in and day-out confirmation of the goodwill and good intentions that stand behind all the operations of the culture, and especially the difficult communication about oneself; and, second, an unshakable trustworthiness at the top, the knowledge that one's leaders congruently walk their own talk.

If you're working in a DDO and you accept the invitation to make your own personal learning public, you must believe that you've entered into a kind of contract, explicitly or implicitly, that places as many responsibilities and demands on those eliciting and engaging your personal learning as it does on you. This contract must feel like a sacred one. Even one violation—even one experience of someone using your weakness against you, that presenting your whole self, warts and all, diminishes rather than enhances your standing—is enough to compromise the trustworthiness of the community, for you and for others as well. If the community cannot redress its wrong (acknowledge and apologize for its violation, take effective action to repair itself), then the community, and the DDO, will turn toxic. Two of the greatest glories of the organizations we studied are that they have many brave members willing to do difficult work, and that they have trustworthy communities, honoring their sacred contracts with these members, so that the members can do their hard work.

Central to the creation and ongoing cultivation of this special kind of community must be the organization's leadership. If the leader is not deeply committed to the full dialectic of the DDO mission—organizations and their people being each other's greatest resource for flourishing—then the DDO will never launch or will not long survive. The leader needs a passionate interest in the business success of the organization, like any leader, *and* she needs, first, a passionate interest in supporting people's unfolding, along with a recognition that this is not a secondary goal but rather is inextricably tied to the goal of business success, and, second, she herself needs to be a full participant in the program.

Someone once said we admire people for the strengths they show us, but we are personally drawn to them for the vulnerabilities they show us. We admire the leaders we've spent time with at Decurion, Bridgewater, and Next Jump for the clarity of their commitments to fashion workplaces where people can grow. Christopher Forman: "Decurion's purpose, the fundamental reason it exists, is to provide places for people to flourish." Ray Dalio: "Bridgewater supports a person's most fundamental motive, which is to evolve." Charlie Kim: "We use business as a platform to build people of high character."

But we find ourselves personally drawn to them because each of them, in his own way, has also done us the honor of letting us in to his fuller humanity. The best way to ensure that a DDO is what it is meant to be might be to have leaders like these, people who are as hard at work on themselves as they are on the performance of their business and the reliability of their cultures.

If you want to move now from this aerial view of the DDO and its twelve general features back down to ground level, to learn more about the specific practices each of these organizations has created to bring those features to life, we invite you into chapter 4.

In the Groove

Practices and Practicing to Create an Everyone Culture

In this chapter we show you specific ways individuals in DDOs are continuously engaged in getting over themselves—identifying their weaknesses, seeing deeply into the ways they're stuck, and having regular opportunities to move past their limiting patterns of thinking and acting. We describe the practices each organization has developed and continues to refine that help everyone become a better version of herself. It may be tempting, therefore, to scan for the practices to import into your own work culture, following them like a recipe.

But we hope you don't read the chapter in that way.

Instead, we invite you to first consider the idea of practice in terms of the larger context, purpose, and outlook in these DDOs. Understanding a DDO's approach to practice will give you a much better sense of how to think about bringing practices into (or creating new practices for) your own organization. We refer to all the developmental tools, habits, formalized behaviors, and types of meetings in DDOs as *practices*, because the word reminds us that we're doing something in a certain spirit, with a particular intention.

Consider what it means to practice, to have a practice, and to be practicing. Perhaps the central idea is that we're doing something repeatedly, with the intention of becoming better at it. In other words, when we're practicing, we are not expecting (and others are not expecting us) to perform perfectly. In naming what we're doing *practice*, we signal that we're experimenting, trying something on, working at improving. And we clarify that practice is what we're supposed to be doing—trying hard at something to get better at it. We're creating conditions in which we won't feel pressure to demonstrate expertise, conditions that will allow us to experiment, that will allow us to gather feedback, that will help us learn.

Practice also suggests we're doing something routinely, regularly, as a normal part of our lives. We think that the way to get better at something requires us to make learning it part of our routine. We expect to be practicing today, tomorrow, and on into the foreseeable future. Although we're trying to become proficient, we never reach completion. Our practicing, and therefore our learning, never stops.

When you think about practice in these ways, what type of practice comes to mind? Practicing a sport? A musical instrument? Meditation? It isn't a coincidence that most people don't think this way about their jobs. The culture of most organizations is not designed for practice; it's designed for performance. Everyone is trying to look good, display expertise, minimize and hide any mistakes or weaknesses, and demonstrate what they already know and can do well. In a culture of practice, in contrast, everyone is learning and growing.

Simply copying DDO practices doesn't work, therefore, because it's not sufficient to give people time and space and rules for practicing. You must also pay attention to creating a culture of practice, helping people adopt the spirit, intentions, and mind-set of practice, rather than those of performance.

When we talk to people who've been immersed in the culture of practice in DDOs for at least a couple of years, they describe the ways their own mind-set began to change from one of performance to one of practice. They tell us how hard it was to receive feedback until they realized that the feedback was being given to help them get better. They describe how hard it was to admit and accept their own weaknesses and realize that the sooner they could see them, the sooner they could learn to improve them. And they explain that the more they could see others accepting feedback, practicing, learning, improving, and growing, the more their own resistance to this type of learning began to dissolve.

Another reason that copying DDO practices will not work is that effective practice depends on many factors. The literature on deliberate practice shows that improvement depends on how frequently we practice tasks that present increasing challenge. Improvement also depends heavily on how we practice. Ideally, practice sessions are designed and supervised by experts who break down our performance to give specific advice about how to practice and who give us feedback about what needs to improve. Perhaps that is one reason all three DDOs are quick to create and try new practices, gathering information about how well they work and help people learn.

Instead of looking for what you can simply copy, we hope you will read about these practices and ask yourself questions like these: Under what conditions could this practice lead to learning and improvement? What type of improvement? For what purpose? How would someone need to practice to begin to see that improvement? We hope that, like all three DDOs we describe, you will want to try things for yourself and experiment with instituting new practices at work as you also step back to gather information, assess the practices, and experiment again.

As we look deeper into the groove of daily life in the three DDO exemplars, we hope you'll see what distinguishes the practices in each company: that they form a system of routines and tools for exposing, exploring, and transcending people's limiting assumptions and mind-sets. Each practice plays its own part in the life of the company, but no practice stands on its own. In each of these companies, practicing is constant, immersive, and layered at multiple levels and time scales.

In an everyone culture, these practices make up the important patterns of working life that everyone participates in—as individuals, in small teams, within divisions, and across the company. It's that saturation of practices that produces a uniquely rich culture for developing people.

Bridgewater: Tools for Getting in Sync

Your earlier visit to Bridgewater's campus in the woods of suburban Connecticut has given you a sense of the kind of dialogue that happens every day there. In every conference room and corner, people are working to get in sync about what is true. Radical transparency can happen face-to-face, as people strive to apply the principles, exposing their reasoning and performance to continuous scrutiny. A practice unthinkable in most companies—recording and sharing the recording of every meeting (including those with visiting researchers like the authors of this book)—is standard practice here.

What other routines and tools does Bridgewater use to bring this thick culture of radical transparency to life? How does the collection of daily workplace practices create a machine for better business results and increasingly effective employees through the search for truth?

An App for That: Dot Collector

In talking about the idea meritocracy that Bridgewater aspires to be, CEO Greg Jensen describes the need for an ecosystem of practical tools to support the challenging work required.

> You build the habits of principled people into the everyday work. So there's no difference between doing the work and managing the work. It's all the same stuff . . . And therefore, [we] embed those habits in the technology and the tools, so that the way you are doing things is consistent with those principles. You're building the habits, and you're building the muscle memory to operate in a certain way. It's very hard to teach people to be fully transparent, to be all of those ways, and so you really need to help them by creating the ecosystem that almost forces them to in doing their work.

To see how this interpersonal ecosystem works, let's power up the standard-issue tablet device. In a key practice for building muscle memory, everyone shares a continuous stream of feedback about people's behavior using an application called the Dot Collector. This custom tool allows people to record their assessments of any other person in two ways: summary ratings—thumbs-up, thumbs-down—and candid, specific comments about the person's actions or inaction.

The dots are individual data points, which are aggregated to reveal larger crowd-sourced patterns to connect the dots. Think of it as Big Data meets human development. The accumulated dots create, in Bridgewater's phrase, "a pointillist picture of a person" over time—one that employees and managers can use, as one of several tools, to generate inferences about what people are like (WAPLs) and identify the developmental work individuals need to do to be more successful in given roles.

Everyone's getting and giving feedback on how he's doing in his job. Jensen is not exempt; there are no exemptions. A sampling from a day's accumulated dots from June 2014 shows the kinds of feedback he gets from across the company, including from his own subordinates, in evaluative categories such as creativity, conceptual thinking, managing vision and purpose, and process management. Some of the live feedback Jensen got that day reflected frank assessments of his leadership:

- Let WGOITW meeting ("What's Going On in the World" meeting, which Jensen is responsible for) devolve into a bit of chaos.

- Good WGOITW meeting.

- Greg, you're too slow in finding a sustainable design for Nella's responsibility set.

- Not prioritizing finding a replacement for Nella.

The Issues Log

The flow of data about people via the Dot Collector is supplemented by other practices that Bridgewater can use to get at root causes of problems. One tool for perceiving, diagnosing, and preventing problems is the issues log, a digital tool for capturing, from a first-person perspective, questions and evidence about errors, mistakes, and problems. Jensen told us that the issues log "is like our evolution machine" for "watching the progress on any problem that's ever been raised in the company."

At Bridgewater, making mistakes is expected—and disclosing and reflecting on the causes of errors are a job requirement. Ray Dalio describes the way big and small problems are diagnosed through the issues log.

> A problem or "issue" that should be logged is easy to identify: anything that went wrong. The issues log acts like a water filter that catches garbage. By examining the garbage and determining where it came from, you can determine how to eliminate it at the source . . . The log must include a frank assessment of individual contributions to the problems alongside their strengths and weaknesses. As you come up with the changes that will reduce or eliminate the garbage, the water will become cleaner.

Dalio goes on to explain how people will resist using the issues log if it's seen only as a way to cast blame on others.

> A common challenge to getting people to use issues logs is that they are sometimes viewed as vehicles for blaming people. You have to encourage use by making clear how necessary they are, rewarding active usage, and punishing nonuse. If, for example, something goes wrong and it's not in the issues log, the relevant people should be in big trouble. But if something goes wrong and it's there (and, ideally, properly diagnosed), the relevant people will probably be rewarded or praised. But there must be personal accountability.

Let's take the example of one such entry. Rohit, a junior staffer in the research department, notices that a department is experiencing problems, and he questions how Alex, the department head, is overseeing the work. Here's a part of Rohit's issues log entry:

> We've been struggling to keep up with all of our needs, and it's gotten to the point where Alex now has consultants managing consultants. For a place so synced in its culture, how could this be? How could we have all these outside people managing these other people without having gone through all the necessary things to become a Bridgewater citizen? . . . How is Alex ensuring the consultants acting as managers are managing in a principled fashion and holding the bar high enough?

In raising this issue, Rohit is doing exactly what every person, regardless of rank, is expected to do at Bridgewater. In fact, it's called an act of good citizenship to call out things, even the smallest things, openly and directly if you believe someone is acting inconsistently with one or more principles guiding the company. Then diagnosis can begin interactively via the issues log, and everyone can determine what is true and act accordingly.

In response, Alex pushes back on Rohit's believability.

> Not sure how Rohit is believable in the organizational design at all. This is a well-probed design and a much longer discussion of the use of CM [consultant-managed] resources in all sorts of roles of staff augmentation. As you recall, I was a CM myself at the start of my tenure here.

In reviewing this unfolding back and forth in the log, Jensen sees a classic managerial problem, one that applies to Alex and to many others. "We would take that as a response from authority, rather than a response that we would expect from logic," he explains. "Okay, maybe the design does make sense, but *why* does it make sense? So, we see Alex deflecting the question instead of dealing with it. Alex is saying, 'Just believe me because a lot of people have looked at this decision.' That's not an acceptable answer at Bridgewater."

What is someone in Rohit's position expected to do in response? Certainly not just let it go. Rohit sees Alex's response as unsatisfactory, and so he uses the Dot Collector to share feedback on Alex's actions. He indicates that Alex is violating one of the key principles: being "assertive and open-minded at the same time." Rohit writes his reason for this assessment:

> When I issue-logged Alex regarding consultants acting as managers, he was deflective, and he didn't help me understand the issue at hand. Instead, he focused on my believability and [my] severity rating of the issue.

At this point, Brian, who is Rohit's manager and the department head for research, reads the exchange in the issues log, sees Rohit's dots about Alex in the Dot Collector, and intervenes.

As always, of course, I don't know what I don't know, so
I am just calling out what I see. I'm going to write a lot here,
because I think it is important. I doubt you will agree with my
perceptions below in their entirety—please take them in the
helpful spirit in which they are intended.

One, the specific issue that was logged—I don't know if
it's a problem or not . . . I certainly don't know, Rohit doesn't
know (and he seemed to acknowledge that).

The more important thing to me in terms of "what to take
from this" is that . . . you [Alex] are taking an issue log in a
way that is far different than it is intended to work. It is not an
attack that needs to be defended. An issue log is a question—a
perception that someone is generous enough to share with you
rather than holding to themselves so that the right RP [respon-
sible party] can use it as "fuel for improvement" . . .

Rohit doesn't need to write this. He can keep his head down
and do his job. But we ask him, beg him, demand as a BW
citizen that he call out badness when he thinks he perceives it.
We don't ask him to be perfect—we ask him to do his best to
balance open-mindedness and assertiveness . . .

The last thing I ever want someone to feel when they
issue-log me, my responsibilities, my people is that I or my
people are being defensive . . . because that is most likely to
shut down the improvement fuel pipe I desperately need.

After going into greater detail to analyze Alex's and others' original responses, Brian then circles back to explain what the payoff
might be for Alex, if he can turn this interaction into an opportunity
for improvement:

Because I could imagine that if you make change at this level
(less defensiveness, in fact a real focus on taking input and
understanding it), you will not only get better faster, but
you will create better, more-dynamic, engaged, and fruitful
relationships with your customers.

As we see this dialogue ripen, it's worth taking a moment to ask,
What's really going on here? What does this exchange tell us about
how people at Bridgewater work, as a habit? Brian is aware that he's

expected to help Alex address what Brian sees as a recurring pattern of defensiveness. Part of Brian's job at Bridgewater, through the practice of issue-logging, is to expose evidence about Alex's limiting behaviors and mind-sets so that Alex can grow. Alex's job requires him to participate in that process with an open mind.

And what does Alex make of all this? He reflects on what Brian has said and pushes himself to step back from the situation to diagnose what may be going on and understand how it relates to other patterns of behavior that may limit his effectiveness:

> Brian, thank you for the feedback. As a colleague and fellow department head, I appreciate the rapport we share and your perspective. I am totally open to my not seeing this in a good way . . . Here's what I heard you say in your feedback to me:
>
> Consistent with my style and what is in my BBC [baseball card—more on that in a moment], my initial "amygdala" response tends toward defensiveness and overconfidence in the moment with other watch-out-fors including [the lack of] encouraging others to probe, more assertive than open-minded, [not] seeing multiple possibilities . . .
>
> So let me reflect on the potential "take-aways" of this case which I now see more clearly represented by the following questions:
>
> - What is true in the information I'm receiving?
>
> - How can I use the information, if true, to iterate my machine (people and design)?
>
> - What does this information tell me about my clients and the quality of service that [we] share with the community?
>
> - Is this possibly a teaching moment?

Alex is now framing this exchange in terms of what Bridgewater would describe as the higher "you" of "two yous." There is the you that is in the middle of the action, experiencing the triggering threat to the self, reacting to the threat defensively; and there is the *higher you*, a part of yourself that can step back and reflect on your actions as part of an ongoing self-system that consistently generates those actions. In our language of adult developmental psychology, we would call the insight of the "higher you" a case of moving what was subject (what we can only look through) to object (something we can now look at). Alex sees that even though he has a pattern of acting this way—a documented pattern—he does not have to be always in its thrall. His questions do not conclude his process of learning, but recognize that there is another way of being that he can construct if he can answer those questions.

The Baseball Card

What is the baseball card (BBC) Alex refers to as a source of information about his pattern of behaviors? What can it reveal to us about another essential practice at Bridgewater? Together with collecting dots, issue-logging, and other tools, the digital baseball cards for each employee form a dynamic system for spurring people to wrestle with their limitations.

A baseball card, as Jensen describes it, forms "a map for how to get you from where you are to where you want to be." The baseball cards, electronically accessible to everyone, integrate all kinds of data about what a person is like—testimonials, the feedback dots, personality inventories (like the Myers-Briggs), surveys of what people are good and bad at (which include forced-ranking exercises). And as you might expect at a successful hedge fund, the company doesn't place all its eggs (or data points) in one basket. Jensen explains: "We're connecting information from multiple streams on people. You can't rely on any one piece of information, or any one information source, to tell you the truth about people." The baseball card allows anyone at Bridgewater to see where a person's demonstrated capabilities stack up against all the principle-driven qualities required for success in any role, benchmarked for the person's given level of responsibility in the organization.

What jumps out, at the top of the display of every baseball card, is the crisp synthesis of what the employee has demonstrated she is reliably good at doing (her "rely-ons," shown in the BBC in green) and her areas of weakness (her "watch-out-fors," shown in red). Alex's baseball card, like all BBCs, lays out succinctly where he can be trusted and where there are concerns, crystallizing in a few top-line points all

TABLE 4-1

Alex's rely-ons and watch-out-fors

Rely-ons	Watch-out-fors
• To be determined	• Synthesizing the situation
• To have the level of skill and experience consistent with his job	• Seeing multiple possibilities
• To be a practical thinker	• Matching people to the job design
• To manage his time	• Logical reasoning
• To have self-discipline	• Ability to self-assess

Note: In the Bridgewater baseball card, rely-ons are shown in green, and watch-out-fors are shown in red.

the accumulated data that runs through the data visualizations and evaluative comments of the whole baseball card (see table 4-1).

You might think that seeing a description of one's "watch-out-fors" so openly documented could be anxiety-provoking. You'd be right, according to people at Bridgewater. Jensen explains, however, that the card is essential for helping match people to roles and that a baseball card is not a fixed description:

> [We] build out that picture [of a person], so that you can know, every time we transfer somebody or move them through the company, you get this baseball card, so you can know if you put this guy in a circumstance, here's what he's likely to be like. And you can connect people with jobs [based on] what they're capable of doing . . . Some people see their baseball card as their destiny—like, "Oh my God, I'm bad at this. I'm screwed." And that kind of person will never get the most out of life . . . There are two ways to deal with your weaknesses. One is to try to learn and get better at them. That's one path that you could be pursuing. The second path is, How do you get around them? How do you use others to get around your weaknesses so you can get to your goal? And so if you can stare at reality, accept what's true about yourself, have others helping you do that, you have a map helping you get to success. And that's really what our baseball card is intended to be.

For Alex, then, the baseball card serves to reflect evidence about what he is like, how he does his work, how he leads, and where people feel they can count on him and where they can't. He can take this source of evidence as grist for the two kinds of self-improvement Jensen proposes. He can overcome those limits through learning, or he can develop ways to use others' help to compensate for his weaknesses (what people at Bridgewater call "guardrailing").

More broadly, the cultural practices we've discussed in this section close the gap between how a person sees himself and how his colleagues see him. This is one way that a DDO can create the conditions for people to feel at home with the work of self-improvement. If having weaknesses is normal—universal and documented for everyone—then acknowledging and working to overcome those limitations are much less frightening. Every senior leader at Bridgewater also has a baseball card openly shared with the entire company. There are usually as many or more watch-out-fors as rely-ons in each of those cards, too.

Other Practices: the Daily Update, the Daily Case

In addition to probing and diagnosis, which happen constantly around the campus, and the use of the Dot Collector, baseball card, and issues log, Bridgewater makes a daily practice of learning and reflection in other ways.

One practice is the submission of daily updates to one's supervisor. Although regular supervisor check-ins aren't unusual elsewhere, the Bridgewater daily update makes each employee's process of getting in sync with his manager a public act. Anyone can see anyone else's daily update. What kinds of updates are shared in this daily communication? Above all, the updates give people an opportunity to reflect on what they are learning about themselves, any pain they're experiencing, and ways they're grappling to improve their application of the principles. At their best, these updates prevent gaps from forming between an employee's interior struggles and a manager's understanding of those struggles.

Another practice is part of every employee's learning each day. Called the "daily case," this process is, according to Bridgewater leaders, "the calisthenics of our culture." For about fifteen minutes every day, people review an actual multimedia case study of a teachable moment in the life of Bridgewater's culture; the case combines video and snippets of digital documents, e-mails, or other artifacts.

Cases are something like teaching cases in a professional school. For example, the details of the case of Rohit, Alex, et al., described earlier in this chapter, are the perfect material for a Bridgewater case.

What happens in the fifteen minutes of daily practice with a case? Employees are asked to review the materials and are asked a series of questions about what they would do in the situation and why. For Jensen, this is both an opportunity for people to exercise and also a chance to gather data about what people are like: "[The daily case] reinforces the exercise of connecting the day-to-day to management," he says. "It's a quick case study where people get a bite of the culture. We see how they react to it. And that helps us fill in an understanding of how they would be in those situations." The result is an entire organization engaged with a similar professional curriculum, one that encourages practicing the application of the principles and collects yet another source of evidence about the mind-set of every person in the company.

From the individual experience of probing in every one-on-one meeting, to the technologically integrated processes for discussing dots, issues, and baseball cards, to the companywide practices of daily updates and cases, Bridgewater has built an ecosystem to support personal development. The system helps everyone in the company confront the truth about what everyone is like.

Next Jump: "Character Is a Muscle"

When Next Jump studied how things fail, the leaders concluded that the number one recurring pattern was the inability of people to manage their emotions, what the leaders call "character imbalances." This inability, they observed, leads to poor decision making. Chief of Staff Meghan Messenger says, "Most companies have super-competent execution people, not super-competent decision makers."

Next Jump discovered that the imbalance between the character traits of confidence and humility led to emotional tantrums, outbursts by the overly confident (or arrogant), and paralysis by the overly humble (or insecure). The growth in the company's leadership took off as leaders discovered and consistently practiced the development of character as a muscle that could be exercised, helping

TABLE 4-2

Next Jump's wallet card for practicing your backhand

	Overconfident/Arrogant	Too humble/Insecure
Better me	Listening more (being last to speak in meetings)	Speaking up more (being first to speak in meetings)
	Being less aggressive (slower to launch)	More aggressive (sooner to launch)
	Being more vulnerable	Being more courageous
	Being more disciplined	Being more optimistic
Better you	Take more advice	Give more advice
	Nurture more	Coach more

people become more humble or more confident. (They even created a wallet-size card with tips or reminders for practicing your less-developed sides. See table 4-2.)

Next Jump leaders believe in the transformative potential of carefully designed rituals. These are not rituals for their own sake, but for the sake of keeping people in the groove of working on their character. Let's take a look.

Talking Partners

As we've mentioned, a typical day at Next Jump begins with people checking in with each other in pairs known as talking partners (TPs). If you were to listen in on these discussions, often held while the partners eat breakfast provided by the company, you'd quickly observe that they don't have a structured agenda, although there is a common purpose for the meetings, which CEO Charlie Kim describes as "co-mentorship."

Each TP meeting is organized around a triangle: meet, vent, work. *Meet* signals the need for the consistency of meeting every morning, getting into a daily ritual of the practice. *Venting* involves "getting the toxins out," as Next Jumpers say. Anything from your home life or work life is fair game for discussion; the theory is that to admit yourself as a whole person, warts and all, into the workplace, you need a place that honors feelings of frustration and anxiety as part of who you are. Venting also gives you a structure for lessening the hold of negative thinking on your attention.

The *work* component of the TP triangle is one that many Next Jumpers describe as having the greatest impact on their growth. Partners are expected to push each other for greatness, set high expectations, and help each other see pathways, both in general and for the day's work, to greatness.

For example, let's look at talking partners Nayan Busa and Lokeya Venkatachalam. Recall that you met Busa in chapter 1 at Next Jump's Super Saturday, when he welcomed a room full of job candidates to Next Jump's headquarters. Now we join him in a different context, as he describes his talking partnership with Venkatachalam.

> In some ways, we are brutally honest with each other. We are past that stage where we are patting each other on the back and saying, "Okay, good, good." And we actually care for each other. And each knows that the other cares. If she was going in the wrong direction, I would just say, "You're going wrong." . . . So, I am honest with her and giving critical feedback when necessary. And I point out the things that I like that she is doing. She is making systematic improvements, and I make a point to tell her that, so that it doesn't go unnoticed to her. And it's the same in return.

Venkatachalam confirms the importance of her morning routine with Busa. We interviewed them on a day when Busa was scheduled to give a presentation at a monthly development event called 10X. (We return to the important practice of monthly 10X meetings shortly.) Venkatachalam gives us a glimpse into the way the TP relationship can provide a context for growth.

> So, this morning, I was telling Nayan as he was preparing for the 10X, let's not worry about it. And I told him, "How about you practice your storytelling, which you've been struggling with? Just pick two stories you want people to take away." And that kind of eased his mind, as he was worrying about too many things. "Hey, work on the concise presentation and your storytelling. That's all you can do. Don't worry about anything else." And I think that kind of guidance we provide to each other, those are the moments we feel, "Oh my God, if

we didn't have this, I would miss a big thing in my life." The peer talking partners understand each other's struggles, which we wouldn't get otherwise . . . It's kind of ongoing weakness correction and how we work on it.

Certainly not all talking partner pairings are as successful a developmental match as Venkatachalam and Busa have turned out to be. These pairings are not permanent, though, and managers regularly reassign members of TP pairs. As they do, they make sure that people are paired with others who will push them, making every effort to match someone who leans arrogant with someone who leans insecure.

The Weekly Situational Workshop

Talking partner pairs become the building blocks of another practice at Next Jump: the situational workshop (SW). The leaders believe that this workshop is among the most effective things they do. Every week for one hour, five people meet: two different pairs of talking partners, along with a more experienced colleague acting as a mentor and coach. SW is a scalable program. Each recipient of coaching is expected eventually to coach four others; the students become the teachers.

Kim identifies what makes this kind of weekly workshop structure powerful.

> At this weekly workshop, each of the four of you describe some challenge you've met in the week and what you've done to meet it—or not. You might not be sure if how you handled the situation was optimal or not—SW is a reflective exercise. The mentor-coach is there to encourage you to reach a higher level of self-awareness, so that you might identify new options for responding to similar future challenges and so avoid reacting in the same old way. You share your situation, and the coach can say, "You thought your choices were this and this? There were *a lot* more choices you didn't see." Over time, you see people growing immensely from these weekly sessions. We've even replaced most manager meetings with situational workshops.

The dilemmas that people raise in an SW are varied but typically deal with people's backhands (limitations). We've heard people talk about a range of specific challenges that point to different potential limitations or triggers: whether to give another person unsolicited advice, how to get over the desire to have a perfect result rather than an acceptable result, how to be more effective in managing time, how to not choke in a high-pressure situation, and more.

As Kim explains, an SW's purpose is to focus "on the training of judgment, rather than on technical training." As a result, the discourse and pace of an SW can be a bit surprising to a first-time observer. People identify problems of practice, but the coach's response is rarely direct problem solving. All Next Jump practices seem to be designed with an awareness that if you solve a problem too quickly, it is certain you will be the same person coming out of the problem as you were going into it. You won't change. And if you don't change, you'll most likely reproduce new versions of the same problem you think you solved earlier.

Accordingly, the coach in the SW is more likely to let the problem "solve you" rather than the other way around. The coach might say, "What does it tell you about yourself that you froze in that kind of situation?" The emphasis is on hearing numerous situations rather than spend a long time on any one of them. Keeping in mind this is happening every week for every employee, the result is something more like Bridgewater's dot collecting. A great many data points are being assembled; no one of them is a big deal, but the cumulative experience is that everyone becomes aware of patterns they would not otherwise see.

From a developmental perspective, an SW has several important features. First, it builds on the relational foundation of the talking partnership, giving people someone to listen in on their learning who will hold them accountable and look for opportunities to help apply their learning. Just as important, SWs are about cases drawn from the flow of your own work life, and not lessons from fictional exercises or abstract business concepts. Situations are meaningful to the person seeking coaching, growing as they do from live preoccupations or nagging recent experiences of discomfort, triggering, or failure. Moving their thinking, feeling, and behavior from subject to object, people are helped to look at lenses they were formerly able only to look through.

At the same time, the SWs strengthen the dimension of home (the developmental communities that support a particular, personal kind of learning on the job). It is not lost on Next Jump participants that the most senior leaders are full participants, investing the time they are, every week, to be helpful to everyone. Keep in mind, as well, that you go through a weekly SW with your daily talking partner, someone who stands to give you better counsel over breakfast each day if she better understands the range of feedback you're getting in the workshop. To be sure, there are lots of places someone at Next Jump can get coaching—at the end (or during) any meeting, in reply to an e-mail, over breakfast. The SW is a regular part of the rhythm of the workweek, ensuring that it will happen predictably for everyone. Before you know it, Next Jumpers become more mindful, traversing their week looking for situations to be brought up in their weekly SWs. And if SWs have begun to replace many management meetings—even though they're not "progress checks" or "behavior resets"—it may be that managing the interior is a powerful way of managing the exterior.

The Monthly 10X Factor

Another companywide practice follows a predictable monthly rhythm: the 10X Factor. Each month, for ninety minutes that command the attention of the entire company, ten Next Jumpers give a short presentation on their contributions to the company. The name of this developmental opportunity started as a play on the television show *The X Factor*. Graphics circulating within the company and posted on the walls announce, "The World Will Be Watching," a play on a meme from that show. In fact, the entire staff at all four global offices is watching, in person or via livestream.

10X presentations are public, shared opportunities for growth. In the five-minute presentations, a Next Jumper can talk about his contributions to one of two things: the company's revenue or its culture. Then everyone rates the presentation on a 1 to 4 scale via mobile app, and then a panel of judges, often including Charlie Kim or Meghan Messenger, scores the presentations and gives live feedback.

Although the feedback from the judges can sometimes be pointed and harsh, it is tied to helping each presenter get better at talking to others about his struggles in ways that help everyone learn. Here is a real example of one judge's feedback:

> Your results are clear. You've taken an evaluation process that used to take three months or more and gotten it down to ten days, with better quality. The visual evidence you show is compelling, the getting rid of the old paper process. But tactically, you missed opportunities here. You should have focused less on what you did and more on how you did it. You should be helping to educate people at 10X. *How* you did it. I think this was all about you having the courage to fail in iterating and training. You robbed everyone of an insight that could have helped them see how to implement that courage to fail.

It's crucial that people aren't being celebrated at 10X for their literal outputs or results on the revenue or culture side. The results matter, of course, but they aren't why the company comes together once a month to focus intently on ten employees' stories. Instead, the Next Jumpers with higher scores earn those scores because they reveal through stories how they're working to overcome a personal limitation in order to generate better results in the business and its culture. It's a reward for bravely revealing your process of working to transcend limits, the work of shifting your mind-set, and not a vote on the outcomes (exactly the same as Bridgewater redirecting its admiration to "struggling well").

This experience feels high-risk for all the presenters. For any individual, it's not a part of the regular workweek, and so even though it is a chance to reflect on and share work on yourself, it's a big enough event to make your heart beat faster and your palms sweat. Harsher feedback is reserved for presentations about culture projects. After all, contributions to the culture are designed to be practice grounds for learning and self-improvement. Next Jump uses the metaphor of projects that are above the water line (the culture) and those that are below the water line (the revenue). If you steer an ocean liner through an icy sea, an iceberg strike above the water line won't sink you, but a strike below the water line can cause the ship to founder. Although practicing is an everyday mantra, cultural initiatives present greater personal risks and greater free-dom to fail in pursuit of excellence. And 10X itself is a cultural initiative, one that was started by twenty-something employees, who (taking off on a talent-oriented reality television show) led the design, implemented the process, and coached others to take it over and improve on it.

In chapter 1, you saw other Next Jump practices that connect to the work of daily talking partners, weekly situational workshops, and monthly 10X meetings (recall Jackie's 10X presentation about her cultural contributions, and lack thereof). These practices include the Super Saturday hiring process, the Personal Leadership Boot Camps for onboarding new staff and developing experienced staff who are struggling, and the many forms of work on Better Me—giving back to people in order to enhance every employee's feeling of doing meaningful work. These practices operate together to create an environment where working on one's character, as Next Jump describes adult development, is a habit for everyone.

Decurion: "Ten Times More Capable Than You Think"

When you spend time in meetings at Decurion, you quickly dis-cover that setting the context is crucial. Decurion leaders talk openly about the need to "align intentions" up front, especially before tricky conversations—ones likely to heighten people's sense of vulnerability or to reveal conflicts.

Aligning intentions is more than being sure people know the meet-ing agenda or even the meeting's goals. It is those things, but it is more. It is a signal that people are about to practice doing something hard, something they may want to avoid because of fear of loss. And so, rather than enter that work on autopilot, carrying forward your state of mind from another setting or task, it's a time to connect to the deeper purpose that calls those around the table to the conver-sation. In a moment, you will see how Decurion uses a subset of its practices to enable people to stay connected to the needs of the busi-ness and to their own flourishing.

As you explore the practices of Decurion, you will take a close look at how the ArcLight cinemas specifically create these conditions. We think that focusing on the practices in the theaters—even if other parts of the company could offer similar insights—offers you a unique perspective. In the knowledge economy industries where Bridgewater and Next Jump operate, highly educated employees work in high-wage jobs. In contrast, working inside the theaters is, for most, a different kind of role, but employees' personal growth is no less powerful. ArcLight crew members create meaningful guest experiences, and their roles are part of a service-oriented, retail sector.

But what distinguishes industries, contexts, and roles in their potential for developing people, we think, is far less important than what transcends those boundaries. For us, and we hope for you, it is just as instructive to understand how a company can create a rich culture to support the psychological development of young people working in a cinema as it is to see similar work for engineers and financial analysts.

Touchpoints

An ArcLight location on a Saturday night is buzzing with activity. Guests stream in, passing through a grand lobby to enjoy the latest blockbuster or independent film. They take their reserved seats in theaters designed for comfort, minimal distraction, and heightened attention to the quality of sound and image. Shows begin and end at regular cycles.

Amid this activity, just below the surface of the guest experience, a series of interlocking practices helps keep workers' development at the center of a thriving business. In quick daily meetings with each crew member, called "touchpoints," managers try to connect members' daily work experience to their personal growth and larger goals. In regular pulse-check huddles throughout the evening, groups of crew members and managers give and receive feedback on how the floor operations are going and how they can be improved.

In the crew offices hang huge "competency boards," where colorful plastic pins hold evidence of every crew member's level of demonstrated competency. The competency boards are modified to show individual areas of growth in the capabilities of the crew members.

Earlier, the theater general manager and other shift supervisors spent time scheduling for the next week, matching business needs to new job rotations and checking in about each person's level of readiness for new challenges or continued practice.

A touchpoint, then, is a frequent, focused opportunity to connect your own growth to the work you're doing. Touchpoints are held for senior executives and for theater crew members alike. Decurion leaders believe that work is inherently meaningful, for everyone, and these touchpoint conversations are like the daily needlework of development, threading the personal through the fabric of working life.

Think for a moment about how rare it is in most organizations to have a conversation about what is meaningful about your work, review any struggles you're having, and discuss aspects of your growth. For nearly all of us, this might be, at best, a quarterly or annual conversation as part of a formal review process. At Decurion, "developmental performance dialogues" (as they are called) also happen, but they are in addition to the more-frequent touchpoints.

Crew members told us about the regularity and importance of touchpoints. Often, they talked about the ways that the conversation helped them see how their work connected more clearly to their own hopes for future growth.

ArcLight crew member Cristina, for example, told us that she shared her goal of becoming a film set decorator. After that touchpoint, her manager gave her the chance to join a team to create the decor for special events held at her location. In Cristina's eyes, ArcLight valued giving her opportunities to connect her own goals for the future to her present work in the theater.

Cristina's manager, Michael, sees touchpoints, in part, as a way to help crew members appreciate what they can learn at ArcLight, knowledge that can help them realize their own aspirations. Even if someone does not stay at ArcLight for a career, Michael says, each crew member can learn many of the aspects of running a successful business, and these skills are transferrable to almost any pursuit. Whether starting from the personal goals of a crew member or from the sincere belief in Decurion's business as a laboratory for more-general self-development, managers like Michael draw on various means of connecting the growth of subordinates to opportunities in the business.

Line of Sight

As in meetings at all companies, sometimes touchpoints get squeezed for time, and sometimes an individual touchpoint isn't particularly productive. But touchpoints, at their best, have a deeper design that simultaneously serves the interests of the business and the employee. Decurion leaders call this deeper design "line of sight." This metaphor is another image of alignment, related to the call for aligning intentions at the start of meetings. Decurion managers look for line-of-sight opportunities every day to help members "connect the why through the what to the how." In other words, built into the style of touchpoint coaching is a practice of questioning, rather than merely giving status updates.

For a crew member, this may mean that a dialogue with a manager enables her to see that her progress in, say, cash management competency (the how) was reflected in shorter guest lines and greater accuracy (the what), and that this contributed to a markedly better guest experience and therefore a positive impact on the business (the why).

Pulse-Check Huddles

If we return to the floor of the theater's Saturday night operations, we find another of ArcLight's practices, "pulse-check huddles." The fast pace of the changes between show sets makes the conversations in the theater especially energetic. In some ways, pulse-check huddles are quintessential experiences at Decurion, and they make salient the way people can work on themselves at the same time that they're working on improving the business. (In chapter 5 we explore in detail the way the DDO treats these two goals as one thing.)

A huddle happens regularly during a shift. Managers and crew members come together for about ten minutes before or after a series of theaters is being reset for the next round of screenings. As they meet, the participants typically do things employees in other businesses might do—make sure that everyone is aware of operational conditions (such as big movie premieres), ticket-sales targets, and the percentage of filled seats throughout the location. But these participants are working on additional skills—giving and receiving feedback effectively and connecting their own roles to the larger organization.

What happens in a huddle? Here's a typical example. After the group members come together, one gives another feedback about the negative impact on guests of not having the largest theater ready to open at the anticipated time, asking that the two of them work together to speed the turnaround for the next set. A shift leader notes that someone—let's call her Angie—is working on getting her "blue pin" (a mark of competency for a specific role) and asks that everyone support her tonight, including giving her feedback about how she's doing.

When the huddle breaks, as people move to different parts of the location to quickly resume their ticket scanning, cleaning, ushering, and other duties, the general manager and the shift leader stay behind for on-the-spot feedback. The manager explains that in the future, it's important to say exactly what competency Angie was working on ("usher scout") so that everyone knows how they can be more helpful. It's about making sure the feedback is as useful as possible, and not only about supporting Angie in general.

For developmental purposes, the most attractive aspect of the huddles is that the conversations operate on at least three levels. At the first level, crew members are talking about how to learn from and improve operations on the spot, while the data is fresh and course corrections can be made. A second level is the direct practice of giving and receiving feedback, crew member to crew member. Like many people in other workplaces, most crew members, on arriving at ArcLight, have little experience in giving feedback to someone at work. The huddle provides a routinized way to practice this skill in the context of a regular structure where that behavior is safe and expected. Finally, there is a third level: getting feedback on the feedback. Crew members involved in giving feedback get coaching from their managers on how to improve.

Huddles put crew members in the position of looking at the operation as a whole, coming together often to take stock of the entire theater as a system—much as a general manager would be expected to do on a walk-through of the location. In this way, huddles allow crew members to be businesspeople first rather than be embedded in their assigned roles. The huddles put into practice what ArcLight means when it says "the crew runs the business."

The Competency Board

The aforementioned competency boards are literal poster boards hanging on the walls of every theater's back-of-house area, prominently displayed as one of the first things people see when they arrive at work, take a break, or duck behind the scenes during their shift. Every crew member has the potential to gain certified competency in a series of about fifteen roles. As they achieve each competency, theater managers publicly honor it by placing a colored pin in the relevant space for that crew member on the competency board. Confirmation with a blue pin comes only after a crew member demonstrates competency over multiple shifts and asks to be evaluated for possible pinning. (A green pin marks an interim step of growth for a competency not yet formally certified.)

Early in a crew member's tenure, some roles serve as a first tier with a shallower gradient to getting pinned. Other roles involve more complexity and integration of theater operations, and getting pinned for those roles offers both a sense of capability and, to Decurion's leaders, data about the pipeline of potential leaders.

Standing backstage near a competency board feels a little like hanging out in a communal watering hole—a place where attention and conversation are focused as people stop to look at the board, seeing whether anyone has gained a new pin. The message is unmistakable: growing people into greater levels of skill, at the very least, is a focus of this community. Moreover, that growth is not a private set of goals between you and your manager but rather a public resource. Everyone knows what others are working on, and, as a result, everyone can step forward with support and feedback. Everyone also knows what kinds of capability, manifested in the roles, are required across the organization for the business to run effectively.

The competency boards are part of a system of tracking data about learning and development that saturates the company. At weekly meetings of theater management, in addition to traditional business metrics, the group tracks the share of crew members who are ready to enter a management role. Knowing clearly where each person is in his development is part of Decurion's commitment to the stance that "everyone is on a developmental path" and "everyone is teaching and learning."

An essential part of tracking individual growth is the creation and calibration of developmental pulls. By "pull," managers mean a kind of challenge that, in itself, motivates growth. A person having a certain level of capability is matched with a demand (such as the skill requirements of a new project) that exceeds the person's current level of capability. The conditions for a strong developmental pull are created when someone is placed in a role or responsibility she hasn't mastered or for which the complexity of the task is slightly above her current capability. With the right amount of support, along with the challenge provided by the pull, growth is a natural process, one in which the person (or group, or division) must improve in order to meet the demand. This is part of assuming, as Decurion leaders say, that "people are ten times more capable than you think they are." In other words, the leaders hold a fundamental belief that people will grow, and can do more, with the right structures and conditions available to them.

The competency board works hand in hand with a scheduling practice that maximizes opportunities for developmental pull. Each week at every theater location, the location management team collaboratively plans the work schedules for every shift and role. As a general matter, Decurion executives believe in the value of frequent changes of responsibilities ("Don't let things settle," they say).

Decurion Business Leadership Meetings

A final practice brings all parts of the company together. Once every three to four months, depending on the need, the entire business leadership—every manager—attends a daylong DBL (Decurion business leadership) meeting. Most of the meeting takes place in one circle, with everyone able to see everyone else.

A DBL is a slower, more deeply reflective version of a huddle. There are no outside facilitators.[1] A DBL usually begins with individuals checking in, sharing the worries and excitement that have a hold on their attention, so that they can acknowledge these concerns and ideas and allow others to better understand what's going on interiorly. Senior leaders align intentions by foregrounding the issues that now require the entire community to act together as businesspeople first, rather than in the guise of their roles—for example, a real estate deal that will stretch the company by its scale and complexity, a national expansion of the theater circuit, the plan to launch a new business line the company has no direct experience in (yet).

Throughout the day, there are whole-group discussions of the requirements of business goals and the ways that parts of the company will need to stretch in capability to achieve business growth. The DBL may also include small-group discussions arranged by division, and celebrations of individuals who exemplify the values of the company. Leaders may share and lead a discussion of an evocative work of art, such as a poem, that heightens members' awareness of the challenges that lie ahead and encourages them to take heart in believing that they can grow in the ways that are required.

Life at Decurion, as at Bridgewater and Next Jump, provides a range of opportunities for development. The opportunities span various scales of routine—the hourly, the daily, the weekly, the monthly. They provide safe, trusting, and consistent places for this work within widening circles of community—from personal coaching, to team developmental dialogue, to shared organization-wide learning experiences. In that spirit, we borrow the idea of a "crew" from Decurion in observing something more general about DDOs. Working on oneself as part of a job requires that everyone, from the CEO to entry-level workers, has a crew to practice with—a trustworthy group of people who can be counted on as a source of challenge and support.

Five Qualities of Practicing in a DDO

Let's step back now from the practices you've seen in each of the DDOs. It's easier to see the differences rather than the similarities, so at this point let's quickly highlight several deeper commonalities in the developmental practices in these companies.

- *Practices help externalize struggles that are interior.* In each of these companies, the practices provide access to what we call the interior life. When the routine assumptions of the business world do not allow people to articulate and examine their limitations, there's little hope they can ever overcome them. The practices at Bridgewater, Next Jump, and Decurion represent a range of ways to allow people to disclose and work on parts of themselves that would typically be off-limits. Only by revealing to others and ourselves how we think, what we feel, and where we're stuck can we construct, over time, new ways of being.

- *Practices connect the work of the business to working on ourselves.* From issues logs to scheduling at ArcLight, practices in a DDO provide tangible ways for people to improve as the business grows. Rather than separate development activities (such as external coaching or sending high-potential employees to an executive MBA program), the DDO practices give people opportunities to work on improving themselves as part of meeting their job requirements. These activities are one in the same, rather than two things.

- *Practices move us from focusing on outcomes to the processes that generate outcomes.* In the practices we've surveyed, feedback is oriented not toward correcting an instance of behavior but toward shifting the mind-sets that produce the behaviors. Practices in a DDO do not reward or punish results independently of the processes that produced them; instead, they target improving the thinking that generates the results. When you're practicing inside a DDO, you are less concerned with the final score in any one game and more concerned with improving the way you play. Charlie Kim of Next Jump is often heard saying, "We focus on the long game, not the short game."

- *Language is a practice, and it creates new tools for a new paradigm.* DDOs are meaning-making cultures—cultures of dialogue. (In these organizations, you'll find many fewer PowerPoint slides and one-way presentations in meetings.) DDOs also develop their own insider language of practice (*backhand, dots, pulls*). Practices can seem opaque to outsiders, especially as a DDO matures and its increasingly fine-grained, coachable distinctions around practices become more elaborated. We don't see this as obfuscation. After all, you can't coach someone without a language for the coachable elements of performance. And remember, a DDO's priority is to strengthen its culture. These communities are making a trade-off. They will give up some of the default language of business in order to help people engage in practices they see as more powerful. To many outside, this makes the organization's discussions of its practices sound peculiar or even cultish, but they might miss the unique power that's released when an organization develops its language of practice.

- *Systemic stretch involves everyone, every day, across the organization.* DDOs get traction with their practices because the organization is saturated with them. As shown in table 4-3, practices are consistently implemented at multiple scales of time and community: daily, weekly, monthly; individual, pair, team, division, company. Rather than a few people having stretch assignments at any one time, we think of the constant all-level, all-the-time nature of practices in DDOs creating *systemic stretch*. Everyone in the culture is being pulled by challenges generated through the DDO's practices to keep acknowledging and trying to overcome the assumptions that limit them. Borrowing Bridgewater's metaphor, every job is a tow rope.

TABLE 4-3

Systemic stretch: integrating practices at multiple levels

Level	Bridgewater	Next Jump	Decurion
Micro (personal)	Daily updates Getting in sync	Talking partners	Touchpoints
Meso (team)	Issues log Dot Collector	Situational workshops	Pulse-check huddles
Macro (organization)	Daily cases	10X	DBLs

The Pan-Developmental Culture

Every practice rests on theory, even if the
practitioners themselves are unaware of it.

—Peter Drucker

How well do the practices work in supporting adult development in the more theoretically rigorous and research-grounded sense in which we define it in chapter 2? We weren't sure ourselves about the answer to this question until we fully immersed ourselves in the day-to-day life of these companies. Our conclusion stunned us: whether or not they were familiar with the theory of adult development (and only people at Decurion were deeply familiar), each of the organizations has come up with an evolving set of practices that ends up making their culture the most pan-developmental incubator for the growth of personal capability we have seen.

We realize this is a big claim, especially because, collectively, we have viewed many remarkable work cultures. What leads us to say this? Developmental researchers have long agreed on the most general characteristics of a human context that is especially supportive of development, whether the setting is the relationship of a parent to a child or a work culture. Technically referred to as a *holding environment*, the setting must deliver well, and at the appropriate time, on three broad functions that can most simply be named holding on, letting go, and sticking around.

Holding on refers to the need for the setting to receive and welcome the person exactly as she now is, with no requirement, at the moment, that she be anything different from who she is. The person is given ample opportunity to exercise the capabilities she has currently developed, and those capabilities are recognized and appreciated.

At the same time, the experience of engaging the world, and especially the encounter with difference and challenge, will eventually bring people to the limitations of their current way of constituting themselves. They may defend against these provocations by locating all the difficulty outside themselves, or—the growth alternative—they may begin to sense the need to become a more developed version of themselves. A good holding environment is itself a source of such provocation, even as it accepts who the person currently is.

In *letting go*, sometimes the holding environment acknowledges the person's own emerging sense of the need to reconstitute himself (and his relationship to the world, including the holding environment); at other times, the holding environment promotes that emerging sense. (Probably, in the best of circumstances, it is a combination of the two.) A parent who holds too tightly to the child-as-he-is-now rather than sponsor the adolescent-he-is-becoming, for example, is now "overholding" and no longer is best serving that person's development. Similarly, a company that holds people in the same job for too long, rewarding reliability and dependability as a means to encourage people to be the same people they have been, is not optimally developmental.

When, by letting go, the holding environment acknowledges that the worker no longer need depend on the environment the way she has or the environment no longer needs to hold her as it has, an important question for the developing person becomes, "In pushing away from the holding environment (my parent or my current job), do I lose you, or do I form a new relationship with you, one that recognizes the bigger person I have become and accords me a greater sphere of influence?" Asking this question begins a new form of holding, with the person ready to repeat the cycle. This is the holding environment *sticking around* to be reconnected with in a new way.

Long-term relationships (in families and at work) that cultivate our growth, rather than ending because of our growth, are precious, and they're necessary for the continuity and wholeness of our lives. Sometimes, at work, our need to find a bigger job that matches the bigger person we have become necessitates our departure. But if, every time you grow, your work setting is unable to stick around and "re-cognize" (literally "reknow") who you are, it is a terrible loss, both for you and for the work setting, which does not benefit from the very development it has fostered.

An optimally developmental work culture not only does an especially good job of holding on, letting go, or sticking around, but also does an especially good job of all three—and it does this good job, not only for people who occupy one particular place in development but also for those who occupy various positions in the entire trajectory of adult development.

Now you know the fullest meaning of "everyone" when we refer to the DDO as an *everyone culture*. It does not simply mean that everyone (and not only a chosen few) gets developmental support; it means that the culture works developmentally—supports you and challenges you—wherever you may be in your developmental journey. It works developmentally for everyone.

"Whoa," you might say, "that sounds like a tall order." And you would be right. Probably every DDO, including the three we studied, finds, at any moment in its evolution, that it is falling short of this ideal in some respect. Developmental organizations must be allowed to develop, too.

But what is remarkable to us, in surveying the practices of each of these companies, is how pan-developmental they really are. *Pan-developmental*, then, means two things: the company does all three things a good holding environment needs to do—holds on, lets go, and sticks around. And it does this for everyone at every stage in adult development.

Holding On, Letting Go, Sticking Around—for All Stages

As headlined in table 4-4, each of these companies' sets of practices serves to hold on in a way that is unusual for work organizations. As you learned earlier, the experience of vulnerability is a wellspring in a DDO, but to be willing to be vulnerable you must trust that the community will still receive you, include you, and value you. Everyone has experienced the kind of vulnerability that leaves you feeling cast out, more alone, unworthy, and ashamed. *Well-held vulnerability* is our term for feeling simultaneously as if you are the furthest thing from your most well-put-together self but you are still valued and included.

Well-held vulnerability is an experience people do not feel often enough. When asked where they have ever felt it, most people

TABLE 4-4

The DDO as holding environment

Holding on

- Workers experience well-held vulnerability.
- Workers are valued for revealing their mistakes and weaknesses.
- The culture invites the whole person in (life is not divided between work and away from work).
- The culture acknowledges and genuinely listens to and for the whole person.

Letting go

- Workers continuously receive feedback.*
- Workers continuously give feedback.*
- Workers have ongoing encounters with differences.
- Workers regularly lift their heads beyond their locality.
- The culture says, "The best job is the one you don't yet know how to do."

Sticking around

- A series of work roles, of increasing scope and authority, is the rule, not the exception.
- Rank does not have its usual privileges (upward feedback is encouraged).

*Being invited to continuously give and receive feedback can also be a form of good holding.

reference their intimate relationships or an experience in therapy or perhaps in a faith community; some people who have been in combat with their band of brothers and sisters, or part of a particularly intense sports team, will think of those settings. Rarely—almost never, outside a DDO—do people reference their place of work.

At the same time that these companies hold on in a rare way, they are also about letting go. "As soon as I really got my legs under me and began to feel comfortable in this job," we heard in all three companies, "I was invited into a new one." But the provocations to "leave home" go beyond what you're doing; they are continuously about crossing borders in the way you're thinking.

The most general pattern we see is that the practices stretch people to step back from a narrow (less complex) focus to a larger (more complex) one. For example, the pulse-check huddles at Decurion stretch crew members to look beyond a defined task or function, beyond their own individual performance, and to embrace a larger, more complex system, focusing on how the specific parts relate to the whole operation. Similarly, the talking partner practice and the situational workshops at Next Jump, and the root cause analyses at Bridgewater, challenge people who are giving feedback to focus not only on a colleague's particular decisions and the quality of the

outcomes (less complex) but also to look for the patterns across decisions and outcomes, thereby helping the colleague identify the mind-
set that produces the pattern (more complex).

The desired shift to greater complexity is not necessarily about
handling more information (more specifics) but about meaningfully
organizing the information into a larger system. The individual must
step back from the concrete to conduct a more abstract, higher level
of analysis. The more the practices stretch people to make these types
of "meta" moves, the more people move beyond the limits of their
current developmental mind-sets.

But perhaps the fullest expression of these cultures' pan-
developmental nature has to do with the way their most pervasive
practices serve their members developmentally wherever they may
be in their development. A practice—for example, continuously
receiving feedback—can provide a different experience across a host
of developmental positions (see table 4-5). Moreover, each of these
can be usefully supportive or usefully challenging. (The same can be
said for other practices, such as the experience of continuously *giving*
feedback.)

For an individual moving toward the socialized plateau, for example, the stretch is to subordinate one's concrete needs to identify with
a larger (external) collection of ideas or people. An adolescent crew
member working in one of Decurion's ArcLight movie theaters, for
example, might likely be making this developmental move. And the
motivation to be aligned with and working to support the effectiveness of the larger team and the larger operation that occurs during
pulse-check huddles can stretch that adolescent to grow toward the
socialized plateau.

In turn, giving and receiving feedback can stretch an individual
to move beyond the socialized mind toward self-authorship when
the external sources of authority are no longer ultimate, when alignment with them is no longer unquestioningly one's goal. Instead, the
individual develops a more complex system that can put external
authorities in relationship to one's own growing internal authority.

For example, at Bridgewater, employees are not expected to
embrace another's opinion unquestioningly. Rohit, whom you met
earlier, is a junior staffer and yet is expected to challenge (via the

TABLE 4-5

The pan-developmental benefits of continuously receiving feedback

	The socialized mind	The self-authoring mind
Supports and confirms	In receiving feedback (listening, not immediately rejecting it), I align with, am faithful to, and feel included in and respected by my community for properly observing a core value.*	In listening to feedback, I have opportunities to read and manage my own defensiveness or triggers; in evaluating it, I have opportunities to exercise my own independent perspective; in accepting it, I have opportunities to modify and improve my independent perspective (within-the-frame adjustments to make it stronger, shore it up; remodeling vs. big architectural restructuring); in rejecting it, I have opportunities to flex the muscles of my own perspective or filter.
Challenges and stretches	In receiving feedback less defensively, I have opportunities to be less identified with it (wiped out by it; made up by it); in evaluating it, I have opportunities to explore whether there is an internal seat of judgment that can stand in relation to it (decide about it, push back on it, choose to accept it). In pushing back on it, can I risk possibly not meeting the other's expectations? I can ask myself, "Am I out of alignment, violating the faith, for not agreeing?"***	In listening to it and considering feedback, I have opportunities to be bigger than my own current perspective, filter, or machine; opportunities to hold that frame more tentatively, to bear what initially can feel like a loss of self or control, to more fully take on a growth mind-set (continuous practice) vs. a fixed mind-set (continuous series of performances); opportunities to be more identified with the process of rearchitecting than with any one building.

*Note: Although the same could be said for the faithful performance of any value, practice, or attitude endorsed by any coherent culture—for example, making no mistakes in a high-reliability organization, or "always be closing (ABC)" in a sales-oriented culture—the important difference here is that you are aligning with a value and practice that is more likely to move you *beyond* this developmental position.

**Note: Of course, the answer in a DDO, from an objective position, is "Not necessarily," but in this developmental position, that is only an emerging recognition.

issues log) what he sees as the department head's overreliance on consultants. When Alex deflects Rohit's concern by claiming the company's practice with the consultants is "well designed" without justifying why he sees it that way, CEO Greg Jensen's view is that Alex's deflection "claims authority" without providing his logical reasoning so that Rohit can assess Alex's thinking.

In this way, the Bridgewater culture actively encourages individuals not to blindly accept opinions from authorities (its own leaders). Instead, each individual is expected to ask for and assess the logic and evidence independently. This is an especially developmental provocation to anyone who has begun to experience the limits of her socialized mind. These Bridgewater practices are meant to be used to develop one's own independent (self-authored) conclusions based on assessing and coordinating the views of others (using criteria such as logic, evidence, and believability).

But just as true, the self-authoring individual is stretched to move beyond her internally generated authority and system of beliefs when the feedback she receives shows her how the theories and metrics that make up her system are preventing her from embracing entirely new (and formerly "other") systems. For example, the canary in the coal mine feedback that Nora Dashwood received was that others felt the air get cold when she disapproved of an idea that did not align with her thinking. That feedback led her to uncover the limiting assumptions that had been guiding her leadership and to explore whether they were always accurate. Through a series of experiments and reflections designed to test her assumptions (the process for overturning an "immunity to change," which you will see in chapter 6), Dashwood came to see that being more open to others' views and others' ways of working not only produced good results but also gave her deep satisfaction in this very different approach to leadership. Thus the same cultural practice—giving or receiving feedback continuously—can both hold on, and let go of, a variety of adult developmental positions.

Putting It All into Practice

Let's pause to survey the path you've walked through the daily landscape of these three companies. You've seen the wide variety, intense pace, and careful design of routines for pushing people to work at their growing edge. What is the source of energy and discipline that these practices provide in a DDO? What makes them effective rather than merely add-ons to working life? We wonder whether any of the following ideas resonate with you.

- "You can't work on yourself and help others to do the same (edge) without the safety of a supportive community (home) and routines that name and normalize the work (groove)."

- "It takes everyone playing the same game, by the same rules, to encourage people to take real risks."

- "If there's a more growth-oriented alternative to a culture of celebrating 'talent' or 'performance,' it might be celebrating constant practice and the way it pays off for people and the company."

- "Practicing can help people feel over time something like this: 'If I risk showing my weaknesses, nothing too bad will happen to me, I'll probably learn something, and I'll be better for it in the end.'"

- "Helping others practice (Better You) has its own special satisfaction, and everyone—not just the managers or the leaders—has the chance to experience it."

We suspect you've been making your own sense out of these practices, even trying them on for fit as you encountered each one, resonating deeply with some and finding others a little cringe-inducing. (If you did recoil a bit at a practice we shared, you might ask, "What about it made me most uncomfortable, as an outsider looking in?" Did it make you feel like something would be at risk for *you* if you were in the shoes of the participant? Might your reaction be different if you were in an organization in which everyone was in it together, engaging in that practice regularly?)

In the end, there is nothing magical about these specific practices. They aren't recipes or checklists, and we don't present any of them as ripe for emulation in every context. Rather, we hope you see the deeper structure that lies behind systems of practices in different companies in different industries—deliberately developmental organizations with no prior contact with one another before we introduced them quite late in our research.

What their practices share is not about the surface-level features—whether a given kind of dialogue always happens in pairs, follows a weekly or biweekly rhythm, happens via mobile app or face-to-face across a conference room table (although it is features like these, understandably, that jump out to the implementers among us as being the most tangible).

Rather than skip directly to implementing a particular practice out of the box, you might think about the ways these practices emerged over time in their original organizational test-beds. They evolved through experimentation and trial and error, through setting aside practices that were not working, and through sticking to difficult new kinds of conversations long enough to witness the payoff.

They grew, most importantly, when leaders counted on the fact that people could become better versions of themselves directly through the work challenges facing them every day—that people could practice getting better even while doing great work. The leaders of these companies paid careful attention to and adapted their approaches in light of the constant stream of evidence about whether the business was doing better because people were making better decisions, were growing faster, were taking greater levels of responsibility for increasingly complex tasks, were spending less time protecting their favored images of themselves and more time doing the real work, and were able to work more effectively together.

What's more, they understood that the culture they were shaping through these practices had to be an everyone culture. There could not be practices that applied to the rank and file, and a different set of rules and expectations for the leaders. Everything they were asking people to do required people to be transparent, vulnerable, and trusting with each other. Without systematic transparency and trustworthiness—clarity about the intentions of the company and its leaders—the practices could end up being meaningless charades, things people pretended to do to keep their jobs but nothing more.

As you consider what it would be like to take on practices like these in your organization or one you could imagine shaping, we invite you to think about the deeper intention of practicing daily at work: to uncover, explore, and transcend the limiting assumptions of individuals and businesses. We encourage you, too, to use that deeper foundation to imagine what practices like these might look like in an entirely different setting or industry. What kinds of routines would help you and the people around you, as part of your daily flow of work, feel enough trust and structure to look directly and without fear at your individual and collective barriers to change?

Like most things in the life of a DDO, practices aren't static, and these organizations continue to fine-tune small things and redesign entire systems. We think of DDOs at any stage—from the earliest efforts at culture shift to the maturity of our featured three companies—as works in progress. We mean to use that phrase in two senses. First, DDOs are unfinished and never-finished products. As you will see in chapter 5, DDOs are built on the assumption that the continuing growth of the business comes through the continuing growth of its people. With changing people, practices, business opportunities, and market and industry conditions, organizations are constantly adapting.

But there is a second meaning to a work in progress. A DDO, as it evolves, is always a human creation (a work) that, at its core, generates progress. This progress can be seen in business results, in the unfolding potential of individual lives, and in the growth of collective capability. How does this new kind of human creation actually become an engine that can generate progress? As we hope you have experienced in this chapter, the structures for constant, immersive, layered practicing hold the promise of shifting mind-sets throughout an organization, wherever workers may be in their personal evolution. With a coherent system of practices like these, the tools for generating a new kind of human progress through business are within reach in each of our offices and meeting rooms.

5

But Is This Any Way to Run a Business?

The Strictly Business Value of Being a DDO

One of the easiest ways to misunderstand a DDO is to conclude that these people are not serious about being a business. When hard-boiled businesspeople see the most senior people in the company spending hours with employees half their age on what they would call mere "personnel issues," their most charitable reactions are along the lines of, "Nice impulse; lousy way to run a business."

"I'm not going to call their leaders naive, or their companies cults, as I've heard some people do," one business analyst told us, "but it's clear these folks are playing a fundamentally different game. The leaders have the souls of teachers more than businesspeople. If you want to use your business as a kind of prop to run a university or Human Potential Center, well, that's very nice. All power to you. But you better have deep pockets or a product that sells itself—some way to pay for all this fooling around—because otherwise bankruptcy is right around the corner. This may be a good way to help Jake or Jennifer find their voice, but it's no way to run a real business."

The most interesting question along these lines for us is not, Is it possible to run a successful business (as *success* is conventionally defined) while, at the same time, giving so much attention to the work of developing people's capabilities? We think that question has already been answered. The *Economist* credited Bridgewater with having made more money for its investors than any other hedge fund in history. Decurion's combined theaters have the highest gross per screen in North America. *INC Magazine* called Next Jump "the most successful company you've never heard of."

Of course it's possible to succeed as a DDO. In 2008, the United States, and much of the world, suffered the biggest economic collapse since the Great Depression. Forecasters, financial advisers, and strategy consulting firms either wrung their hands over failing to anticipate so great a downturn, or consoled themselves with the thought that no one else saw it coming either. But it's not true that no one else saw it coming. Bridgewater leaders warned anyone who would listen, followed its own analysis, and protected its clients' investments.

As for Next Jump, the industry average annual turnover among coders in high-tech companies is a whopping 40 percent. The visible and hidden costs of replacing even a single employee are significant. If you imagine paying those costs for nearly half your enterprise every year, you begin to glimpse the volatility of this sector. Next Jump's annual turnover before it matured into a full-fledged DDO was no different from its high-tech competitors—40 percent for 2010 and 2011. Now its year-on-year turnover is in the single digits, while the sector remains at 40 percent.

The senior living industry, providing residential facilities and care to senior citizens, is a highly regulated one, as you would expect. Decurion, with no prior history in health care, made its way through the maze of approvals in California and entered the industry in a matter of weeks.

A more interesting question is this one: Do these companies succeed despite, or *because of*, their unusual cultures? Are their success and their DDO-hood mere coincidences, or does being a DDO contribute to their success? This is the question we explore in this chapter.

The leaders of Bridgewater, Next Jump, and Decurion feel certain that their cultures create their business success. As friendly skeptics, we asked them to convince us. To apply Bridgewater's medicine to itself, we said, "You believe it, but is it true?" *Post hoc ergo propter hoc* ("After this, therefore because of this") is a cardinal fallacy in logic. The question is this: "You created a certain kind of culture, and, after that, your business flourished. But how do you know one caused the other?" Maybe Ray Dalio is just a genius investor.

And Next Jump, which had annual growth of about 30 percent, evolved to a full-fledged DDO and then had growth of more than 100 percent for three years running. Their leaders believe that one thing caused the other, but do they have good reason to? Maybe, as an e-commerce business, Next Jump is riding the crest of an economic recovery; people shop more in a recovery.

Having given the question of causation a lot of thought (which we share with you shortly), we've come to a view similar to that of these leaders. In telling you this, you may feel we've spoiled our ending—but we don't think so. We still have a little surprise in store. It was a surprise to us what shows up if you take seriously the assertion that these companies' business success may be more because of, than in spite of, their unusual cultures. But we will save that surprise for the end.

Next Jump's Success and Its DDO-hood

When we pushed Charlie Kim and coleader Meghan Messenger to convince us that Next Jump's leap to 100 percent annual growth (from 30 percent), and to a turnover reduction to single digits (from 40 percent), was because of its explicit commitment to being a DDO, they didn't have a fast answer. (And, by the way, although Messenger, by nature, is more circumspect, for Kim not to have a fast answer to anything is unusual. As you've learned, everyone at Next Jump can tell you whether they lean toward arrogance or insecurity, and Kim will tell you easily he leans toward arrogance.)

The only way for them to answer our question was to unpack what it means, in practice, to say that they led Next Jump into becoming more deliberately developmental. In retrospect, they see it as an evolution, and not a revolution, that started well before 2012, the year leadership "ripened," leading to the financial outperformance.

In the early years, many of Next Jump's leadership training programs did not cover the entire company. Its culture was not an everyone culture. The programs targeted specific individuals who showed the most promise and invested in them early in their careers. The executives told us that this ultimately led to enhanced retention, as it became evident Next Jump would commit to growing leaders from within and at an accelerated rate. The company then took what worked in small teams and scaled it into programs across the entire company. Kim says, "Financial performance showed up last. It's the lagging indicator of our culture; it takes time to grow people. It's not an overnight task."

What did they think was the most important change in the way the company operated? They came to two things.

1. *They continuously transferred authority downward.* Starting at the top, the two most senior leaders gave much of their jobs away to their most talented lieutenants. For years, Kim and Messenger had literally run their business, as you would think the leaders might. They were the "revenue captains," each week monitoring the dashboards that kept track of every aspect of operations and taking actions accordingly. Today two of their groomed associates are running the week-to-week operations of the company. (One of them, by the way, is thirty-two, and the other is twenty-eight. Their e-commerce sales last year were in the billions.)

   The transfer of authority was accelerated in 2012 when Messenger had her second child, experiencing the time constraints that come with being a working mother. She recalls a conversation with Kim when she said, "I don't want to work these hours. I want more time with my children." Kim responded, "I don't want to run the company alone. The only way this will be possible is to have everyone else own everything. We need to create more leaders."

   Transferring authority downward gives people a dramatically more complex job, with wider responsibilities and new demands, on both their learning and their performance. Those who have made the transfer are freed to turn to a different kind of work. What should they do with that windfall of work's most precious commodity—the time of its senior people?

2. *They reconceived the role of the coach.* Messenger and Kim devoted a huge proportion of the freed time to coaching— coaching their direct reports, coaching other leaders to coach. Their reconstitution of the coach's role became part of the company's DNA right down the line. Most business-related coaches, if they're honest, admit they know only a slice of their client's full work reality—the slice the client makes available to them. This is not the case with a Next Jump coach. You can't coach a person at Next Jump unless you've done that person's job and know it inside out. The coaching role is not outsourced; the company's full-on commitment to continuous teaching does not add to the workforce. Rather, it is hardwired into the way people on the line spend their time.

Business and School

As it happens, the authors of this book are professional educators. We work in a graduate school of education, and not business or management. We have studied learning and schooling. We think about what it takes to significantly alter the quality of learning in a classroom, a school district, or a university. In looking at these two key features of the change Next Jump made, we have only to turn our heads a little to see something familiar.

The twin pillars that hold up school are the curriculum (what is to be learned?) and the pedagogy (how will it be taught?). Slight adjustments to either element might lead to modest changes in the nature, depth, and quality of people's learning. If you want to transform the learning enterprise (in a school or at work), you need to reconstitute both the curriculum and the pedagogy. This pretty much amounts to what Next Jump has done. In continuously moving the work down the chain, the company keeps giving people a qualitatively bigger job (not just a quantitatively bigger scope of responsibility); the work becomes more complex. The company continuously ramps up the challenge of a job's curriculum.

By itself, though, this change is not enough. To give people a qualitatively more complex curriculum, you must qualitatively alter the nature of the teaching support you provide them so that they might master it. You begin by expecting them not to be able to do the work successfully. In a conventional work context, this may seem like an odd qualification for a job. But in a school, if you could master the year's curriculum on the first day, you wouldn't belong in that grade level.

So you begin by expecting that workers cannot do the work successfully, and you provide them a teaching staff that will help them gradually grow into the job. By hardwiring the coaching activity into the line leader's job responsibility—a line leader who has himself done this very job—you alter the sourcing, credibility, and quality of the teaching. In short, Next Jump radically altered the nature of work's curriculum and pedagogy.

Improving Retention and Productivity

We've described the essence of what Next Jump did. Why should we believe that these actions might have had a direct effect on retention and productivity?

Let's start with retention. If you ask people what they like about working at Next Jump (or Decurion or Bridgewater, for that matter), the two most common answers are, "I'm doing things here I would have had to wait years to do somewhere else" and, "What I like most about working here is the same thing I could tell you I hate most about working here. Whenever I come close to mastering a job, they give me a new one, and I am in over my head again, grrrr."

It's an honest answer, that second one, and it deserves a pause for consideration. It reflects the tension that all of us struggle with, between our own internal longings for both the progressive and the conservative. Work settings that will let you stay in a job you've mastered, and that appreciate and reward the dependable, high-quality output you consistently deliver, are a good match for those who prefer to settle this tension on the side of the conservative. The conservative impulse places a high premium on maintaining equilibrium. It doesn't make you a bad person for having this preference. But ordinary organizations typically favor the conservative (even when they talk about innovation and entrepreneurship) and may deprive their employees of the opportunity to discover their true preference.

When people in a DDO curse the very thing they've come to love, they're acknowledging the pull of the conservative but reaffirming that they've found something they experience as more precious. It's messy and tumultuous to undergo so much disequilibrium. Status, certainty, predictability, and control are never permanently in hand. Like anyone, of course, people sometimes prefer a little less stimulation, thank you; but in the main, being rewarded for reliably and repeatedly performing a role we have mastered comes to feel like coasting, and we fear we may be missing out on a clearly preferred alternative. Any honest person working in a DDO will tell you there are times she would like a holiday from the DDO experience, but after you've worked in one, an ordinary workplace becomes for many the nice place to visit and not the place where you want to live.

How strong is this preference? What if the ordinary workplace offers to pay you a much bigger salary or give you more of the perks and goodies highly sought-after high-tech employees have come to expect and demand? What if it continuously tempts you with these offers? Next Jump gets several thousand early-career applicants a year and hires about ten. The typical hire is a standout from MIT, Carnegie Mellon, or Georgia Tech. Her services are in high demand. No one who found the pressures of a DDO not to their liking would have any trouble finding a new job. Kim and Messenger tell us it is not unusual for their employees to receive a serious solicitation every week.

In 2010, just as Next Jump became a top recruiter of engineers from East Coast universities, its turnover skyrocketed. The shortage of engineering talent in the industry was (and still is) severe. Next Jump became a hub of engineering talent, and technology companies found that the fastest and best way to recruit engineers was to poach from Next Jump. Engineers exited the company, easily trading up for better compensation and often doubling and tripling their salaries.

But then Next Jump matured into a full-fledged DDO in 2012, and now engineers rarely leave. Before the Next Jump transition, engineers weren't finding the person above them regularly passing his job down to them, and now they do. We don't know whether the one thing contributes to the other, but to us it seems like a compelling hypothesis.

Probably everyone wants to work where he feels he's getting the greatest income; it's just that there are many kinds of incomes. There are external incomes and internal incomes. There is money, and there are opportunities to experience your own unfolding. Each of the incomes may have some value for most of us. We differ in how we prioritize them.

How else can we account for the sharp reduction in turnover? The alternative offers did not suddenly stop. Next Jump didn't soup up its salary schedule at the same time it became a DDO. It didn't start giving people leased sports cars. It changed one big thing: it increased the intrinsic, internal incomes. And, over time, it has clearly done a better job in its hiring processes, finding people for whom this form of income shows up as highly valuable. That combination—being a DDO and doing better at finding people who will feel well paid in a DDO—seems to us the most plausible explanation for the way Next Jump solved the turnover problem.[1]

It's easier to draw a direct line between the way Next Jump altered work's curriculum and pedagogy, on the one hand, and the increase in its productivity, on the other. Its productivity can be directly tied to the number of revenue-generating projects or initiatives it can launch and capably captain.

Being a Good School

Another way of describing Next Jump's transition to a DDO is that it turned its business into a captain-creating machine. In a company full of engineers, the leaders' proudest engineering feat is that they've created an engine that cultivates captains.

Cultivating captains means more than just giving more people opportunities to lead initiatives and projects. It also means providing them with an ongoing coaching, mentoring, and teaching wraparound that increases the chances the captain will succeed. By making the person who has done the job the coach, they increase the quality of the teaching. By deriving the coach from their existing workforce and deriving coaching time from the benefits of delegation, they increase the economic sustainability of the teaching. The arguable formula is that (a) more captains, taking on (b) more revenue-generating projects, working with (c) sustainably continuous support, leads to (d) dramatically higher productivity.

And, of course, the reduction in turnover is related to the increase in productivity. It takes time to cultivate a captain. If you're losing too many good people, no one is staying in your school long enough to return its benefits.

We're not suggesting that what is unusual about Next Jump is that it brought the fundamental features of schooling to the world of work. Every workplace is a kind of school and can be assessed by its curriculum and pedagogy, whether or not it is a DDO. It's just that—to be blunt—most workplaces are not very good schools.

In most cases (particularly in mature companies) the workplace is a poor school because people take the same curriculum over and over again. Instead of feeling that they're failing, being forced to repeat the class rather than be promoted, people find their reliability and dependability labeled a form of success that earns them rewards.

In some cases (more commonly in start-ups, or during enterprise-wide shifts in mature companies), workplaces are poor schools for the opposite reason: they present people with extremely challenging curricula but do an inadequate job of providing sufficiently talented and pervasive teaching support so that they can master the curriculum.

So, in one way or another, most organizations are poor schools. It would be understandable for leaders of such organizations to say, "Well, we don't care how good a school we are; that's not why we exist. We only care how good a business we are." And that would be a fine response, if being a good "school," in the way we're talking about it here, were not crucial to being a good business in a volatile, uncertain, complex, ambiguous (VUCA) environment.

Just how valuable is it for a company to be a good school? We have only begun to explore that question, using Next Jump as a first point of inquiry. In becoming a DDO, Next Jump altered its work curriculum and work pedagogy by transferring authority downward and by providing systematic forms of support to help people master a more complex job. We've suggested that these shifts may have had direct benefits for the company. Now we want to generalize this point by saying what any employee from Decurion or Bridgewater has been thinking while reading this chapter: "Well, that's exactly what we do, too!" Pushing the work downward and helping people successfully handle the way their work lives have changed are not just basic elements of Next Jump's architecture. Given their robust presence across all three companies, they are likely fundamental elements of the DDO itself.

Bridgewater's Success and Its DDO-hood

Bridgewater CEO Greg Jensen could not be clearer about his answer to this chapter's question: "We do not think of our culture as a 'contributor' to our business success; we do not think of it as a 'factor.' We think of it as, literally, the cause of our success. We are successful because of our culture. We think of the culture as itself our business strategy. Full stop."

You already know that challenging every belief is a watchword of the Bridgewater culture, so you will not be surprised that Jensen has given thought to the basis for this belief. It begins with a consideration of what it takes to succeed in the investment management business. "First, you need to have an independent view, because you are trying to beat the market, and the general consensus is already priced in to the market," he says. "Second, you need real insight; that independent view has to be worthwhile. Third, you need the humility to survive being wrong, because you are going to be wrong a lot of the time. Finally, you have to be more accurate than not, over the long term."

Jensen draws a direct line from the Bridgewater culture to these attributes.

> How do you get a genuinely independent view that is not based on, or a reaction to, the way someone else is thinking? How do you be more often right than wrong? How do you remain humble enough in the face of your success so that you can survive your success? For us, we connect the fact that we have been the most successful investment management company in the world—in terms of return for our clients, largest hedge fund in the world, etc.—to being independent, insightful, accurate, and humble; and how do we achieve these? When we look at what we have invented, to us it all

comes from a focus on what could be wrong, meritocracy of ideas, argument about the best way to do things, and getting out the ideas that other people didn't have. If you look at our inventions—first investment company to systematize human intuition, first investment company to split off alpha and beta, the first to sell pure alpha to institutional investors because that was the best way for them to access alpha, totally redefine how people put together their passive portfolio with our "all weather" approach—those inventions didn't exist in the world, and no one person at Bridgewater could have created them. They came out of an idea meritocracy that allowed us to have totally different ways of doing something that thousands of people were doing similarly.

Improving Employee and Client Retention

You cannot create a culture like a DDO unless you can retain people for long periods, and we've mentioned that, after the first two years of trial by fire, few leave Bridgewater.

Low turnover of the right people is itself a positive business indicator, but does Jensen believe it can be attributed to Bridgewater's culture? "Without the culture, without the kinds of relationships total honesty brings, I don't think we would have those kinds of [retention] numbers," he says.

> I can see this just personally. When I joined I certainly never thought I would be here for twenty years. The reason I am here is these relationships that are a function of the total honesty; the amount I have grown from the kind of feedback that I get; all my weaknesses being illustrated to me; the reflectiveness that has allowed me to move forward in life. But that is just me. We survey our people every two months, and anonymously every year. The vast majority point to the culture as the absolute key to what keeps them here.

What can matter more to the success of a professional services firm than the quality of its relationships with its clients? Bridgewater is proud of having a distinctive relationship with the majority of its clients, and Jensen ties that distinction directly to its culture.

We are unlike any other hedge fund in the world in that our clients look at us as a strategic partner. When we survey our clients and ask them to describe us, more than half do not call us a hedge fund or an investment manager; they call us a strategic partner. This is radical in our industry. For the most part, the relationship between investment managers and their clients is more of a *quid pro quo* relationship. They are out hiring managers, trying to get the best return, trying to negotiate the best fees, and so on. In our industry it is very rarely a deep, trustful relationship.

Interestingly, when asked where he thinks the company's distinctive relationships come from, Jensen returns immediately to the culture and not to the economic return clients enjoy. "It comes from twenty years of relating to them in ways consistent with our culture, being totally honest with them, bringing them ideas that no one else had, never thinking in terms of a product to sell but thinking in terms of what is the best way to do things, working with them to do that, getting our client advisers to form these kinds of relationships—it all comes from the culture inside Bridgewater, brought outside to them."

In considering the strictly business value of a DDO, we can't discuss Bridgewater without returning briefly to one of its most distinctive business accomplishments. In the midst of the worst economic crisis since the Great Depression—in 2008, the worst year of the ensuing recession, when individuals, companies, and countries were reeling from downward lurching markets—Bridgewater earned 9.4 percent for its investors. It would have been an extraordinary accomplishment to have held losses to a minimum, but Bridgewater made money for its clients. Throughout the several years of the recession, 80 percent of Bridgewater's trades were winners, and CEO Ray Dalio was on record, years before the downturn, warning of an impending crisis.

All this is testimony to some kind of special edge, to be sure; but is it reasonable to attribute this success to Bridgewater's being a DDO? One thing you learn when you spend time with Dalio or Jensen is that they are full of passionate convictions about how wrong we can be in our passionate convictions. For all the credit Bridgewater receives for having known something and having been right about it when others didn't know and were wrong, Dalio and Jensen naturally present themselves not as great seers, but as people who must stay continuously mindful that they frequently do not know, that they are frequently wrong, and that knowing *this* may be the most important thing they do know.

As someone who wrote an e-mail to the entire company with the subject, "I fail every day," Dalio will tell you that the company's success in the economic crisis stems from the same source as the company's culture. The e-mail included this line.

> These results were due to Bridgewater's way of being, most importantly because deep, independent thinking and debate about what is true allowed us to understand deleveragings and hold a well-thought-out view that was different from the consensus.[2]

Jensen is far less impressed than outside observers that Bridgewater predicted the economic downturn. It seems to be his view that, like a stopped clock that is right twice a day, someone will always come up with a correct prediction. It's more important to plan for the things you anticipate as well as things you're wrong about. From Jensen's point of view, this is the real accomplishment, and it came about, first and last, because of Bridgewater's culture.

> How did we have a game plan for banks failing, for a financial crisis of this magnitude, and how could we successfully manage money through it, even though none of the principals in the firm had ever personally experienced anything like this? Through our process of always probing what could you be wrong about, always writing down what we believe, stress-testing all of our thoughts, getting beyond our own experience, what can we learn from prior situations, thinking through what happened in the Great Depression or Japan's bubble collapse, we force ourselves to think better about how do you manage through a real financial crisis. As we managed through it, we made lots of mistakes, saw lots of ways we were wrong, and learned through that, compounded that understanding as well, improving our model.

This may sound like a paean to the value of steely-eyed analytic judgment and rigorous stress-testing of the logic and evidence for every cause-and-effect proposition. But that is only half of what it means to "go deep" at Bridgewater, whether the discussion is about the credit-lending pattern of a bank or a manager's third consecutive inability to deliver his work product on the day he promised. Dalio is a well-read aficionado of brain science, and in both cases the analysis is not the work of the neocortex (the analytic part of the brain) alone; it's also about the amygdala (the more primitive, reactive part) and the relationship between "thinking slow" and "thinking fast," to use the words of psychologist Daniel Kahneman.[3]

How does our aversion to loss—threats we may feel about losses of status, control, predictability, affection, respect, and the like—incline us to cognitive distortions that cloud our judgment and lead us to poor performance as managers of people or managers of money? In both cases—in all cases, Bridgewater's culture suggests—we are managing only one thing: ourselves. This is what the banking expert meant when he told us on our first day visiting, after we asked him how Bridgewater's culture had anything to do with the work of an investment adviser: "The culture is not a 'piece' of how I do my work. It is the whole context in which I do my work. I get up every day, very clear what I am working on—myself."

Earlier we mentioned Jensen's observation that people need humility to survive being wrong. You can get a sense of what he means by humility if you look at something Bridgewater has not yet succeeded at. In 2009, founder Ray Dalio announced he was ready to vacate the role of CEO. How does a company whose distinctive profile is so much the expression of its founder survive his departure, carrying that distinction to the next generation? This is a living question for Bridgewater, but, in one form or another, it is a widely recognizable question many young companies face. "This will be a great test," Jensen says, "and it's not a test it is clear we will pass." He continues:

> How much can you create a very unique culture and get it to carry on beyond the person who created it? This is Ray's last vision, to make the way this culture works *perpetual*. Obviously, our thoughts will change as we continue to learn and improve; no one expects that to be perpetual. But this process

by which we do learn—focusing relentlessly on how we are right and how we are wrong, as individuals, and collectively, how to sustain an idea meritocracy; all of these things—how to make that perpetual. We are six years into a ten-year process. It has been bumpy; it has been difficult, because we—the leadership team, including me—have struggled to do the things necessary to make that work.

It would be premature to say, in this instance, that the culture is the cause of the successful solution of this business problem, because it hasn't yet been successfully resolved. But it is clear that Bridgewater, unlike other companies, is putting its bets on its culture here, as it has for every other business challenge it has faced.

Listen to Jensen on how he, and his peers, are using their culture as the strategy to successfully receive the mantle Dalio is passing to them.

We've done this radically transparently. Everyone in the company knows about our struggles. The people involved are evolving as a function of going through this in an extremely open, caring, transparent, logical way. That seems unique, for the whole community to have a complete window into this process, to provide feedback on how we are doing and what we are doing. When you look at transitions of founders, I don't think there is anything like this—in terms of declaring it will be a ten-year process, knowing it will be a struggle, doing the struggle in a completely open and transparent way. We will see. I'm certainly not saying our culture and process will solve every problem, so we may not succeed, but if we don't succeed, we will have failed openly, transparently, logically, and that's being true to applying our culture as a strategy for everything, even the succession challenge.

We asked Jensen how it was going, how he would even judge how successfully things were going. After all, six years is no small time sample.

It has been an incredible learning journey, so at one level that is already a kind of success. Because we are going through it transparently, logically, we are all learning an unbelievable amount by struggling with this huge problem. We're learning about each other, and what works and doesn't work in terms of culture and company. That part has been a great success, in the sense that it is extremely meaningful work, the learning is incredible, and I think most people involved feel very connected to, and like they own, the process, and that they feel the benefits of meaningful work.

But, to bring us back to where this chapter began, Bridgewater is not a university. Jensen again:

> Of course, the goal is not just the learning—although that is a huge part of why the people who work here live, so that is a good in itself—but in terms of the business outcome, twenty years from now, thirty years from now, will Bridgewater be unique in these ways that have made it successful? As we look at that, we'd say, "Boy, six years in, incredible progress, and still, the probability is lower than we are comfortable with"— meaning that, because we haven't filled some of the leadership roles we need, because we have found weaknesses in myself and others that we have not yet overcome, it means there are still gaps, we are still missing some of what we need. From that perspective the odds of our succeeding in having this very unusual culture survive another twenty years, might be, say, 40 percent. This isn't the number we want, but six years ago, when we began this process, the odds would have been close to zero. So we have brought the odds from near zero to 40 percent in six years, and we are fighting hard to get them closer to, say, 60 percent.

It may strike you as interesting, as it did us, that Jensen makes no reference, in assessing how well the transition is going, to how the company has performed during this period as the leadership has transitioned from Dalio to the next generation. Certainly Wall Street and other observers would be answering the question on the basis of return to investors, and whether such patterns suggest Bridgewater can "do it" without Dalio at the helm.

In fact, by any conventional business metric, the company has performed brilliantly over this period, a period that obviously has been challenging, given the global economic situation. In terms of the company's profitability, return to investors, and client satisfaction, "we are better than we have ever been," Jensen says. But, again, he does not seem to us impressed by glittery indicators that catch other people's eyes.

> You are right, that is not how we think about how we are
> doing with the transition. To be clear, we think there is a much
> higher probability the company will be around and be reason-
> ably successful in twenty years. But that is not our goal. Our
> goal is that it remains a unique, inventive place, and not what
> it could easily become—a mediocre investment management
> firm living off the reputation that has been built. We don't
> look at those things [how well the company is performing
> currently, as a business], because we know they are a lagging
> indicator, not a leading one.

From Jensen's point of view, the culture is at once the very means, or strategy, by which the leaders hope to succeed with the transition, and it is, at the same time, the goal of the transition. For the business to survive without the culture would not feel like victory, nor, given Jensen's belief that the culture is the cause of the success, would he expect it to be successful in the same way. Ultimately, it is as true of Jensen, Dalio, and the world's largest hedge fund, as it is true of Forman and Ungard and Decurion, as it is true of Kim and Messenger and Next Jump, that the culture and the business are part of a single whole, that each is seen to depend on the other, that each is both means and end.

"Whenever it is looking like a choice between the culture and profitability," Jensen says, "the culture always wins." But even this is not because Bridgewater (or any DDO) is putting culture ahead of the strictly business motive. Jensen told us about regretfully having to fire a tremendously successful employee from a strictly business point of view. "This is a client guy who is really, really amazing, clients loved him. But he was not building the same place we were building. And you face these hard choices: Are you going to put the profitability and business metrics first, or are you going to put the culture first? I don't know how you could do it if you didn't always put the culture first. It can't be half-done." (More about this example in a moment.)

Referring to the injunction of Mustafa Kemal Atatürk, the founder of modern Turkey, that some changes must be 100 percent, all in, such as changing from driving on the right side of the road to the left side, Jensen says, "If someone is only halfway in, you are always trying to figure out, 'So is this the time they aren't telling me the truth?' That's why it is important to say the culture is the cause, not just a contributor. Once you say it is just a part of things, you're balancing it with other considerations, then I think you are lost. And if that means that some people can't be here, then that's hard, and we have to figure our way through that, but otherwise the cost of giving it up and sliding away from it is too great just for the short-term benefit. It seems uncompromising, but it is necessary."

The culture always wins, but not because it is put above profitability; profitability is the oxygen that keeps the company alive. The culture wins because it is seen as the route to profitability. The superstar client guy had to be let go, it seemed to us, not because the culture was put ahead of profitability, but because it was put ahead of short-term profitability. "That's right," Jensen says. "The benefit is a mirage, a short-term benefit that will end up killing you. The culture creates the success, and the success allows you to further invest in the culture. It's a circle. It's all one thing." (As you will see shortly, the Decurion culture will help us to better understand this notion of a circle, the culture and long-term success being "all one thing.")

Moreover, Bridgewater gives us another way of inquiring into this chapter's main question: Does being a DDO coexist with the drivers of business success, or is it a contributor, even the cause, of success? We had a friend who was about to accept a senior position at Bridgewater, and we asked him what attracted him to the company. He was a senior partner at a global strategy-consulting firm, earning a seven-figure salary, highly regarded by his peers.

His answer had nothing to do with Bridgewater's culture, which he seemed to view more as a challenge he was preparing to withstand. This is a person who had spent twenty years, for a living, being brought deeply inside the inner workings of a multitude of companies. He has become, without exactly planning to be, an expert evaluator of the way complex businesses throughout the world are run, so you might want to consider his answer carefully: "I have never seen a better-managed company."

Countering Two Corrosive Dynamics

There is a way in which, if you look only at the DDO itself, it is not possible to fully answer how being a DDO makes a company a better company in the strictly business sense, because the answer may have as much to do with what does *not* happen in a DDO. You need to bring the ordinary organization alongside the DDO to make some of its features stand out.

Consider those familiar bottlenecks and logjams besetting organizational life, obstructions that people come to take as the inevitable cost of doing business with human beings: "Same old, same old." "Same shit, different day." "Situation normal, all f—ed up" (which is what the acronym SNAFU stands for).

Bridgewater's radical transparency is a vivid example of the way many derailing processes we resignedly accept as inevitable in normal organizational life rarely get enough oxygen to survive in DDOs. Bridgewater also shows how different it is, when people do screw up, to be able to count on an entire system—rather than a rare, brave individual—to engage the error in a productive way, one that is productive for both the organization and the person who is screwing up.

Let's consider two of the most widespread, pandemic dynamics in organizational life, which damage business effectiveness every day in nearly every organization. The first of these familiar realities is something you've read now in nearly every chapter of this book: that everyone, in the usual organization, is doing a second job of hiding her weaknesses, uncertainties, and limitations; managing others' favorable impression. What is the cost of this second job to the company?

Companies have become very aware of the cost of downtime—lost days when employees are out sick, lost time when people flee into the internet for nonwork distractions. These losses are so enormous that companies now make huge investments in wellness and employee engagement.

But we have news: this kind of lost time and energy, large as it is, is puny compared with the daily, constant diversion of employees' attention to covering up and looking good. Imagine if you could redirect that energy to the purposes of the company. What if it were possible for people to give up this second job they would rather not have in the first place? What if it were possible for them to work full-time at the job they were hired to do? What would it mean for the performance of the organization?

This is what happens in a successful DDO, where people are rewarded for demonstrating what they don't know and can't yet do, as much as they are for what they do know and can do. At Bridgewater there is only one kind of mistake that is not acceptable, and that is failing to acknowledge your mistakes. At the end of every day, anything you had a hand in that didn't go as it should you enter in the issues log. It's not a catalog of shame, a paper trail to justify your eventual firing or loss of bonus. Instead, it's a living text (the curriculum again) from which you and your colleagues will have the chance to learn and get better.

And this idea—that more of the energy flows into the actual work, rather than to hiding out—is not just a New Age abstraction. If it were a real phenomenon—more energy going into a common enterprise per hour—you would literally feel it if you were there. If you were to spend a week, or even a couple of days, at Decurion, Bridgewater, or Next Jump, you would experience the "compression phenomenon" they all talk about—Decurion calls it "Decurion time." At all three companies we heard, "A day here feels like a week," in terms of how much happens (inside and outside a person).

The second dynamic is the widespread, corrosive, trust-destroying practice of speaking negatively about coworkers behind their backs. Twenty years ago two of us wrote a book (*How the Way We Talk Can Change the Way We Work*) asking this question: if everyone says this is unprofessional behavior and if everyone says they value being professional, then why don't we think about creating work cultures where people try to live by their agreements—including the agreement to take their difficulties and disappointments with coworkers directly to the parties involved? Everyone said this was a lovely idea, and we could look forward to seeing this real soon, right after people stopped cheating on their income taxes and gave up all vestiges of racial prejudice.

People at Bridgewater don't believe they're saints, but neither do they think this means they must be hypocrites. If you agree it's unprofessional to talk behind people's backs, and if you agree you aspire not to be unprofessional, and if you want to experience—maybe for the first time in your professional life—what we call the "collective integrity" of an entire work community living by its principles, then why wouldn't you welcome a practice that enables you and all your colleagues to stay aligned with these agreements? If every conversation is available for everyone to hear, then there is no back to talk behind. This space is gone. Everyone who first hears that Bridgewater tapes every conversation thinks it's crazy. No one stops to think whether it's crazy to believe it's unacceptably unprofessional to talk behind people's backs but still be party to such conversations.

The issues log and universal taping are two Bridgewater practices—features of what we call its groove—that address two widespread, corrosive dynamics that hemorrhage value every day in the usual organization. Whereas the first dynamic has to do with things people don't say and do that they should say and do, the second dynamic has to do with things people say and do that they should not. People waste time looking good, and they waste time making others look bad.

Worse than just a waste of time, these corrosive dynamics disarm a company's ability to effectively address and improve any and all of the suboptimal practices from which the organization suffers. Here's a quick example. We are currently trying to help a company that is not a DDO but wants to become one. The company has a great mission, and its people are dedicated; it has outperformed its competitors, is growing rapidly, and is very profitable. Still, the company is running far below its own targets, leaving on the table hundreds of millions of dollars each year because it is not managing itself as the leaders know it should. The reason? People will not call each other out, across ranks and divisions, when someone is screwing up (although they can clearly see it and are happy to complain about it to others); and people will not call themselves out when they know they're falling short. In the non-DDO organizations we work with, we regularly ask, "On a one-to-ten scale, how frank are you with each other on matters of importance to how the business is run? 'One' equals 'not at all,' and 'ten' equals 'completely.'" We gather the scores anonymously (because otherwise they wouldn't be frank about this either).

The averages are usually around 6—a pathetic score. Imagine your doctor, your attorney, or your spouse telling you just 60 percent of what she feels you need to know. If we had to turn this whole chapter into a Tweet and were required to address the strictly business value of being a DDO in 140 characters, this might be our best shot: "Q: Why should a business become a DDO? A: To move its Frankness Score from 6 to 9 or 10! A business w/ a 6 runs at 60 percent efficiency."

It's easy to see how these two pervasive dynamics collude with each other. We make a sort of bargain: "I won't take you on directly, if you'll give me the same pass. I won't interfere with the work you're doing to look good, if you won't interfere with mine." Each of us is free to keep hiding our weaknesses and letting off steam about others' shortcomings behind their backs.

Bridgewater is an object lesson in the error the rest of us make when we settle for less in defining human nature. People will tell you it's only human nature for coworkers to talk behind each other's backs. It's only human nature to hide your weaknesses and show only your strengths. Asked to explain why she wouldn't want to work at Bridgewater, a Harvard student said, "I want people at work to think I'm *better* than I really am. I don't want them to know how I *really* am! That's just human nature, isn't it?" What if what she regards as "only human nature" is exhausting in both senses of the word: it is personally exhausting, and all that wasted energy is exhausting resources that could be brought to the work at hand?

If it's only human nature to hide in plain sight (covering your weaknesses) and regularly violate your own sense of what is right (talking behind people's backs), then the folks who work at Bridgewater, or any of the other DDOs, have some serious explaining to do. If they are not human, where did they come from? How many freaks of nature would it take before we'd begin to change our view of nature?

Decurion's Success and Its DDO-hood

As we have said, it would be easy to return to Decurion for the purpose of again illustrating the business benefits of passing the work down the chain, seeing the work as a curriculum, engaging in radical transparency, or looking closely at weaknesses, for all these are as much at the heart of that culture as they are at Next Jump or Bridgewater. But Decurion can also help us break fresh ground in telling the story of the relationship of DDO-hood to business performance, through a theme we will call integrity.

If you ask any of the Decurion leaders, "Which aspects of your developmentally oriented culture do you think are actually contributing to the business in the strictly business sense?" they either will tell you, "All of them," or, if they have more time, they will explain their problem with the question itself: "Sorry, but your question already suggests a way of dividing up the world that we would challenge. 'Which aspects of light are waves, and which are particles?' That question wouldn't make much sense, right? Light is all one thing, and only one thing. Particles and waves are not divisible constituents of light; they are different ways of looking at one unified thing." Decurion leaders begin with "the light," not the particles or the waves; they begin with the "one thing" and are more inclined to see different dimensions as differing reflections of it.

"Pursuing human development and profitability emerges as one thing—nothing extra is required" is one of Decurion's axioms, as explained in "Decurion's Ends and Means," an internal document:

> Decurion's axioms are statements about how we choose to
> view and live our lives. They are decisions about how we act
> together. They reflect a choice to see wholeness and possibility
> rather than separateness and trade-offs. Our axioms join work,
> people, and development as one unified possibility rather than
> as separate pieces.

We have come to see this theme of "making one" running through the whole of Decurion, whether we're looking at the single individual or the entire enterprise. *Integer*, the Latin root of *integrity*, means "one." "If I had to sum up the single biggest difference between working here and anywhere else I have worked, the thing I appreciate most," the president of Decurion's Robertson Properties Group, Jeff Koblentz, told us, "it is this: at Decurion I am not living a divided life. I don't have to check some piece of my humanity at the door. I am the same person inside the company that I am outside the company."

Whether it is the individual overcoming the divided life, or the company overcoming the choice between profit and people, starting "at one" is the company's first principle. "For us, pursuing profitability and human development emerges as one thing," Decurion's Christopher Forman says. "We do not see a trade-off, and the moment we consider sacrificing one for the other, we recognize that we have lost both."

It may be easier to see more immediately how this core orientation to wholeness redounds to the benefit of people development than it does to business development. We focus here on what wholeness means in the strictly business sense. We can imagine our friends at Decurion even cringing a bit because of our willingness to single out one-half of the whole, but we have few qualms in doing so; in testimony to this brand of integrity, you will see there is no way to avoid the obvious implications for people development in every instance of business advantage we're about to suggest. If it really is all one thing, there should be no way to pick up half the stick without moving the other half, and this turns out to be true.

So let's take a look. Advancing "wholeness and possibility over trade-offs and separateness" may sound like the business equivalent of Camelot. But if you were to spend a few days at Decurion, you would quickly see that you're not in the gauzy clouds but down on messy ground, where there is always hard work to do in acknowledging and engaging (and mining) the persistent gaps that derail integrity (and, as a result, dampen optimal business performance).

Tensions between divisions and their leaders beset every company. Most try their best to work around the difficulties and accept the attendant losses of time, efficiency, and creativity as the cost of doing business with imperfect humans and differing personalities. The most enlightened organizations may try to effect some kind of truce. To a DDO like Decurion, however, that "problem solving" would squander an opportunity to "let the problem solve us." Why? "Because that's where the money is," someone at Decurion might say.

When Decurion took over management of its first senior living facility, the leadership team decided to put two high-ranking members (Jeff Koblentz and Bryan Ungard) in charge, intentionally pairing two people who think, talk, and operate in highly different ways. "I have no idea what he's saying half the time," one of them will say. "The way he thinks and talks can drive me nuts," the other rejoins. "We can really get on each other's nerves," both agree. Still, as they continuously confront each other's different assumptions and framing of issues, each of them, as well as the operations of the company, have benefited.

Decurion brings together unlikely partners at every level of the business. "From all my past experience in the movie theater business," Nora Dashwood told us, reflecting on the hourly-wage workers who make up the bulk of the employees, "having a nineteen-year-old work with a sixty-five-year-old would be a sure recipe for disaster. They couldn't relate. There was no common humanity. I can't remember one situation where it was successful, not one. I look at our theaters [where we do this all the time], and it actually makes the community healthier. The diversity of people that can come together—and Decurion gives them the tools to be human first, and then to engage in the business—is something that I know helps our business."

Another way to explore the business value of Decurion's integrity is to look at something that has an obvious business advantage and then work backward to discover its source. The movie theater business is a classic example of a high-volume, customer-oriented, retail-service enterprise. Hundreds of thousands of people pass through a given theater annually. You are certainly familiar with the retail customer's experience. Have you ever stayed at a hotel or shopped in a department store, for example, where you are attended to, not by an ordinary staff, but by what can only be called an inspired one?

We're not talking about service-providers just being friendly and helpful, and we're not talking about being oversolicitous. We're talking about being served by people who bring such a level of engaged vitality to their work that it makes your experience memorable. Decurion's ArcLight theaters have a number of qualities that make the moviegoing experience memorable—including the comfort of the seats and the quality of sound and the image on the screen—but surely this experience of an inspired staff is an indispensable element of its appeal, and the strictly business value of that dimension is enormous.

Where does engaged vitality come from? There is only one way for a workforce in a retail business to be inspired, day in and day out. It can't come from daily pep talks or external rewards. These are like willpower; their oomph always runs out. Rather, it must come from a genuine, internal sense of the meaningfulness of one's activity. It's not something you can "put in" your people; it's something they themselves need to be able to create, from within, every day.

You've seen the idea of developmental pulls in action, with theater managers carefully planning job rotations as part of a weekly, focused process. The theater leaders continuously align individuals' learning needs—and the next challenges crew members are ready for—with operational requirements. Managers like Matt Kauwe (of Los Angeles) work to ensure the systemic stretch of their locations, moving crew members into positions that create pull for them, adding to the overall capability of the crew. At the same time, they maintain a culture where people are not limited by or overly identified with any one role. Everyone at Decurion, from ArcLight crew members to the senior leaders, is a businessperson first, and only second a concessions cashier, property manager, or chief information officer.

Managers and leaders think every day about how to structure development into tasks, roles, projects, and systems. When they talk with other corporate leaders about the ways that the pursuit of development and the pursuit of profitability are really one thing, however, they report something being lost in translation. (We confess it took us, as a research team, a long time and lots of on-the-ground experience to appreciate the subtlety and power of this insistence on oneness.) The initial response of leaders from other companies often goes something like this:

> So, if I understand your philosophy right, I think what you do is certainly admirable. You're making sure that people get the training experiences they need and want, and as a company you're doing that intentionally. That kind of dedication to your

employees is good for your employment brand and must help you attract and retain talent. More than that, it seems like this is part of how you do well by doing good. Decurion sounds like a good place to work, even a very special place to work, and I'm inspired by the way you really walk the talk when it comes to being a socially conscious company.

The point these appreciative outsiders often miss, however, is that this approach to business is not first about attracting and retaining talent, or merely doing the right thing by people in an abstract sense, making principled sacrifices in the name of corporate social responsibility. Rather, it's a choice, fundamental to the company's identity, to see the pursuit of profitability as requiring the continuous growth of the people joined in that pursuit. At the same time, it's a choice to see that people grow—even flourish—in the presence of the individual and collective challenges that the pursuit of profitability generates.

Business growth requires people who are developing; developing people requires the rich context for growth that business provides. Both are true at once. Neither is true without the other.

Learning from the Hawaii Project

If we hold this concept of oneness, as we ask you to do here, it invites a clear-eyed approach to gathering evidence about the business impact of Decurion's focus on development. Put simply, we should be able to observe repeated, specific instances of the way that focusing on people development is essential to creating value within the company.

Let's look carefully at the results of several strategic bets Decurion has made in its portfolio of activities, from the real estate business, to senior living, to the theaters. As we do so, consider the ways that the business advantages you see depend on unlocking the potential of Decurion's people.

Long after ArcLight's model had transformed the theater business, Decurion's real estate unit operated quite differently from the theaters. Although ArcLight was led by a leadership work group that held collective responsibility for the health of the unit, such a structure seemed improbable in the real estate business. Progress

had been made, but the relationship between all real estate functions was one of silos at best, and it was especially bad between
property managers and accountants. The real estate managers saw
the people in accounting as rigid paper-pushers, slowing them down
with demands to attend to boring details and inflexible deadlines.
The accountants saw the real estate managers as careless, unprofessional, and unreliable.

Professional stereotypes by role also beset every company, and
again, most would try to work around their difficulties and costs.
Instead, Decurion set about unlocking potential for business growth
in real estate by making accounting and property management even
more dependent on one another for success.

Decurion was in the midst of a massive real estate development in
Hawaii, an ambitious project encompassing three residential towers,
a shopping center, and a hotel. The company needed to develop a
new model of entitling, developing, leasing, operating, and reporting
on a project that was larger than anything it had built previously.

The project's complexity called for a new level of collaboration
across all functions of the real estate business—development, leasing, finance and accounting, legal, and property management. Jeff
Koblentz, who leads the real estate business, saw the necessity of a
new way of operating, one that represented the wholeness of people
development and business growth. He saw the Hawaii project as a
good business opportunity in traditional terms, one that also had
the potential to transform the business if members of the real estate
community could overcome their internal barriers. The demands of
the project offered an opportunity to create pulls for the entire real
estate team. But Decurion couldn't develop more projects like the
one in Hawaii until its people learned how to develop the first one.

Koblentz created a real estate work group modeled on the community that governed the theater unit, and he carefully worked to
strengthen the interdependencies of its members. Koblentz held hierarchical accountability for decisions in real estate, but the work group
shared responsibility for running the business. The members needed
to learn to work together to understand the entirety of the business
and to think, decide, and act in unison. In Decurion's language, "This
is what the business required." As Koblentz put it, he made clear to

the group that "there were new business demands, and as a result, there were new demands that the working relationship among all disciplines develop to a more sophisticated and integrated level."

Decurion made it a business requirement that people in the work group grow into a learning community whose members saw things first as businesspeople rather than through their limited expert roles. Over time, they also worked to recognize that the present state of their capabilities was not sufficient for the challenge of the Hawaii project and the promise of what lay beyond it. But if the group members came together to both push and support one another to take collective responsibility for the health of the real estate business, individuals could grow in the very ways the business required, and people could use the business challenge as a practice ground for their own self-improvement.

As the group's members continued to focus on overcoming their individual and collective limitations, something started to happen, something that Decurion leaders had seen earlier in the theater business: the members of the real estate work group began gaining skill as a group in evaluating new real estate deals, identifying and assessing opportunities faster, with more coordination, with clearer discussion of trade-offs, and with better-quality recommendations. The technical experts—architects, in-house counsel, and the heads of property management and accounting—started to act more consistently as a trust on behalf of the company. This didn't mean that their meetings were easy, tidy, and nice, or without tension and occasional rancor. But supported by Decurion's assumption that people and the business grow together and that growth requires commitment, patience, and daily effort, members of the work group began to feel responsible for the whole of the real estate business rather than only their respective bases of expertise.

Considered on its own, the developmental value of a move like Koblentz's in creating and nurturing the real estate work group may seem obvious by this point. Clearly it helped individuals develop complex, less-role-bound thinking about real estate. Koblentz explains:

> People want to stretch and grow. When you talk to the head of
> accounting, she'll tell you she's got accountability for the work

of the accountants, but what she really wants is to function more like a CFO. She wants to be more involved in the business decisions around acquisition, leasing, development, and property management. She wants to move beyond the numbers, and this holds true for almost everyone in accounting. The property managers are in a similar spot. The bottom line is that their careers will be better served by operating as asset managers rather than property managers. And in order to be a good asset manager, they really need to understand the financials and the structure and details of transactions. Along the way, as they learn more about the whole of the business, they make better decisions.

On one level, having accountants and property managers who understand more about the business improves the quality of work within their existing groups. But the even more hard-nosed value to the business's success was just as essential to Koblentz and other senior Decurion executives. He explains this in terms of cost structure, something everyone in business can relate to.

We could have solved our issue by hiring more accountants and property managers. But adding more bodies to an inefficient system, where functions acting in silos are creating tension and ineffectiveness, hasn't proven to work in the long run. Management can "focus" on the situation for a while and maybe see incremental improvement, but I don't think anyone who tells you that this is sustainable is being honest.

I want to build the capability of the organization. I want to get upstream of the issues so that the work is structured for people to perform better. In this case it amounts to being accountable for more of the business earlier in their careers and making better decisions along the way. If I build this capability across the organization, the conversation about adding employees to solve the "problem" is moot—we can actually work with fewer employees rather than more. My cost structure is lower, because the employees are more capable and are earlier in their careers, earning less than more-seasoned employees but more than their less capable peers. This requires more than just throwing people into the deep end and hoping they can swim. It requires a conscious structuring of the work to get it right. When we do this, I don't have to enter the conversation through the human-development door. If someone doesn't want to talk about development, that's fine. We can talk only about the results—I'm getting better performance at a lower cost structure.

What lessons about the value of the DDO approach can we take, then, from the Hawaii project? First, Decurion leaders take a sophisticated business play as an audacious goal the business must meet, one that exceeds the current limits of the business and its people. Both the business and the people must be in a little bit over their heads.

Second, the leaders spend time building a shared understanding that the project can be accomplished *only* if people overcome their limiting assumptions, individually and collectively, to get to the needed level of capability.

Third, the company creates community governance, forcing individual technical experts or subject-matter stars to think relentlessly about the whole of the company—to see all of its elements coherently and understand how value is and could be created, not only by their unit but by the interplay of all the units. Finally, and under these conditions, the pursuit of profitability provides the way for an individual's desire for growth to be one with, and not competing with, the needs of the company.

In this way, focusing on development creates business value across many activities and strategic bets.

Learning from the Senior Living Business

Let's take another example. Decurion got into the senior living business with a long view: to learn how to translate its corporate strengths and values to a new type of business, and also, very clearly, to make a profit, as an expression of its purpose as a company that creates places for people to flourish.

From the beginning, the company's leaders struggled to break free from many aspects of the standard practice in such facilities.

Over time, they identified a number of practices that would integrate individual development and business success. For most of these practices, they realized that something that "at first seemed innocuous," in one person's words, "was actually a key to addressing the big-picture issue: exceptional, affordable care."

For example, in their facility operations one practice they found hiding in plain sight was scheduling. In a typical facility, senior executives take care of scheduling, and schedules remain fairly static. But Decurion leaders realized that rotating more people at lower levels through the responsibility of scheduling work shifts would require people to learn more about the entirety of the business. To schedule the right people with the right skills at the right time in a facility requires an understanding of how the whole business operates. People with this knowledge make better decisions, are more effective, and progress faster in their careers. Decurion also requires the function to be fluid, and, as the organization learns how to operate more efficiently, changes are made immediately.

"It's just pragmatic," Koblentz explains. "We use scheduling and other similar tasks differently than others in the industry. When a quarter of our workforce can hold the whole of the business, we get better results on the floor. For the employees involved in the process, the business knowledge they are gaining and using is going to progress their careers, either with us or at other operators in the industry."

As in the real estate business, the need for a lower cost structure called for people to develop in ways not typical of the industry. The company structured a way for people to overcome their limited perspectives and see the complexity of the business as a whole. As a result, it gets more capacity out of fewer people earlier in their careers.

Rethinking Roles

As you've seen earlier in their theater business, creating a big stretch goal for the company is explicitly about both growing the people and growing the business. But let's focus for a moment less on the developmental outcomes for individual crew members, managers, and senior leaders. What about the success of the business? At ArcLight, top-line growth goals for revenue are tied to strategic bets that assume people's growth and the business results of the theater circuit are interdependent. One of these goals is especially worth spotlighting: a different kind of respect for the entry-level employee, part-time workers, and retail work.

Nora Dashwood knows from her decades of experience that our default assumption about the growth possible for people in retail jobs stifles the people in those jobs. "It's an entry-level job, whether it's popping corn behind the concessions stand or tearing tickets," she says. "It's something somebody does until they can go do something else. But what is possible in that role versus what most companies think is possible in those roles are two very different things."

The success of the theater business depends on the quality of the guest experience, and the way each crew member shows up in the business each day is directly related to guest engagement. To measure this aspect of the work, ArcLight is data-driven. It carefully tracks financial metrics that are standard in the industry, but it also monitors in every operational meeting two families of metrics that are closely tied: guest engagement and crew development. Decurion leaders draw a straight line between the theaters' profitability and crew members' experience of the meaningfulness of their work. That line goes through the quality of the guest experience, something that depends on every crew member upholding standards of excellence.

Practices and principles you've seen earlier form a workplace culture organized to connect people to personal meaning. Via check-ins, the company welcomes people's humanity in the workplace; you're a person with dreams and dignity, and not the human equivalent of a widget. During pulse-check huddles, the crew members come together, giving and getting feedback constantly during a busy evening of screenings, and, in doing so, the crew is at the center of running the business. Crew members repeatedly describe discovering they were capable of more than they knew, because they were treated, and invested in, like budding businesspeople. And this discovery often extends outside work to family life, relationships, college study, and new life ambitions. At ArcLight, hourly employees can learn to read the profit-and-loss statement then make decisions about show scheduling the very next week, opportunities other companies in their industry do not provide. Crew members' identities are not pegged to the duties they might perform in a given shift, but constantly are oriented toward workers' seeing themselves running the business as a whole.

Dashwood sums up the impact of all this on the business: "We see a big difference in our revenues and the experience of our guests *because* we focus on people's development and their critical thinking. What's right for the business actually creates meaning and confidence for the crew members. We have had breakthrough results in every category. This is not just fun and games."

Exploiting the Power of Pulls

Integrity, oneness, and pursuing profitability and employee growth as one thing, indivisible—these features of working life in the theaters are emblematic of the way Decurion supports a kind of agency for individuals. It does this by creating conditions where the requirements of a growing business constantly pull people toward higher expectations for what they can do and who they can become.

Those developmental pulls, like the ones you've seen in the real estate, senior living, and theater businesses in this chapter, use the demands of business growth to inspire individuals to overcome their limiting assumptions. From the walk through Decurion you've just taken, we hope you might even now see its metaphor of the developmental pull with fresh eyes, more aware of both the business side and the personal side of the pull. The metaphor, after all, requires something that pulls and something being pulled; we can't understand the physical concept without holding on to both parts simultaneously. A pull creates tension over a distance that must be closed. In the developmental sense, when we work to close the distance between where we are and where the company needs us to be, we overcome our current limits. We are developing, and the business shares the benefits fully.

Even if you still worry that the focus on people development in a DDO is a lavish expense of time and energy, we hope you'll at least take away the notion that there's nothing charitable about it. At Decurion, the drive to develop greater capability requires greater challenge supported by strong communities. Greater capability in turn enables things like lower cost structures and more talent ready for leadership positions.

People at Decurion might even turn the questions around and ask skeptics, "How much potential growth in your own business are you leaving off the table by not assuming that your employees' growth and your business's growth are really one thing?"

A Surprise Conclusion

We've dedicated this chapter to the frequent question we hear as we begin to talk with people about the DDO: "Okay, I get it that this kind of culture can make a big difference for its employees, who become a more capable version of themselves. That's a wonderful thing. But a business is a business, not a university. What I want to know is, what does it do for the business?"

We thought we had the answer to this question after first gathering our data, but gathering data and analyzing it are two different things, and the analysis you see in this chapter led us to a much stronger answer. Our initial answer, after gathering the data, was along these lines: if you're asking whether we think we've learned some secret to running a more successful business (in ordinary business terms— greater profitability, maximization of shareholder value), then perhaps we're misunderstanding each other right from the start. We grant there are many ways to run a successful business, and you would have no trouble pointing to very successful businesses that are nothing like a DDO. We aren't saying, "To be successful, you have to be a DDO." We are saying, "If you care deeply about people development (for the good of the company, or the good of the planet, or both), this might be the most powerful way to organize your culture—and it is possible to do so, and still run a very successful business."

In other words, we were happy to imagine our audience limited to people who already place a premium on people development. We felt we had something exciting to show our colleagues, who have a burning interest in adult development. These are people who find themselves wondering more than once, "With all the other dramatic knowledge development we have witnessed in the past fifty or sixty years—in the sciences and technology—have we learned nothing that would permit a similarly dramatic reconceptualization of the way

198 An Everyone Culture

organizations and work life can support human capital development, leadership development, and talent development?"

At that point, this was the only audience we thought we were writing to, and that was fine with us. For people who needed to be convinced beforehand that this would be the superior route to running a successful business, our sense was that it is exciting to see how successful, even in the conventional sense, these DDOs turned out to be—if for no other reason than they prevent the dismissive rejoinder, "I can see why people might get a tremendous amount out of working in such a place, but they aren't going to get it for long, because these businesses are unsustainable and headed for dissolution." But if the only reason you'd want to become a DDO in the first place were to be more profitable, then it is probably just as well your interest is going to flag, because it looks to us as if you need both passions—business excellence and an interest in developing people—in order to make a DDO work.

Although we weren't so explicitly aware of this when we began our analysis, once it becomes clear that being a DDO does not have to be a drag on business success (a kind of "cost" one might be willing to pay on behalf of a nonbusiness agenda), there is a continuum of positions one might end up taking on this issue.

1. Being a DDO can *coexist with* being a conventionally successful company.

2. Being a DDO can *contribute to* what makes a successful company successful.

3. Being a DDO can be the *cause of* what makes a successful company successful.

Before we did our analysis we were squarely in position 2. As we said at the outset, we felt Decurion, Bridgewater, and Next Jump constituted an existence of proof for a position at least as strong as position 1. They are clearly very successful companies. We wanted to use the chapter to see how persuasive we would be in arguing that these companies were not only successful, and happened to be DDOs, but also that being DDOs made a difference in their success (position 2).

But as anyone who has ever put pen to paper (or fingertips to keyboard) knows, the act of writing is not simply a matter of producing a written version of the script that is running in your head. It is not merely recording thinking. It's a way to examine your thinking and figure out exactly what you do think.

You will have to decide how persuasive you find our analysis here, but one surprise for us is that we conclude the chapter prepared to take a stronger position than when we entered it. At least as it concerns these three companies, we find ourselves closer to the view that being a DDO is not only a contributor to, but also the cause of, these companies' success (position 3).

What is the implication, if we are not the only ones who find themselves thinking along these lines? We had taken the position that there are many ways to climb the mountain of business success, and, if you had an interest in making your company a powerful incubator for people development, this might be the path for you. If people development was not your thing, we expected that you would try a different path, and all the best; we'd see you at the summit. Let a thousand pathways bloom.

But now we are not so sure. When we consider the range and nature of business challenges that we see these companies better able to meet for being a DDO, we find ourselves leaving this chapter with a question that surprises us.

The companies have come up with novel and effective means to meet a host of challenges—how to increase retention, profitability, coaching support, readiness to learn, speed to promotability, frankness in communication, effective delegation, effective downsizing, acceptance of responsibility; how to reduce political maneuvering, impression management, behind-the-back disparagement, downtime, and disengagement; how to anticipate crises no one in the company has experienced and manage successfully through them; how to invent future possibilities no one has experienced and realize them.

There are still many pathways to the top of the mountain of business success, but perhaps companies should ask themselves before they set out, "For my particular business, at this moment in history, will the challenges we face be largely technical ones, or largely adaptive ones?" This important distinction comes from our Harvard colleague Ronald Heifetz: technical challenges require new skill sets, like new apps or files for an operating system. In contrast, adaptive challenges require changes not only in skill sets but also in mind-sets: changes at the level of the operating system itself, precisely what we mean by development.[4]

If the challenges your business faces are largely technical ones, there exist a number of workable paths to success, and every one of them may be an easier climb than the path of the DDO. But Heifetz says that the most common mistake organizations and their leaders make is to try meeting adaptive challenges with technical means. What if, in a VUCA environment, companies' challenges are pre-dominantly adaptive? If that's true, then *most* companies—whether or not they are initially enthusiastic about people development—will need to consider the path that may best equip them to meet adaptive challenges. This is what we believe the DDO to be: the jet engine culture for meeting adaptive challenges when most organizations are still flying a prop plane.

We should thus all perhaps think twice before assuming that a DDO must always be a rare flower, limited to those places whose leaders begin with a burning passion to combine business develop-ment with human development. DDOs may be the first adopters, the ones who turn an eccentric path into a blazed trail.

Most companies, nonprofits, government organizations, and other public institutions (like schools and hospitals) may never take on all the features of a DDO as you have learned about them in this book. But just as the twentieth century saw one kind of recasting of the healthier workplace from being an exception to being the rule (regarding child labor, length of the workweek, industrial safety, health and pension benefits, and the like), might it not be that the twenty-first century may witness a new recasting on behalf of a more interior kind of health—for the benefit of individual workers and their organizations?

6

Uncovering Your Biggest Blind Spot

What You'd Be Working On in a DDO

Now that you have a picture of the growth fostered by DDOs, we want to give you a direct experience of one dimension of the culture: edge. Remember Jackie from Next Jump, the marketing manager who was voted off the company's leadership group? Although people told her that her backhand (weakness) was arrogance, she knew that she had truly zeroed in on her backhand only when she felt the pain of saying out loud her own version of arrogance: being selfish. In her words, "What is the thing that is more meaningful, that is actually painful to say, that is embarrassing to say? I think that's when you really get to your true backhand." That's what we want for you by the end of this chapter—self-awareness of your genuine backhand, not to trouble you, but to enable you to identify and experience your own version of the personal learning curriculum you'd have the chance to take up in a DDO.

We'll help you by guiding you through the *immunity to change* (ITC) exercise.[1] To start, you identify a personal growth goal, a self-improvement issue that is important to you. (We often call this our *one big thing*, or OBT for short.) Then you answer a series of additional questions to reveal how you're unconsciously getting in the way of achieving that important goal and becoming your best self. This is the quickest, most powerful practice we know for illuminating current blind spots. If you allow yourself to be completely honest throughout the exercise, you'll discover your personal version of your backhand. (And it may not be painful or embarrassing.)

You will then have both a picture of how you're limiting yourself and a glimmer of what it might mean to upgrade your own operating system. We also hope you will experience the sense of freedom and possibility that comes from seeing your limits in the bigger, more spacious context of your unfolding development.

If you're a leader, we wouldn't be surprised if you want to skip this chapter. Maybe you're questioning its relevance to you or, more honestly, feeling daunted by the prospects of looking at yourself in this way. "Do I really want to feel such discomfort?" you might be asking yourself. If so, you might find it valuable to remember that (for example) Jackie's world expanded when she embraced her backhand. She couldn't have known that her tacit assumption—something like, "Spending time to help other people would diminish my success"—was wrong if she hadn't squarely faced the truth. She couldn't have known that helping people might actually lead to her greater success. What a revelation for her to discover not only that people actually were grateful for her time spent helping them but also that there was a whole different income awaiting her when she did!

You'll also see in the pages ahead how someone you have already met, Decurion's Nora Dashwood, who by all standards was an extremely successful leader, became an even more effective one by facing her limiting assumptions through the very process we invite you to engage in this chapter.

Creating an ITC map shines a light on what a person needs to work on to become, in Next Jump parlance, "a better me." It will allow you, in Bridgewater terms, to touch the nerve that must be touched for you to face reality. You will see the ego attachments that need to be worked through in order for you to flourish (a favorite word at Decurion). If you want to do something bigger with yourself, your life, your leadership, your organization, this exercise will reveal something important for that journey.

Our two recommendations for getting the most out of the chapter. First, do the exercises! Don't just read the examples; apply the ideas to yourself, your own mind, your behavior. The ideas themselves, as novel and intriguing as they may be, will not help you identify your growing edge. You'll experience the ideas of this chapter only cognitively. You won't feel them, or fully understand them, until you apply them to yourself. Second, we strongly recommend that you write your responses into the map (see figure 6-1). (Alternatively, you can download a map template from www.mindsatwork.com if you'd rather type into the template or print it and handwrite your responses.)

Writing your responses down will ultimately help you see something that just answering the questions in your own mind will not. You may also benefit from finding and doing the exercise with someone you feel comfortable with and trust (a tiny instance of the DDO dimension of home). Being in conversation with such a person may help you dig deeper.

Let's look in detail at using the ITC map to find your edge.

FIGURE 6-1

The immunity to change map template

1. Commitment (improvement goal)	2. Doing/not doing instead	3. Hidden/competing commitment	4. Big assumptions
I am committed to getting better at . . .			

Column 1: Your Improvement Goal and Starting Commitment

We hope and expect that your experience with this tool will be interesting for you. We suggest that you think carefully about each entry you make, pushing yourself to be as honest as possible.

To begin, you need to identify your improvement goal. Because the rest of the process stems from this goal, it's important to choose a good one. How do you do that?

Here are a few avenues to explore.

- What would you need to get better at in order to be more effective in your current role? What would you need to get better at in order to make a bigger contribution to your organization, or to a current high-priority initiative?

- What would you need to get better at in order to bring your organization or department closer to operating as a DDO? What changes would you need to make to your own behavior?

- Choosing any aspect of your life—work, family, friendship— what single thing is most important to you? Now, having identified that, ask yourself one more question: What one way of personally improving yourself would make the biggest difference for this most important thing?

- Is there some improvement goal you have already tried to accomplish, perhaps many times, but you have never been happy with the result or its staying power? What is it?

Generate a few possibilities, and then decide which one feels like the most powerful one to focus on. The more self-aware you are, the more likely you are to generate a good goal using this approach alone. However, we have found that individuals do not always, all on their own, choose goals that are most likely to impact their leadership effectiveness. Even among the leaders we have spoken with at each of the DDOs, where there is quite a bit of focus on helping individuals get better, we hear stories of how difficult it can be to identify the improvement goal that is right for each person.

We therefore recommend that you seek lots of input from others. Ask your supervisor, your colleagues, your direct reports, your friends and family: "What improvement would make the biggest difference in your evaluation of me and my potential in this organization? What contribution could I make that would have the most impact? What would I need to get better at in order to make that contribution? What would enable me to serve you better? What would I need to get better at to do so?" As you sift through this feedback, look for patterns, issues that hit home for you, and areas that feel most important for your own growth.

The best goal for this exercise should meet the following criteria:

- It should be about *getting better at* something, and not itself be a result or an outcome. "Being less controlling" is not an improvement goal; it is a result or an outcome. "Getting better at being less controlling" is OK, but "Getting better at giving more control to others" is an even better example of an improvement goal, because it names what you can do to become less controlling. And it identifies what you want to actually get better at, something that leads to the next criterion.

- It should be stated *affirmatively*, if possible. Saying that you want to improve by stopping some behavior or tendency is often less powerful than naming what you want to do instead. Consider what success will be for you.

- It should feel *quite important to you,* so that you imagine its realization—if you can achieve it—as personally valuable, desirable, or powerful.

- It should be something you have *not yet accomplished* or turned the corner on, meaning that there is plenty of room for improvement and future growth.

- It should be clear how getting better at this commitment means that *you* (and not someone else) must make changes to the way you live, think, and act.

Nora Dashwood, Decurion

In chapter 1 you met Nora Dashwood, who identified her personal challenge as "being with" people better, letting them learn how to do things in their own way rather than be directed by her. She wanted to stop withdrawing her goodwill, making the air in the room turn cold, when others made different decisions than those she would make. Rather than approach this improvement process as one solely focused on behavior change, the DDO approach is to look more deeply into the person's mind-set and belief system, which for Dashwood were the roots of her unwanted behaviors. An ITC map, such as the one she actually constructed, helps us encapsulate this complex dynamic system in a single image (see figure 6-2).

Dashwood's ITC map begins on the far left with her improvement goal:

> I am committed to getting better at "being with" others, to being less controlling, to being more open to others' ways of doing things.

Bob Prince, Bridgewater

Bob Prince, co-chief investment officer at Bridgewater, struggled with a large project Ray Dalio gave him that involved a particular type of exploration and analysis of the bond market. The project presented Prince with a complex and challenging problem; Dalio simply explained the goals of the project and then left it to Prince to lead a team to achieve it. The project took many years, entailed many failures, and required lots of reflections and changes on Prince's part. He came to be seen as someone who was highly creative but who struggled to make things happen reliably. Greg Jensen's synthesis of Prince (available for all employees at Bridgewater to see) was that Prince was a "mad scientist archetype: experimenter, great ideas, but unreliable/sometimes blows up lab."

This characterization is one that Prince agreed with and also wanted to change. He acknowledged, "I'm really bad at getting in sync on the goal and coordinating the parts. [On the bond market project] I would tend to get off track, get in rabbit holes, stay in rabbit holes, do things that [led down] unproductive paths. It was not a well-directed process."

FIGURE 6-2

Nora Dashwood's immunity to change map

1. Commitment (improvement goal)	2. Doing/not doing instead	3. Hidden/competing commitment	4. Big assumptions
I am committed to getting better at "being with" others, to being less controlling, to being more open to others' ways of doing things	• I don't listen to others • I talk too much to try to convince others that my way is the right way • When someone presents an idea or plan that doesn't correspond to my own view, I constantly ask questions and follow up too extensively, micromanage • I freeze them out with a stony face, withdraw from conversation, lack of encouragement • I solve smaller problems or challenges that I know I can control • I don't consider alternatives • I spend time on things I don't want to • I don't delegate	Worry box: alternatives will emerge that I can't accomplish; that these ideas might be better than mine, and I won't be seen as valuable; that they are not and I'll have to do more work to fix things since I didn't veto the idea in the first place; that I won't like leading in a different way; that leading in a different way means losing who I am; that if I try to lead differently, I might fail at it; that I'll be taken advantage of or walked over. I am also committed to . . . • Avoiding alternatives from emerging that I don't think I can accomplish • Avoiding being shown up, or my ideas being seen as less valuable • Not having to do things twice • Staying interested in doing by "leading" • Not losing my sense of self • Not showing that I will fail at being able to effectively support others • Avoiding being taken advantage of or walked over	• I assume my accomplishments and talents might be more about my good fortune than about my abilities, hence I am out of my league • I assume that I have contextually developed (in Decurion's structure) but have not been truly developing (across all contexts) • I assume that I am a leopard trying to change its spots • I assume that I care more about myself than I care about others • I assume that a lot of my value comes from having the right view, that things done by others will likely not be done right—in other words, not the way I want them done • I need a certain kind of stimulus to be effective • My prime source of enjoyment in this role is having the right view

Eager to overcome these weaknesses, Bob set out on a path of improvement (see figure 6-3). In particular, he was looking to get better at creating clear strategic plans for a team, specifying, for example, "what type of people are required for what roles and laying out the attributes of what's required in spec sheets" and to "use this information to assign people to suitable roles, help them find ways to succeed, and guardrail them and us against their weaknesses."

Here is Bob's column 1 improvement goal:

> To get better at making things happen reliably in projects by getting in sync on the goal and coordinating the parts.

Your Turn

Review your various ideas for your self-improvement goal, and choose one that meets all of the criteria. When you're ready, write your starting commitment in the first column of your map (refer again to figure 6-1). We've started it for you: "I am committed to getting better at . . ." As you continue the exercise, you'll need to return to this page to add new entries.

Column 2: What You Are Doing and Not Doing

Your next step requires brutal honesty. You need to develop a fearless inventory of all the things you do that work against your improvement goal, as well as the ways you're working against that goal by what you are not doing. In other words, we're asking you to fess up to your own bad behaviors. Your list will be a picture of you screwing up, working against your improvement goal. What are the things you're doing and not doing instead? What do you do, or neglect to do, that derails, undermines, or sabotages your improvement goal?

Again, your list of behaviors in column 2 will be much more robust and accurate if you draw on feedback from others. If you do get regular feedback, supervision, mentoring, or formal evaluation, consider that input as a potential source of column 2 entries. Go back to the same people who gave you input about your improvement goal, and ask them to identify any behaviors in your repertoire that work against that goal.

FIGURE 6-3

Bob Prince's immunity to change map

1. Commitment (improvement goal)	2. Doing/not doing instead	3. Hidden/competing commitment	4. Big assumptions
To get better at making things happen reliably in projects by getting in sync on the goal and coordinating the parts	I regularly make plans and act on them without seeking input from people (especially those more skilled at strategic planning) I regard my plans with too much confidence I tend not to question the plans I generate	**Worry box:** not being able to do what I want to do; won't know how to engage with others to get in sync; being held back by others; not adding enough value to Bridgewater I may also be committed to: • Doing what I want to do, when I want to do it • Not being held back by, or having to depend on, others • Not having to experience my own inability to get in sync with the others • Not continuing to feel I am adding insufficient value to Bridgewater	I may be assuming that: • If I try to get in sync on what I want to do, I won't know how to do it, others will "say no" and hold me back from doing what I want • I know best, that my plan doesn't need any external input, that nothing especially valuable will come about from getting in sync • Once I have figured out what I want to do, others are more of a drag on me than a source of improved design • I am not adding enough value to Bridgewater • I need to significantly increase the value I add • My best route to significantly add greater value is to unilaterally jam through my plan • "Outsourcing" some of the work is no way to significantly add value

There are two criteria for this column.

- Be sure that the entries you list are *behaviors*, and the more concrete you can be, the better. For example, rather than write, "I get bored when I mentor direct reports," write something like, "I stop listening when a direct report explains his or her problem" or, "I immediately solve others' problems before hearing the full story," both of which are behaviors stemming from an inner experience of boredom. If you find yourself naming something that is more like a feeling, a state of mind, or an attitude, ask yourself, "What do I *do* (or what don't I do) that leads to, or follows from, these feelings or attitudes? What do I do (or not do) as a result of these feelings or attitudes?"

- Each item is something you're doing that works *against* your improvement goal. Our bet is that you're doing lots of things in order to move toward your commitment, as well, but here we're asking you just the opposite. We also imagine you could make a long and detailed list of how *others* are undermining your improvement, but we aren't asking you to do that here either.

The more behaviors you can list, the better your chances are of coming to powerful insights later in the process. So give yourself plenty of time to think back to the times when you've vowed to improve and maybe even started to change your behaviors but then slipped back into old and familiar ways of being at work.

Write all of your behaviors in the second column of your ITC map. Review your list of behaviors carefully to make sure it is thorough, that all the entries are concrete behaviors, and that all the behaviors listed work against your improvement goal.

Nora Dashwood

Improvement goal: I am committed to getting better at "being with" others, to being less controlling, to being more open to others' ways of doing things.

In column 2 (Doing/not doing), Dashwood listed, honestly and candidly, the things she was doing that were undermining her improvement goal:

- I don't listen to others
- I talk too much to try to convince others that my way is the right way
- When someone presents an idea or plan that doesn't correspond to my own view, I constantly ask questions and follow up too extensively, micromanage
- I freeze them out with a stony face, withdraw from conversation, lack of encouragement
- I solve smaller problems or challenges that I know I can control
- I don't consider alternatives
- I spend time on things I don't want to
- I don't delegate

It is a long, courageous, vulnerability-producing list, one that doesn't paint Dashwood in a glowing light. Of course she had already had a long and successful career, one that had brought her to the top of her field. At Decurion she was widely admired and beloved for her compassion, expertise, ability to teach others, and high standards. But she was unwilling to rest on that or hide behind it; she was open to remaking herself, as a way to continue to grow and learn.

Bob Prince

I am committed to getting better at making things happen reliably in projects by getting in sync on the goal and coordinating the parts.

Prince had a hard time seeing how he behaved in ways that undermined his goal. Although he wanted to be open-minded and take guidance from others who were strong in the strategic planning areas where he was weak, he regularly made plans and acted on them without realizing that he would do better to seek input from those who were more skilled at strategic planning. At Bridgewater, Prince was sure to get this feedback. Others reminded him of his weakness when they saw him behaving in ways he didn't even realize were problematic. In Bridgewater terminology, they were guardrailing him against his weaknesses. In ITC terminology, they were helping Prince see the column 2 behaviors he engaged in that undermined his progress.

In a meeting dedicated to assessing whether Prince was making progress, Dalio told him, "Two basic things. You trust yourself too much. You don't work it through well. If you had less confidence, felt you could be wrong with the strategic . . . trusting yourself less, you would have been much more successful. But because you are hell-bent to not do that, you went down that path. If you could be more open-minded, and trusted yourself less, you would have done a better job." (Note that the picture this feedback creates, if it is accurate [and Prince felt it was], is one Next Jump would call overconfidence or arrogance.)

The Bridgewater culture is designed so that Prince would receive that feedback repeatedly—to know exactly what he did (or didn't do) that undermined his goals. Painful as that process can be, the culture is also designed to help those like Prince consider feedback not only as a diagnosis of weakness and source of pain but also as the information they need to learn and grow. (Charlie Kim, at Next Jump, calls this kind of feedback "sunshine." It's what helps you grow.)

Prince added these behaviors to column 2 of his ITC map.

- I regularly make plans and act on them without seeking input from people (especially those more skilled at strategic planning)

- I regard my plans with too much confidence

- I tend not to question the plans I generate

Your Turn

What are you doing (and what are you not doing) that undermines your improvement goal?

People tend to go offtrack in this column in two ways. Either they write explanations for sometimes working against their goals, or they list what they plan to do differently. Notice that both Dashwood and Prince listed their undermining behaviors, without explanation or promises for change. If you find yourself adding justifications or new plans for change, you are in good company, but limit your list to just the behaviors.

It's tempting to immediately start vowing and plotting to make things different. People usually feel guilty or embarrassed by their list and want to eradicate it by being stricter with themselves, punishing themselves for their "bad" behaviors, or willing themselves to be more disciplined. Again, the only things that should be in your second column are the things you do and don't do that work against your improvement goal. No judgments, no explanations, no promises to yourself or future plans.

Write your own undermining behaviors in column 2 of your ITC map.

Column 3, Worry Box: Naming Your Fears and Worries

From an ITC perspective, reflecting on your behaviors, even very candidly, is rarely enough to lead to transformational change and learning. It can lead to the sincerest of New Year's resolutions, but how powerful have these ever proven for promoting lasting change? You name the behaviors in order to go deeper, to consider (as you will see) what lies at their root—your anxieties, dreaded images, ego attachments, and patterns of self-protection.

As a result, something intriguing happens in column 3: a dynamic that has been hidden before now—the immunity to change—begins to emerge. Often, the work in this column feels unexpectedly potent and arresting. You start by filling in the box at the top, which we call the *worry box*. (In a moment you'll move on to the bottom half of this column.)

In the worry box, name the fears and worries that come up when you imagine doing *the opposite* of each thing you listed in column 2. Typically, people spend a lot of energy trying to keep their fears at bay, trying to convince themselves and others that they're brilliantly competent and have everything under control. But if that's all you let yourself feel, you won't have a powerful map. For the worry box, try to come up with something that feels scary or a bit dangerous, something that you feel in your gut. The goal is to locate an actual loathsome or fearful feeling, and not just a thought or an idea about an unpleasant feeling.

You may be able to get to a deeper level of reflection by slowing down your reactions and pushing yourself to imagine what is actually the opposite of (and not only different from) your column 2 behaviors. Actually imagine yourself doing (or even trying to do) the opposite of a column 2 behavior. Vicariously put yourself into that movie. Now—how does that feel? What is the fear or loathing (or both) that you feel?

Your Turn

One by one, look at the behaviors you listed in column 2, and imagine yourself doing (or even trying to do) the opposite. What worries or fears come up for you? What might you really hate for others to see in you? What might be a way you would least like to see yourself?

If you have identified something that feels bad but still seems a bit safe, try to push to a deeper level. Ask yourself, "What would be the worst thing about that for me?" If you have named a handful of fears, ask yourself that question about each one. You need to get to a place where the warning bells begin to sound, where you feel the threat of some loss—for example, to how others regard you, or your ability to maintain control, or your sense of yourself as loved, smart, worthy, or whatever.

Now enter your fears in the worry box in column 3.

Column 3, Bottom Half: Uncovering Your Hidden Commitments

Identifying your fears and worries will help you discover something else—what we call a *hidden competing commitment*. Your fears are the raw material for generating these commitments.

A central idea in the immunity to change practice is that we do not merely have these fears; we sensibly, even artfully, protect ourselves from them. No one wants to feel fear or worry. We don't generally enjoy experiencing ourselves as in danger or at risk in some way. We don't often seek that kind of vulnerability. Instead, we usually try to protect ourselves from these feelings. We defend ourselves from what terrifies us. We make sure that we're not standing on the edge of our own personal abyss of anxiety and danger but that we're standing quite comfortably far away—far enough away that we don't even have to be consciously aware that the abyss is there. Hidden commitments are our mental strategies for standing far away from the abyss, our ways of keeping far away from the things we fear.

Although we're actively committed to making sure the things we fear do not happen, we are not usually conscious of these commitments. To be conscious of them would mean we would also have the uncomfortable awareness of our fears. So they usually stay hidden from our consciousness, all the while working hard to make sure the things we fear do not happen.

Nora Dashwood

Dashwood surveyed her list of behaviors in column 2 and began to imagine what she would feel if she were to do the opposite of those things. What if she listened more and spoke less? What if instead of micromanaging, she actually encouraged others to fully develop their own ideas? Here are her worries:

> Alternatives will emerge that I can't accomplish; that these ideas might be better than mine, and I won't be seen as valuable; that they are not and I'll have to do more work to fix things since I didn't veto the idea in the first place; that I won't like leading in a different way; that leading in a different way means losing who I am; that if I try to lead differently, I might fail at it; that I'll be taken advantage of or walked over.

These worries felt terrible and also true for her. They showed her that—like every human on earth—she had powerful, largely unconscious hidden commitments operating against the changes she was consciously striving to make. These commitments protect her from the dangers that some part of her brain felt she would surely encounter if she actually were to change. Could Dashwood fail in this new role? No longer be seen as valuable? Would others take advantage of a less controlling style? Would she no longer even feel like herself?

Because they're usually hidden in our unconscious, these commitments are hard to unearth and name without undergoing the kind of triggering captured in the worry box. But when we uncover them, we can see how we've been preventing our own improvement. Dashwood found she was unconsciously committed to the following:

- Avoiding alternatives from emerging that I don't think I can accomplish

- Avoiding being shown up, or my ideas being seen as less valuable

- Not having to do things twice

- Staying interested in doing by "leading"

- Not losing my sense of self

- Not showing that I will fail at being able to effectively support others

- Avoiding being taken advantage of or walked over

Now Dashwood clearly saw that she was heading into territory that tapped in to deep fears about what she would feel, and what she could find, if she began to lead in new ways.

Across the three columns she saw a schematic of her immune system, a picture that captured the reality: that even though there was a part of her that genuinely wanted to improve her leadership by being more open to others' ways, there was simultaneously another part of her that wanted, actually *needed*, something counter to that goal in order for her to be safe. She had one foot on the gas pedal saying, "Go, go, go" (column 1) while her other foot was on the brakes (column 3), saying, "No way!"

Here's what is going on, in a nutshell. We believe that the mind, like the body, has an immune system—a beautiful, intelligent force of nature that works continuously, beyond our awareness, with one purpose in mind: to protect us and keep us alive. And like our body's immune system, our psychological one can occasionally misread reality and mistakenly see danger that's not really there. Then our immune system itself becomes a source of trouble; as it "protects" us, it rejects what the system needs in order to thrive (think autoimmune attack on parts of your own body here, or the rejection of a donor organ).

Bob Prince

When Prince thought about doing the opposite of what was in his column 2, he imagined what it would be like to seek more input from others and to be actively skeptical of his own ability to make sound plans and follow through with them. A handful of self-protective worries arose for him:

> Not being able to do what I want to do; won't know how to engage with others to get in sync; being held back by others; not adding enough value to Bridgewater.

Prince now saw what he had been unconsciously committed to:

- Doing what I want to do, when I want to do it

- Not being held back by, or having to depend on, others

- Not having to experience my own inability to get in sync with the others

- Not continuing to feel I am adding insufficient value to Bridgewater

In Bridgewater's language, Prince touched the nerve here. In our language, we now can imagine his immune system. By moving from the worries to the hidden commitments, and then connecting the dots between his conscious and unconscious comments, we see a system at play that must produce exactly the results that create ineffectiveness relative to his goal. He had a conscious goal he was failing at (becoming a more effective project manager), but the very behaviors that were causing him to fail (to blow up the lab, as Jensen said) were brilliantly serving the unconscious goal of his hidden commitments (e.g., "I don't want to be held back, to be prevented from doing what I want to do, when I want to do it.")

Like Dashwood, Prince was finally able to see why he was stuck, with one foot on the gas and one foot on the brake. This contradiction was not a sign that he was a bad thinker or illogical. It was nothing to be ashamed of. It was, in fact, a sign that he had created an immune system that took care of him and protected him. This system had helped him in many ways in life. It probably contributed to his being as successful as he was and being seen as an expert. However, his immune system also explained why he was not succeeding on his goal. No one could who was captive of this system.

Your Turn

You probably don't want to experience those fears or worries in your worry box (let alone have them happen). What self-protective, hidden commitment stands behind each of your fears or worries? Don't try to consciously figure this out. Just restate your worries in column 3 as commitments to prevent what you're worried about from happening.

Here are three guidelines to help you come to a good list of hidden commitments.

- *Keep the language of the particular fear, worry, or dread in the worry box when you write the hidden commitment.* For example, "I fear others will think I'm not up to this job" should be converted to "I'm committed to others not thinking poorly of me," or "I'm committed to not being seen as incompetent" and *not* "I'm committed to others thinking well of me" or "I'm committed to being seen as competent." You may need to use a clunky double negative in order to preserve the danger you're protecting yourself from, and that's fine. This isn't an English composition class.

- *Remember that hidden commitments are forms of self-protection.* They protect us from the dangers that may lurk in our fears. If your first attempts at identifying worries yield more noble-sounding, not-so-self-protective entries, keep asking yourself what would feel worst for you, what you are protecting yourself from, what is truly at stake for you, what would feel yuckiest to you—until you land on hidden fears that are deeper, harder to face, and yet ring absolutely true.

- *Hidden commitments should show that the behaviors you've listed in column 2 now make perfect sense.* Paradoxically, powerful hidden commitments mean that those "bad behaviors" are also simultaneously "smart behaviors," making sure that one foot stays firmly on the brake. The problem is not that you can't change your behavior. The problem is not that you are weak-willed. It is not that you're not strong enough, smart enough, or brave enough. You are very strongly taking good care of yourself. Rather, the problem is that your perfectly sensible unconscious effort to take care of yourself is producing the very behaviors guaranteed to keep you from accomplishing your goal.

Write your list of hidden commitments in the bottom half of column 3 in your map (underneath the worry box).

The Immune System

Now that you've identified your own hidden commitments, you should see a whole picture across your three columns—a picture of your personal immunity to change. You should now see how you have one foot on the gas (your improvement goal) and the other foot on the brake (your competing hidden commitments). And you should see why you haven't made progress on your improvement goal before.

Only when you see more deeply into how it is—and why it is—you have prevented yourself from making progress can you enter a new space to begin changing. Only when you have an accurate mental map can you correctly see the obstacles so that you can chart the course ahead. You have created a vivid and powerful, and perhaps painful, map of the problem. Now you can start working on creating your own personally powerful solution.

Where might you imagine doing that? Few people would think about the possibility (let alone weigh the value) of doing this in the public light of the shared workplace. On the contrary, psychological self-protection operates in full force in the culture of most workplaces. As we've said all along, in a typical organization, individuals expend enormous energy protecting themselves. People hide parts of themselves, avoid conflict, unwittingly sabotage change efforts, and subtly enforce a separation between their true, full selves and the selves they allow themselves to be at work. They hide these parts to keep themselves safe, for self-protection. They hide these parts because they (rightly or wrongly) assume that exposing them can only put them in danger. They hide these parts because they work in organizations that allow them to.

We have argued that there is no greater waste of resources in ordinary organizations than the energy spent to hide our weaknesses and manage others' favorable impressions of us. As an organization takes steps to become deliberately developmental, the question is, Who else should know about your hidden commitments? Where else do these commitments undermine your effectiveness at work? What are the costs that you (and others, and the organization) bear because of your immune system?

Asking these questions doesn't mean you will know yet how to solve the problem, how to end the struggling. That will come later. Einstein said that if he had one hour to save the world, he would spend fifty-five minutes defining the problem, and five minutes finding the solution. That is because we can't get to the right solution if we don't truly understand the problem. You will come to a solution, but only after you have gotten the problem right.

People sometimes tell us that mapping their immunity to change gets them quickly to a deep level of insight and awareness about why they're stuck. Others need a bit more time and help to get to something that feels meaningful. We hope you feel you're approaching something that is both powerful and intriguing for you.

So at this point it is worth asking yourself, "On a scale of 1 to 5 (where 1 means not powerful or not intriguing, and 5 means very powerful or very intriguing), how does this map feel for me?" If you answered 4 or 5, that's great, and you should feel free to move on to the final column in this exercise. If you answered 1, 2, or 3, we recommend that you accept a little help to strengthen your entries. If the map doesn't pop for you, there is probably a problem in one or more columns. You'll find help in the box "Making Your Map More Powerful."

Making Your Map More Powerful

If your map does not yet feel intriguing, what might help?

- Make sure that the fear, worry, or dread from the worry box did not disappear when you converted it into a hidden commitment. If it did, it means that the "virus" (the danger the immune system is protecting you from) did not get named in your hidden commitments. Remember, clunky double negatives are fine. (The fear that I won't be listened to becomes the hidden commitment "to not be ignored," or "to not be silenced," "to not become invisible." It does not become a commitment "to be heard.")

- When you look at your hidden commitments, you should be able to see how you have been protecting yourself. If not, ask, "What is the danger lurking for me? In what way am I trying to protect myself?"

- Look to see whether everything you identified as a hidden commitment also shows how the behaviors you listed in column 2 now make sense. You should be able to see why it hasn't worked (and won't work) to try to change those behaviors only through willpower or increased effort. The harder you step on the gas, the harder your other foot will step on the brakes. You will spend more energy trying to go in opposite directions at the same time. If you can't see how your hidden commitments make your behaviors in column 2 look perfectly reasonable, that's a sign that you've gotten offtrack somewhere. You may need to revise your hidden commitments or go back to your fears to see whether you need to get clearer about them.

Column 4: Big Assumptions

The most reliable route to ultimately disrupting your immune system is to identify the core assumptions that sustain it. *Big assumptions* are the core beliefs that hold your immune system in place. They are the root of your behaviors. Assumptions are beliefs—ideas that we have about ourselves and about the world. They are mental constructions, but we tend to take these beliefs as truths, or rules about how the world really is. And we don't know whether or not they are true until we can name them and explore them.

When we treat an assumption as if it were the absolute truth, we allow it to rule our actions. We allow it to shape everything we see. We don't consider or explore other possibilities, and so it continues to hold enormous power over us. That is why it is a big assumption. But when we name the big assumptions underlying our immunities to change, we can consider the possibility that they may not actually be 100 percent true.

Nora Dashwood

Naming her fears and hidden commitments helped Dashwood identify the beliefs she had formed about herself—beliefs that were central to her identity.

- I assume my accomplishments and talents might be more about my good fortune than about my abilities; hence I am out of my league

- I assume that I have contextually developed (in Decurion's structure) but have not been truly developing (across all contexts)

- I assume that I am a leopard trying to change its spots

- I assume that I care more about myself than I care about others

- I assume that a lot of my value comes from having the right view, that things done by others will likely not be done right—in other words not the way I want them done

- I need a certain kind of stimulus to be effective

- My prime source of enjoyment is in the role, of having the right view

There was a part of Dashwood that believed she could not change her spots, that she was not going to enjoy being a different type of leader nearly as much as she enjoyed being the leader in front, the one who has the right answer, and the one driving things. She felt she needed the type of stimulation that came with that style of leadership. And she felt she was the only one who could do it right. For her to make a successful transition into her new role, she would have to find out that this part of her was wrong. She would have to undertake an exploration to find out whether she could do more than she ever thought she could, whether she might be able to become a bigger person than she had been, and whether these transformations would bring her pleasure.

The reason Dashwood's transition was successful was that neither she, nor those she worked with, approached it as simply a technical matter of learning new skills and new information. In fact, that kind of focus would likely have led to an unsuccessful transition, because as long as her fears and attachments were unexplored and untested, they would lead her to hold tightly to her controlling leadership style. Her visible, neocortex commitments (the ones in the first column) would be stymied by her amygdala commitments (the ones in the third column). Brain psychology talks about the importance of "dual processing," of "thinking slow and thinking fast." We're more effective when we bring these modes of thinking into conversation with each other, as the ITC practice helps you do.

The curriculum for Dashwood's learning, a curriculum provided for her in a DDO, was much deeper than the technical approach of skill change alone; it also included the adaptive approach of mind-set change. The ITC map provided a clear image of the way Dashwood's mind-set shaped her behavior and held her back. It helped illustrate this deeper psychological dimension of human meaning-making that DDOs look to uncover for their workers.

But the far more valuable purpose of an ITC map is for you to generate these types of insight by creating your own map. In other words, creating your own map is a reflective process that allows you—in a DDO or in any other context—to begin to uncover the deeper psychological roots of your own limiting assumptions. Dashwood created an ITC map to help her reveal the deeper levels of her challenge and to focus her improvement work on overturning her immunity to change.

Bob Prince

Looking at his immune system, Prince identified several big assumptions that held it in place.

I may be assuming that:

- If I try to get in sync on what I want to do, I won't know how to do it, others will "say no" and hold me back from doing what I want

- I know best, that my plan doesn't need any external input, that nothing especially valuable will come about from getting in sync

- Once I have figured out what I want to do, others are more of a drag on me than a source of improved design

- I am not adding enough value to Bridgewater

- I need to significantly increase the value I add

- My best route to significantly add greater value is to unilaterally jam through my plan

- "Outsourcing" some of the work is no way to significantly add value

Why uncover these assumptions? Remember that we call these big assumptions precisely because they're not being taken as assumptions that are possibly true, and possibly not true; rather, they're being taken as unquestioningly true. By taking this next, crucial step, Prince created a clear and focused curriculum to consider the favorite Bridgewater question—What is true?—at a whole new level, and not only at the diagnostic level. At the diagnostic level he would have explored whether or not it was true that he really had a problem; but at the new, treatment level he had a path for changing his mind. By being conscious of his own big assumptions, Prince is able to search for the truth. His questions can become deeper.

- Is it true that if I try to get in sync with others I won't know how to, and that others will say no and hold me back from doing what I want?

- Is it true that I know best, that my plan doesn't need any external input, that nothing especially valuable will come about from getting in sync?

- Is it true that once I have figured out what I want to do, others are more of a drag on me than a source of improved design?

- Is it true that I am not adding enough value to Bridgewater and that I need to significantly increase the value I add?

- Is it true that the best route to significantly adding greater value is for me to unilaterally jam through my plan?

- Is it true that outsourcing some of the work is no way to significantly add value?

These are questions Prince pursued. Watching the video of his conversation with Dalio helped Prince begin to challenge some of his key big assumptions. As a viewer, he was able to step back a bit and take a third-party perspective, looking for the data that might show him that these assumptions were inaccurate. He reached several insights.

- The characterization of him as someone who "struggles to make things happen reliably" was accurate in this case

- There were others on the project who were very skilled at project management

- Drawing on data about his own weaknesses and others' strengths to determine who should do what would lead to better project outcomes

Realizing how much he hadn't seen before, and realizing that others had seen these dynamics in play, Prince had clear data that his big assumption—that he knew best, that his plan didn't need external input, that nothing especially valuable would come about from getting in sync—was wrong.

As that big assumption began to crumble, he saw that other big assumptions were also falling apart. If understanding and sourcing work according to people's varying strengths and weaknesses would lead to a better product outcome, then unilaterally jamming through his plan was not a good way for him to add value at Bridgewater.

Instead, his great ideas for the project, and the project itself, would more likely be held back—the very outcome he dreaded.

As Prince explains, "I could be much more productive and would be much more empowered to pursue my ideas and add more value to Bridgewater if I operated in a different way; 'outsourcing' management design, learning how to get in sync on the goal and the path with others. This discovery helped me to improve and to add more value to Bridgewater (with less strain), so it was very rewarding to me."

We should note that the video of Prince's conversation with Dalio and Jensen, in which they all reflect on and describe Prince's weaknesses in great detail, was developed into a short case (or tidbit) and published on the company tablet for all employees to view and reflect on. Prince is regarded as a great hero at Bridgewater, someone who has contributed enormously to Bridgewater's success, but he has also struggled. The process illustrates how everyone involved can learn a great deal from that struggle, how everyone is expected to learn and grow from painful feedback.

Prince was "struggling well" in that he openly accepted feedback on his own weaknesses and acknowledged them. In fact, his admired contributions to Bridgewater are attributed to the fact that he struggles well. Viewers of the case are invited "to struggle openly, because it is good for you and good for the people around you."

Your Turn

When you look over all that you've uncovered, and especially your column 3 hidden commitments, what does it suggest about your assumptions—the beliefs you hold about yourself and the way things are—that connect to and support your immune system? Generate as many big assumptions as you can.

Here are guidelines for doing this work.

- Some of your big assumptions may feel undeniably true ("What do you mean, 'an assumption'? I think this is exactly the awful thing that would happen!"). Others you may know aren't really true (although you act and feel as if they were true). And still others you may feel are only partially or sometimes true. However true you believe your big assumptions are, *all of them go in your column 4*, and they will be valuable resources if you decide to pursue working on your edge. (See "Big Assumptions at Decurion" for ways some of the leaders describe their big assumptions.)

- Every big assumption should show why one or more of your hidden commitments feel absolutely necessary. You should be able to trace your map backward and see how the big assumptions make your column 3 commitments necessary, how column 3 commitments lead to your column 2 behaviors, and how these behaviors undermine your column 1 goals.

- Your big assumptions set clear limits on what you must do and what you must not do; you should be able to see that your big assumptions are rules you have for how to live your life, rules you must always follow if you want to avoid danger and disaster and defeat. But you might also be able to see (at least hypothetically) that, like other rules, yours can be broken.

Generate as many big assumptions as you can, and write them in column 4 in your ITC map.

How Was That for You?

Now that you've diagnosed your own personal immune system, understandably you may be eager to learn how to begin overturning it. Before we turn to next steps, we want you to take a moment to think about what your experience of this exercise has been like. We hope you experienced something of the discomfort of stepping out of your mind-set (the root of your behavior)—what it means to be working on your edge.

You also may have experienced a range of emotions through this process—as both Dashwood and Prince did—and as those who work for DDOs experience regularly in their work. You may have felt twinges of pain or shame, which often happens when you gain difficult insights into your own limitations. And you may have also felt something of the joy of having insights that potentially can bring about transformational change in your life, a means to

Big Assumptions at Decurion

When you identify big assumptions that limit you, you experience a different, deeper type of learning than the more common technical learning. Decurion leaders describe the limiting assumptions they are working to overturn.

Bryan Ungard (COO). "My current practice is to start with what's up for me in simple, raw, emotional terms, to be more disclosing about what's behind my thoughts and feelings. My fear is that I'm going to be rejected unless I'm an expert on something, and if I don't pull that off in a masterful way, I will be judged. So I'm practicing letting the real messy me be seen."

Nora Dashwood (ArcLight's COO). "I guess what I'm really practicing is how to just be okay with being me, to trust that I am enough. And to be more—to be more 'needy,' more interdependent. I have a thing about feeling like I have to be strong and independent and take care of myself because nobody else is going to. [It's a] good motto to be instilled into the daughter of loving, immigrant parents, but it's outlived its usefulness."

Jeff Koblentz (President of Robertson Properties Group). "I'm working on not disconnecting from people or closing my heart when results are not good. My driving belief from early in life is that the world can hurt me, and that if I produce excellent results (i.e., am 'competent'), I can protect myself. I'm sure this has served me well at times, but only associating oneself with things that are going 'excellently' is not an effective way to operate in business, to say nothing about how it works as a parent."

become a better you. That possibility exists because—instead of viewing your personal challenge only as it appears in columns 1 and 2 (identifying goals, finding motivation, focusing on unproductive behaviors you wish to change)—the ITC map targets hidden fears, commitments, and beliefs that, once uncovered, recast the personal challenge in a way that involves the whole self. You see how you can, if you're willing, put your whole self at risk for change.

What's Next?

Now that you can both see and feel what it's like to be out on your growing edge, where might you think to pursue the inner learning agenda that's uncovered by an exercise like this one? In a DDO you could share your learning with others in your organization. They could give you feedback to help strengthen your column 1 and column 2 entries. You could begin to test the accuracy of your big assumptions (see "How to Test a Big Assumption" for more on this). You could let your colleagues know the big assumptions you've identified so that they can help you find out whether those assumptions are as true as you have seen them to be. You could provide your colleagues with the same feedback and support so that they, too, can evolve. You could make this part of the work you do every day.

This practice contrasts with the way things are done in a typical organization, where you might be advised to find a private space and a trustworthy coach or counselor with whom to work through the issues and implications the exercise provokes. "I wouldn't want to wash my dirty laundry in public, for everyone at work to see," you might say. And that makes sense if your work setting requires you to continually protect your brand and hide any indication of inadequacy or incompleteness. You can see your coach only an hour a week, however, and you can't actually practice new behavior in the coach's office.

Now imagine if you had coaching continuously, and work were a safe place to practice every day. Imagine if your organization figured out that it should help you overcome your limitations, not only out of the goodness of its collective heart but also because this practice is in its own interests: the longer you successfully hide your limitations, the longer the company has to pay for them. Imagine, then, that you will work out the implications of an exercise like this one, not behind closed doors in your coach's office but in the daily conduct of your work.

How to Test a Big Assumption

Testing big assumptions is at the heart of overturning an immunity to change. The purpose of a test is to learn about the accuracy of your big assumption by seeing what happens when you intentionally alter your usual behavior. When you design and run a test, you act *as if* your big assumptions might not be as absolutely true as you seem to believe. The purpose of the test is not to immediately improve or take a step closer to your goal. Nor are you testing yourself. You're not trying to determine whether you have the wherewithal or courage to do something daring. Here are some tips.

- Rarely is a person's big assumption simply "right" or "wrong." Often, the problem is that we tend to overuse and overgeneralize it.

- No single experiment is likely to be conclusive about a big assumption. Consider the test as the first of several.

- Designing a good test includes planning how to collect data.

- A good test meets SMART criteria.

  1. *SM* means safe and modest. *Safe* means that if the worst-case outcome were to occur, you could live with it. It can also mean you make a *small* change in what you do. *Modest* means that the test is relatively simple and easy to carry out. Ideally, it doesn't require you to go out of your way but rather is an opportunity to do something different in your normal day.

  2. *A* means *actionable* in the near term (within the next week or so) and relatively easy to carry out (you can easily imagine a setting or upcoming situation in which to run your test).

  3. *RT* means that the *test researches* the question, "How accurate is my big assumption?" and, like any good research, it requires collecting data (e.g., how people respond to you as well as your thoughts and feelings). The test doesn't test you; it tests your big assumption and should be designed so that it can generate disconfirming data, if it exists. It shouldn't be a clever way to prove that your big assumption is true.

Identify one big assumption to test. Which one jumps out at you as the one that most gets in your way? Or imagine that you can dismiss any single big assumption in your map. Which one would make the biggest, most positive difference for you? Be sure that the assumption you choose feels powerful to you.

Now design your test. Start with the end in mind by asking yourself, "What data would lead me to doubt my big assumption?" (If you can't imagine what kind of data could challenge or cast doubt on your assumption, then you don't have a testable assumption.) Work backward from there to figure out what action you could take that could generate that data. Your action is likely to be one that is the opposite of a behavior from your column 2 or an action that runs counter to your column 3 hidden commitment.

Following is a form you can use to guide your efforts.

Testing big assumptions workspace

My big assumption says:	So I will (change my behavior this way) . . .	And I will collect the following data . . .	In order to find out whether . . .

(continued)

(continued)

Reflections on your test results

My big assumption says:	So in order to test it I changed my behavior this way . . .	This is what I observed happening . . .	And this is what it tells me about my big assumption . . .

For more information on overturning immune systems, see *Immunity to Change: How to Overcome It and Unlock Potential in Yourself and Your Organization*, Robert Kegan and Lisa Laskow Lahey (Boston: Harvard Business Review Press, 2009), especially chapter 10.

Creating Home

Getting Started toward Becoming a DDO

This is our last chapter, but we want to talk more about beginnings than endings. In the same spirit of chapter 1, where we give you impressions of life inside the mature DDO—plunking you down in the middle of them and inviting you to turn your head this way and that—now we invite you into a similar collection of glimpses into fledgling DDOs with whom we've worked. If leaders of an organization are considering a move in this direction, how would they get started? They may not know, at the outset, how far they will choose to go, but how do they begin?

You can't get out on your developmental edge until you've created practices that bring it into view. And you can't sustain these practices (your groove) without first fostering a setting to support a new level of vulnerability. So, for us, the first moves in getting started always have to do with creating a home to support a new level of personal and collective learning.

There is no one right way to get started, and you won't necessarily find your right way in the glimpses we show you here. But hopefully they'll help you think about what might best fit your setting.

Before we begin the tour, we want to say explicitly that we're speaking in this chapter mostly to people who have some kind of formal authority—CEOs, division leaders, team leaders, managers. That is because we believe you're the people in the most powerful position to decide whether you want your organization (or unit) to head down the path toward becoming a DDO. You can't make it happen on your own, but if you're not on board, it's not likely to succeed in the setting you lead. You'll see in the pages ahead that it's possible to approach the work from the top down, the middle out, or a combination of the two. However, no matter which pattern you use, those in the lead (of the team, the division, the whole organization) need to publicly serve as enthusiastic exemplars of the DDO idea, visibly operating with their fellow leaders as a developmental community for themselves, and demonstrating the requisite openness and vulnerability in their relationship to the rest of the organization. It is no accident that the remarkable set of leaders from Bridgewater, Decurion, and Next Jump whom you met in previous chapters are at once staunch champions of, and full participants in, their unusual cultures.

In saying this, we hope we don't lose you if you have no formal power or authority in your organization but nonetheless are enthusiastic about DDOs. Let us clarify our view: we believe everyone at every level can exercise a form of power and influence in and on an organization. Worthy ideas can spread from one person to another, and, before long, a small instance of positive deviance can develop, and someone with formal authority can take notice. Consider trying some of the practices in the box "Being Deliberately Developmental without a DDO."

Look for opportunities to make your passions and your thoughts known to decision makers. Take the stance that you believe they could join you in your interests and efforts.

Tell them what excites you about imagining being part of a DDO-like community. Share what you've learned from personally experimenting with any of the practices you've tried. Tell them you know that there are places where the answers to the following questions are all positive: Does your organization help you identify a personal challenge—meaningful to you and valuable for the company—that

Being Deliberately Developmental without a DDO

So, you're in the early or middle stage of your career, and you don't work in a DDO. How can you work on growing every day? Try these practices.

- *Become developmental buddies with someone.* Creating a sense of home is important for your development, and you can experience it by mutually sharing what you're working on about yourself. Remember that it's not about giving each other advice about how to solve problems. Rather, it's about giving one another a chance to regularly check in about how your growing edge is showing up on a daily basis. Useful questions to ask a development buddy go something like this: "What did that experience bring up for you? Why do you think you had that response, reaction, thought, or fear?"

- *Seek input about your growing edge.* It's hard to take advantage of all the opportunities to grow at work if you don't have a sense of what you're actively working on. Try this simple exercise to jump-start identifying your own growing edge. Ask three people you trust, who know how you get work done, to answer a question for you: "As someone who knows me and wants to help me keep growing, what do you observe that I could be doing differently that might make me more effective?"

- *Create an immunity-to-change map on your growing edge goal.* Turn to chapter 6 for guidance on creating one. Share your map, as well as your observations and tests of your big assumptions, with your developmental buddy.

- *Seek bite-size, regular, meaningful feedback from trusted observers.* Ask trusted colleagues to watch you during a meeting, a presentation, or other setting and give you a little feedback afterward.

(continued)

(continued)

For example, hypothetically you might say, "I'm working on doing more active listening and less talking, less justifying of my reasoning and sharing my opinions. Can you tell me what you notice about my actions in this meeting?"

- *Bring your manager into your growth agenda.* If you feel comfortable doing so, tell your manager about your goals for learning and growth. When you proactively seek feedback and signal your intention to keep working on your effectiveness, by and large, your supervisors have more room to mentor you. For most managers, it's a breath of fresh air—and a clear win-win situation for the organization—to have employees with a genuine interest in self-improvement.

- *Watch for modeling by others.* Some colleagues and experienced leaders are especially good role models for seizing opportunities to grow at work. Look for evidence of people who seek active input, publicly model learning behaviors, and invest in others' growth. Watch what they do, and ask to talk to them about their day-to-day approach to learning and growing at work.

you can work on in order to grow? Are there others who are aware of this growing edge and who care that you transcend it? Are you given support to overcome your limitations? Can you name and describe them? Do you experience yourself actively working on transcending this growing edge daily or at least weekly? When you become a more capable version of yourself, is it recognized, is it celebrated, and—when you're ready—are you given the opportunity to keep growing? Give them this book, and ask to meet with them after they read it. Let them know we're ready to help you and that resources you will learn about in this chapter can be made available to your organization, too.

Let's jump in and get a first, brief glimpse of a company looking to become a DDO.

XYZ, Inc.

We are sitting in a large, multipurpose conference room on the top floor of the headquarters of XYZ, Inc. (the name is fictitious, at the company's request; all the facts are true). With cameras and light poles scattered about, the space looks more like a TV studio than a corporate boardroom. Seated in a circle before us are the ten top leaders of this multinational company with annual revenues exceeding $20 billion.

We have just finished commending these leaders for their courage. Having inherited a company, some eight years earlier, that had shaky performance and a dismal, eye-rolling regard of its customers, this group has taken a complicated organization and turned it around. They have made XYZ one of its sector's most admired companies by installing a top-down, give-orders-take-orders culture throughout, one that is marked by efficiency, hierarchy, and zero tolerance for mistakes.

We admire their courage because, here they are, about to renounce the very culture that is winning them regular plaudits in the newspapers and the praise of taxi drivers and local lunch companions, whom we have randomly asked, "How do you feel about XYZ?"

"The predictable path for a group of leaders who have received as much credit as you have," we tell them, "would be to ride this winning horse until it drops."

"The culture we created," the CEO says, "might have been necessary to turn around a company in crisis. But we believe, and our people agree, it will not be the best culture for the next twenty years."

"To deal with the world in front of us," the head of HR joins in, "and to bring out the best in our people, we need a much more collaborative, more innovative, more risk-taking culture."

But changing any culture, much less one with over a hundred thousand employees, is not an easy job, as this group knows well. "Everyone might raise their hand," the HR head says, "when you ask who'd prefer to work in the new culture we hope to move to. But when you ask, 'Okay, so who wants to make the first big mistake?' it's a different story."

This is a classic example of an adaptive challenge. There will be new skills and new concepts to learn in order to move to the new culture. But new skills and new ideas alone will never be enough to get XYZ where it wants to go. People will need to change their mind-sets, not just their skill sets. They will need to know what's in their third and fourth columns in their ITC maps. What are the hidden, self-protective commitments that keep a team leader from shifting her top-down style to one marked by significantly more delegating or that enable a team member to push back on an order from his boss? (As you learned in chapter 6, hidden commitments might be, "I am committed to not putting my ability to deliver on my goals in the hands of someone else whom I then have to depend on." Or, "I am committed to not having my boss feel I am disloyal, or not a team player." Hidden commitments must be overcome for people to meet their improvement goals.)

And how important will it be, not only for each employee to know his own immunity to change but also for his colleagues to know—his team members, his team leaders?

A New Kind of Home

What are we doing there, in this circle on the top floor of a building? The simplest answer: we're helping the leaders begin to create a new kind of home at XYZ, Inc., a community where employees can see and value each other as individual human beings and can hold the greater degree of vulnerability that will be necessary for the company to meet its adaptive challenge. We're starting with the leaders at the very top. We're going to take each of them through the experience of creating their own immunity to change maps, and they're going to have the chance to share them with each other.

Weeks later, the HR head will begin to spread home beyond the C-suite. He will introduce us to the first of four groups of 150 leaders we will work with at XYZ—the 600 senior managers of the company, each of whom is running a business unit. He will set the stage for an invitation to greater vulnerability in this large, publicly traded, multinational corporation.

"I've gone through the same experience you are about to go through," he will say. "And so has every member of the top team.

We wouldn't be asking you to do this if we hadn't experienced the power of it firsthand."

The HR head will continue, "I'll give you a little taste of how I experienced this. You know that thing that can sometimes happen with your iPhone, where all the icons start to jiggle? Well, that's what this was like for me. So let me introduce you to Dr. Lisa Lahey. She's here to jiggle your icons."

XYZ employees' concept of home will continue to widen when, months later, the head of leadership development will introduce us to about a thousand employees in twelve countries connected via webinar. Each of the six hundred senior managers has a top team of eight to ten. Home will eventually spread to the more than five thousand team members of these six hundred senior managers via four such webinars, each guiding more than a thousand employees through their own ITC maps, over three or four hours, in the company of their team members and team leader.

As we prepare this book, XYZ is making plans to spread home beyond the top six thousand to tens of thousands, via a highly engaging, highly interactive digital space we have cocreated that will provide several months of online support to XYZ employees who will test and overturn their big assumptions through experiments they will run at work—and, apparently, at home as well. (An XYZ employee came up to one of us during a recent visit to headquarters. "I know you don't know me," he said, "but I recognize you from the videos on that 'immunity' stuff. I just want to tell you, I'm frankly not sure yet how much better this is making me at work, but my wife wants me to thank you for making me a much better husband!")

Early Indications

Will XYZ become a DDO? Will a 100,000-person company ever become an everyone culture? Who knows. Decurion, Bridgewater, and Next Jump are all privately held companies, owned (at least in part) by their leaders, with no more than about a thousand employees each. It is natural to wonder whether a DDO must fit these characteristics. But with XYZ as an example, it's possible to imagine how a huge, publicly traded, multinational corporation begins to create an expanding home that can host the vulnerable-making groove of a practice like ITC, helping thousands of people, out on their edge, meet individual and collective adaptive challenges.

What we do know is that the work pays off. The company conducted an interim assessment of the impact and value after about a year and a half, comparing a group of senior managers with whom we worked with a comparably positioned group with whom we had not yet worked. XYZ decided the internally respected metrics for determining end-of-year bonus—metrics tightly tied to the performance of the units these managers were running—would be a good proxy for assessing impact. "In the aggregate," they asked, "does the group that has been participating in the personal-change work receive a higher end-of-year bonus than the group that has not?"

The conclusion: the group with whom we worked, in comparison to the group with whom we did not, added slightly more than a billion dollars to the company's revenues.

A Multiframe View: The Four-Box Model

Before we give you an extended look at another organization beginning to explore the DDO route, let's step back for a moment. Even in this first brief picture you can see several elements at play at XYZ, Inc.

1. The organization, as a whole, has identified a challenge, which is inevitably some part problem, and some part opportunity. In this case, a large multinational with a traditional culture wants to morph into a twenty-first-century company that is much more innovative and entrepreneurial.

2. As a result, individuals in the organization will find themselves with new challenges, new definitions of their roles, new answers to what constitutes doing the job well. For XYZ, all down the line, people need to be better delegators; people need to step up and take more initiative rather than wait for orders.

Note that these two elements would be intelligible and uncontroversial in any organizational setting or any management school curriculum. The first moves in the journey to becoming a DDO are nothing esoteric; rather, they're firmly anchored in the present realities and future aspirations of the business, as any leader might think about them: "What is going on in our organization and business sector right now? What do we want to be different?" (If the answer to the second question is, "Nothing! All is well and looks to stay that way," it's not likely you would want to start any change journey, let alone something in the direction of a DDO.)

So the first two arenas would make perfectly good sense, whether or not you had read a page of this book. But these are not the only elements signaled in the XYZ example. Let's look at two others.

3. To meet its outward-looking organizational challenge, XYZ has simultaneously engaged in an extensive look inward. Leaders asked, "What is our institutional personality or culture like? What do the most familiar patterns of what we do and how we act say about what we think and believe?" The XYZ leaders characterized their culture as too authoritarian, too top-down, too much giving and taking of orders; the company had been indirectly telling its people it was more important not to make mistakes than to innovate. Then the leaders asked, "What is it going to take for us to change our culture? What collective mind-sets will need to shift? In what ways are we most likely to sabotage or prevent any collective change we might try to bring about?" In XYZ's case, it is going to be a big shift for the system as a whole to get out of the "take orders from above/give orders to those below" pattern. "What risks do we assume, collectively, we would run, for our leadership and our followership, in trading parent-child patterns for adult-adult ones?"

4. Nor does the inward turn stop at the level of the organization as a whole. Individuals too will be faced with new expectations, and meeting these will require new learning. If this new learning constitutes adaptive as well as technical challenges, then it will be necessary to alter individual mind-sets and to understand the dynamics that prevent or undermine personal change. The immunity to change approach, which you learned

about in chapter 6, is only one way of doing this, but it is the one we know best, and the one XYZ used. Pushing back on one's leaders, and accepting pushback from one's direct reports, will inevitably wreak havoc with currently unchallenged personal assumptions about authority, responsibility, and risk.

Our colleague Ken Wilber has created a four-box model, which has been a valuable heuristic for a more comprehensive view of any complicated psychosocial phenomenon.[1] (We express our thanks, as well as apologies for any liberties we are taking with it here.) Wilber's four elements can be arrayed in a fashion that attends to the distinctions between the individual and the organizational and between the exterior and the interior (see figure 7-1).

Wilber's central motivation was to remind people of their tendencies to look at a phenomenon through too few lenses. The psychologically minded, for example, may be inclined to consider a change topic (say, gun reform or healthier eating) too exclusively from the *individual interior* perspective ("How can we better understand the motives and feelings of individual voters or eaters?") and ignore the need to consider more systemic issues ("What is the role of the National Rifle Association in preventing Congress from responding to the 70 percent of the population that supports background checks for gun purchases?" "How are we socialized from an early age to become overdependent on sugar or to take an unhealthy view of the amount of meat that should go into a main course?").

Those who are more comfortable with a systemic, political, or organizational perspective may be prone to the opposite myopia, overattending to the *organizational exterior*. We have seen many efforts, such as those to reform the US public education system, founder on change designs that reflect a sophisticated understanding of the dynamics of organizational change and resistance to change, but a naive understanding of those same dynamics in the individual psychologies of administrators and teachers who must change the ways they think and act, and vice versa.

The four-box heuristic invites people who are thinking about moving in the direction of a DDO to keep their eyes on all four boxes, what Wilber refers to as an "integral," or more adequately holistic,

FIGURE 7-1

A multiframe view of the organization for prospective DDOs

	Organizational	Individual
	What do you want to change or improve on any of these fronts?	What do you want to change or improve on any of these fronts?
Exterior	Our business performance Our business objective or function Our staffing patterns Our recruitment and retention Our value proposition for our people Our leadership Our governance structure Our goals and targets Our known problems and bottlenecks (e.g., execution, scope creep, mission creep, silos) Our resources and resource allocation (e.g., capital, time, people and their capabilities) Our patterns of association (e.g., teams, meetings, people support) Our understanding of our customer Our rewards Our forecasting	My role definition (e.g., leadership mandate, employee responsibilities, accountabilities, performance metrics [what is excellent?]) My individual capabilities (e.g., what I know, what I can do) My known problems or challenges (e.g., I don't delegate, am too reactive vs. proactive, am unreliable, avoid conflict, am too emotionally distant, am disorganized, micromanage, am unsupportive, am a poor team player)
Interior	Mission (deep purpose or soul of the organization) Organizational culture or personality[a] Organizational health (vs. organizational performance)[b] Collective developmental maturity[c] Collective immunities to change[d]	Personal values and motivations Hardwired personality preferences (things unlikely to change, e.g., introversion, extroversion, or any of the MBTI polarities)[e] Individual developmental maturity (a profile that can potentially change, but gradually) Individual immunity to change

a. Lee G. Bolman and Terrence E. Deal, *Reframing Organizations: Artistry, Choice, and Leadership* (San Francisco: Jossey-Bass, 2013); Edgar H. Schein, *Organizational Culture and Leadership* (San Francisco: Jossey-Bass, 2010).

b. Scott Keller and Colin Price, *Beyond Performance: How Great Organizations Build Competitive Advantage* (New York: Wiley, 2011).

c. David Rooke, William Torbert, and Dal Fisher, *Personal and Organizational Transformations* (New York: McGraw-Hill, 1995); Frederic Laloux, *Reinventing Organizations: A Guide to Creating Organizations Inspired by the Next Stage of Human Consciousness* (Brussels: Nelson Parker, 2014).

d. Robert Kegan and Lisa Laskow Lahey, *Immunity to Change* (Boston: Harvard Business Press, 2009).

e. Myers-Briggs Type Indicator. See Isabel Briggs Myers and Peter B. Myers, *Gifts Differing: Understanding Personality Type* (Palo Alto, CA: Consulting Psychologists Press, 1980).

perspective. The model reminds us that it might be easy for the authors of this book to overattend to the two interior boxes in figure 7-1 (the invisible interiors of the individual and of the collective); for line leaders and people trying to meet quarterly targets, it might be easy to overattend to the exterior boxes. We are all prone to one or the other kind of myopia.

We confess, as the authors of this book, that collectively our natural bent has been toward the lower-right box (the individual interior), and from there, to the lower left (the collective interior). We have long been interested in the way the less visible issues (the lower half of the box) have been omitted from the leadership agenda and from the responsibilities management must take up if organizational life is to become what companies and their members need it to be.

In the language of a Bridgewater baseball card, we suggest you "watch out" for us in this respect. The upper boxes (the exterior elements) are not our strong suits. But we ourselves are on a learning journey. Our ongoing experience of the DDOs in this book has deepened our appreciation for the dynamic, interdependent relationship between the interior and the exterior. Still, we, like everyone else, are works in progress. You will see in the examples to follow that we still lean heavily in the direction of our preferences. Even so, we hope that, taken as a whole, the examples will bring to life what it means to keep all four boxes in mind as you consider your own journey in the direction of the DDO. We invite you to fill in your own entries in any quadrant that you feel we are giving too little attention.

Frazier & Deeter

"We need to talk. What you guys are describing about being 'deliberately developmental' is what our firm really needs." Those were the first words that Seth McDaniel, managing partner of Frazier & Deeter, spoke to Andy Fleming (an author of this book). (For more about this firm, see "Frazier & Deeter in Its Own Words.") Thus began an eighteen-month conversation and journey that eventually resulted in the firm hiring our company, Way to Grow, INC., to help design and support a yearlong pilot initiative titled "Lead FD."

Frazier & Deeter in Its Own Words

Founded in 1981, Frazier & Deeter is a nationally ranked, PCAOB registered CPA and advisory firm that helps businesses and individuals succeed in a changing marketplace. We provide a wide range of tax, audit, accounting, and advisory services.

We are a nationally respected accounting firm:

- Top 100 Largest Accounting Firms in the Nation

- #1 Best Accounting Firm to Work for in the United States

- Recipient of the Practical Accountant Practice Innovation Award for six consecutive years

- Top 25 Best Managed U.S. Accounting Firms

- Gold medalist of Top American CPA Firms and an Accounting All-Star by Bowman's Accounting Report and Inside Public Accounting

- The second largest independent CPA and Advisory firm in Georgia

- Second Fastest Growing Accounting Firm among the Top 100 Firms in the United States in 2014

- A firm committed to producing top-quality work, consistently going the extra mile to achieve great results

Source: www.frazierdeeter.com.

Why Become a DDO?

McDaniel explains how he decided to move toward a more deliberately developmental culture:

> On the business side, the math is pretty simple. When we
> looked ten years out, we could see that a lot of our senior

partners who drive the business today will be retired. In most CPA firms, succession doesn't get a lot of focus, so when they lose their business drivers, they wind up having to merge with others. But we had made a decision that we wanted to be a legacy firm and maintain our name and culture. That was important to us. So if we were really serious, either we were going to have to hire a bunch of expensive senior people—and some of them wouldn't pan out and would probably mess up our culture anyway—or we were going to have to get better at growing people who could become business drivers.

Note that McDaniel's picture of F&D's change story begins squarely in the upper-left box (organizational exterior): a clear business problem that needs addressing. And note that his story, beginning here, naturally moves to the upper-right (individual exterior), because collective needs implicate individual capabilities. McDaniel explains:

> In a nutshell, we came to the realization that we needed to put as much attention into people development as we did into business development. In the long term, for a professional services firm, they really are the same thing. What resonates with us about the DDO concept is the idea that our day-to-day culture could serve as a catalyst for people's development. That has a lot of appeal for our firm. We want to help people be better inside or outside the firm. We have a duty to help people progress.

For F&D, development begins at the beginning:

> We also have a duty to be genuine in our recruiting—in our message and in the way we relate to people. If we're going to talk about "growing with our firm," we have to be able to back that up. With the quantity and quality of people we need to recruit, we thought that having a distinctive approach to development could set us apart and attract more of the people we wanted.
>
> Most midsize CPA firms help their people develop technical skills, but they don't do much to help them develop the more adaptive skills. They operate from an assumption that you

either have them or you don't. Every firm says, "We'll help you grow," but they don't really help beyond the technical things you can learn in a book or a class, and I just don't think you can learn something like leadership or "professional judgment" that way. The lessons you learn may stick for a month or two at best, and then you go back to doing what your existing culture says.

The DDO model works well with the industry in which F&D operates:

> Then there's the apprenticeship model, which most of the CPA world is built on, but there are no guarantees with that, and most of our existing senior partners made it on their own anyway. We decided that was too hit-or-miss, too much of a crapshoot. So unless we did something different, we saw a dynamic that younger people we recruited and hired who had the capacity to grow—some of their potential would go unfulfilled.

"Growing our people" for McDaniel, is not only a means of fulfilling the first business objective of creating a new generation of senior business drivers but also an end in itself—in effect, a second business objective: to make development itself an important part of the value proposition of working at F&D. This is the classic, expected profile for early adopters of the DDO idea—leaders and organizations that see people development as both means and ends of the business.

Then What?

McDaniel and his fellow partners collectively agreed that they needed to focus on developing younger people. The agenda was firmed up, but McDaniel knew he couldn't simply mandate that the firm move forward with it.

So McDaniel asked one of us to make a presentation at F&D's partners' retreat on adult development (something McDaniel could have done himself and done it well, but he wanted to participate in the conversation and focus on his partners' responses). He next decided to vet the immunity to change (ITC) method with the few select people who he knew would need to be advocates for the DDO approach if it were to take hold. McDaniel had one of us conduct an ITC workshop with those five people so that they could gain a better sense of what it would mean for the firm to become a DDO.

In other words, McDaniel took actions to build a home for the work to take place: discussing with partners whether to focus on growing younger people; exposing partners to adult development; participating in the retreat; and vetting the ITC method with a few people.

This is also where McDaniel's story begins to move into the lower half of the four-box model. It is not only that he identifies a business problem, or that he sees that the business problem will make new demands on individual members, or even that he has a dual conception of the business problem that includes people development as an end in itself. He could do all these things and still envisage that the road from here to there is essentially a technical one, in which his central need is a good plan to get people on board to shift their behaviors in the desired direction.

But McDaniel's earlier critique of the industry is, in essence, a diagnosis that his business objectives have an adaptive dimension, and this means that focusing on behavior without also focusing on the mind-sets that drive the behavior is not likely to succeed. This move from a focus on the visible behavior alone to the invisible interior is what moves him into the lower half of the model.

A Word on the ITC Map

We would never suggest that McDaniel's chosen means—the ITC approach—is the only tool or must even be one among the various tools an organization will use. The immunity to change approach does play a prominent role, in one way or another, in many of the examples in this chapter, so perhaps a quick word is due as to why. The answer is not pride of ownership (two of the authors invented the approach), nor is it a matter of going with what you know best (collectively the authors might have a hundred years' worth of experience with the method). We like the ITC approach because it is the most focused, most functional, fastest, and least costly way (psychically, for the individual and the organization) we have seen to get everyone engaged with her growing edge, in a fashion that links gut, mind, and hand (how you feel, how you think, and what you can do when you make that connection).

What is the most familiar alternative? It's waiting until people screw up and then mining the valuable lessons therein. With the proper support, intentions, and focus on the interior (instead of mere problem solving), the mistakes people make can be a gold mine for a DDO. But as the central engine for producing internal learning opportunities, it has serious limitations.

First, it takes a long time for everyone to have a rich, working curriculum (you have to wait for everyone to screw up). Second, it costs the organization a lot to build such a curriculum. (Each person's lesson plan is purchased at the cost of some kind of damage.) And for most people, the moment after they've done something wrong is not the optimal moment for learning. In contrast, the ITC approach quickly gets everyone out on his growing edge (aware of at least some of the demons he's fighting and understanding how his way of fighting is producing his ineffectiveness) and without his having to do any damage.

So let's return to McDaniel's story. The outcome of the ITC session was that the group of five agreed to the firm moving further in its exploration to be a DDO; the yearlong pilot was hatched. The subcommittee next created a process to answer questions about whom to involve. In the end, the hope was that the ten people chosen would serve as a best case to test whether it was possible for F&D to accelerate people development in a way that would serve the firm.

The First DDO Practice

The program centered on ten selected professionals, representing many areas and levels, forming a developmental community to work on improving themselves, each other, and the firm. For the first four months, through the height of the busy season for accounting firms, participants focused mainly on developing themselves and each other by conducting and interpreting small, ITC-based experiments related to improvement goals in the context of their regular work. They met weekly in peer coaching pairs, and they talked regularly with an external ITC coach as well as a partner in the firm who served as an ongoing mentor.

In March 2015 (three months into the project), and then later in the summer, Andy Fleming interviewed McDaniel and three other firm members engaged with the initiative to hear their thoughts and observations on their experience so far. Collectively, the ten participants in the initiative reported more than a hundred experiments and twenty-five peer coaching meetings conducted in the first six weeks.

Why was there such engagement? What were they learning? Where did they see things going? Let's hear from McDaniel and also from Beth Newton (director of people and culture), Susan Koschewa (senior manager, audit), and Charli Traylor (manager, tax). McDaniel and Newton are the primary overseers of the initiative—they're the ones who have put their necks on the line to make it happen—and Koschewa and Traylor applied and were chosen to be participants in the group of ten.

The Journey So Far: McDaniel

In McDaniel's words, "My big assumption is that I always have to have the answer, and I've done some experiments telling folks, 'I've thought it through and don't have an answer.'" He describes what happened when he acted against that assumption.

> I've found that people don't necessarily expect me to have the answer. A lot of times they're happier to think through the question themselves or to think it through with me. And when I'm not carrying the burden of having to have all the answers to day-to-day challenges, that frees me up to work on more long-term strategic issues.
>
> Right now, for example, we're looking at a candidate firm for a possible merger, and I'm sending a team on an off-site next week to create a detailed merger and integration plan instead of leading all the detailed planning myself, which is what I would have done before. I've met with our team, and I'll be there later to review the plan with the candidate firm. I'm actually spending the on-site day, instead, with some key people at a university where we would like to deepen some

relationships that enable us to get to know and recruit more of their top students.

As an internal coach in the initiative, McDaniel has also learned about others' big assumptions. One in particular is shared across the culture and has a direct relationship to the development of future business drivers. Here's what he says about it:

> I've learned that more than a few of our younger people have a lot of anxiety and misconceptions about business development. They think they are expected to be continuously networking with a lot of people they don't know and somehow closing deals with them. Because that assumption has gotten surfaced, I'm able to share my experience that business development is not as complicated as it might seem. It really starts with building relationships with the people that you're already serving. As I moved up, I found that the people who I had taken care of along the way were now in a position to hire F&D. I've started talking to our people about this. We don't want them going to a bunch of meetings where they burn a lot of time and brain cells trying to network with people they don't know.
>
> So I'm seeing a lot of how our people think and where their developmental holes are . . . and where some of our cultural holes are, too. I'm excited to see the impact that this first set of ten people can have on the organization. Will they apply what they're learning and help others, too? Will there be a multiplier effect? I like what I'm seeing so far.

Beth Newton, Director of People and Culture

In August 2013, Frazier & Deeter hired Newton as director of learning and development, a visible expression of the firm's deep commitment to develop its people and culture. Newton says she joined F&D because she wanted to work on the DDO initiative, which, she acknowledges, presents a challenge.

> I realize this is not an easy road for the participants or for the firm. I keep getting more confirmation that this is deep change—not just deep exploration. This is about deeply

embedding a new thought process, a new way of thinking for people. I'm seeing that change in people I've known for a year and a half who had been trained to follow the rules and check the right boxes—even when it comes to their own learning and development—and I'm seeing them shift.

In a conference call we had with all ten participants after about a month, I heard them saying, "I'm not getting the process; I'm not seeing the end game. Is this worth my time?" They wanted to be hitting milestones related to their improvement goals immediately. Then at the checkpoint meeting we had a few weeks later, it was very apparent that they were starting to realize that the process was about their own learning at their own pace and using their improvement goals as a way to learn more deeply about themselves and that this was a very different way of learning for them. It was like a light went on for all of them.

Now if you could somehow add up all of the moments they've had with their teammates, their clients, their partners, and their staff when they've been more open, more aware, and more willing to look at things from different perspectives, I think you would come up with a huge impact on the business. As they continue to grow and we involve more people in the process, it will be fun to see where this goes.

Susan Koschewa, Senior Manager, Audit

My first improvement goal had to do with being less anxious and not always having to be in control of every situation. My big assumption about having to control everything at work and at home definitely held me back. My first experiments were at home—asking others in the family to take on some things I was doing. That helped me practice. Then at work I started experimenting with delegating more of what I would typically do, particularly when I feel anxious. And with my coaches pointing out ways that I could think differently about situations that cause me the most stress, I've started processing through difficult situations faster, not letting them keep me down. I limit the time I dwell on tasks—one partner coach says, "Done is better than perfect"—and I'm able to let go much quicker and operate much more efficiently.

In fact, I can directly compare what I'm getting done this year to years past, because most of my projects are repeat engagements. I've been doing them for the last five years and can see where we are in the deadline process compared to the year before . . . or to where we usually are. And right now I'd say we're five or six weeks ahead of where we usually are. We have a lot more projects done; and if they aren't done, they're much further along than they would have been.

That's good for me and good for the business, obviously, because I'm able to do more in a shorter period of time. But from my experience recently with a project that was definitely *not* in my wheelhouse, I can see another benefit for the business in addition to greater efficiency—*more flexibility* in being able to put people on projects where they're needed, even if they don't initially have 100 percent of the qualifications that would make them feel comfortable.

I recently got put on this kind of project, and when I reached different points of aggravation that would have typically slowed me down, I kept using the tools and asking myself, "How would someone else see this?" Without the tools, I would have stayed "locked up" emotionally longer. Instead I was able to project myself into other perspectives and actually deal with the situation.

Charli Traylor, Manager, Tax

In my day-to-day work, it is easy to get bogged down and have tunnel vision and to just focus on what I need to get done in a very narrow sense. It's easy to get self-centered, particularly during busy season when everybody is under a lot of pressure. It's easy to *not* consider the needs of others and how they are interpreting the world, to *not* try to look through other people's glasses. But through "Lead FD" and the coaching,

I have found myself thinking about how others are able (or not able) to do their jobs because of my actions.

For example, last Friday was the day before a tax deadline—my first deadline day as a manager—and everything was squeezed. I was running around like a headless chicken and needed to delegate a task on the fly to an intern (only with us for forty-five days), and I really cut corners in giving her instructions about this task that actually served a distinctive kind of client and need.

After I walked away, I said to myself, "She has no idea why I asked her to do those things; she has no context for understanding the real point of what she's been asked to do." I could have and should have taken the time to explain it—and it wouldn't have taken *that* long—because this is something that would help her long term; this is something that she could be doing again and again. So I did get the immediate work done through her but went home that night thinking that I need to do a better job when I get that way—a better job of explaining things, giving others something they can use in the future.

So this is Monday and I haven't gone back to her yet, but I will. I *have* talked about it with another person who was there who said to me, "I'm used to the way you work, but others aren't." So now I have a clearer view of how others experience me under pressure, and I have a real situation to attach it to.

The process of identifying big assumptions helps you see why you have that behavior—and when you see it, sometimes it seems really dumb . . . One of the big assumptions that drives my behavior is that I always assume that others are ahead of me (I didn't have a lot of guidance when I was younger), and that leads me to set unrealistic expectations for myself. I shared that recently with a senior partner (my partner coach), and she questioned the idea that others are ahead of me and talked it through with me. That was really helpful . . . Now that I'm aware of my tendencies, I can go into stressful situations and be more cognizant of how I approach people and the work.

In the past, when I've had people who encouraged me and helped me do better and be better, that's what has meant the most to me. Now I see the ten of us going forward to make sure that we apply the lessons of this program to developing others—and that this culture spreads throughout the firm.

The Way Forward

You can imagine that each of these people (as well as the other participants, if we were to hear from them) would say "yes" to our three characteristics that point toward a DDO culture: yes, they each have an *edge*—a personal growth goal or one big thing they're working on right now; yes, they have a *home*—a community of people who are aware of what they're working on and who care about whether they make progress on it; and yes, they have *groove*—a practice they are engaged in that allows them to be at work on their edge during their work activities. And because they have these three elements, they have begun to become the change they want to see.

Compared to XYZ, Inc., Frazier & Deeter is taking a slower approach to expanding its edge, groove, and home by using a pilot program. Whereas XYZ is using a top-down approach, starting with the CEO and the top six hundred leaders, F&D is using more of what we would call a middle-out approach.

What is similar, though, is that the two organizations' choice to turn toward becoming a DDO does not mean committing themselves to moving all the way down the path to become a full-fledged DDO; nor does it mean that the entire company culture will one day resemble the developmental intensity of a Decurion, a Bridgewater, or a Next Jump. It does mean that F&D's leaders are committed to enacting certain DDO principles and practices (and to creating some of their own) in a bounded way and to seeing what they might learn and what might emerge as the best next steps. They're building their bridge as they walk on it, and several members of our team have been fortunate to accompany them.

Returning to the four-box heuristic and keeping ourselves honest, this example may bring to life both the upper and lower halves of the box, and the relationship between them, but with respect to the lower half, the emphasis is on the individual interior. Perhaps our next example can correct this a bit.

WellMed

"What's our biggest fear? To be seen by other docs as having gone over to the dark side."

"Yes, and to see myself as a traitor to my calling. To become too corporate."

"I agree with that, but I think there is a whole other issue, too, more internal to our team. I think we don't want to step on each other's toes. We'd rather avoid conflict than surface it and engage it."

[In mock outrage] "I vehemently disagree with that!" [group laughs]

"It's a good list, but I can add another: I think we have way more authority than we are exercising. I think we are reluctant to claim the power we have and to act."

We're sitting in a conference room in San Antonio, Texas, with nine doctors in the middle of a relentlessly candid, daylong, collective self-examination of their performance as the physician leadership team (PLT) of WellMed Medical Management. The company, which specializes in health care for seniors, operates more than one hundred clinics in Texas and Florida, serves more than 250,000 patients and HMO members, employs more than two thousand people, and earned revenues in 2015 of about $2 billion.

What has always been unusual about the organization, since its founding by George Rapier, MD, in 1990, is that WellMed is a proudly physician-led company. Also unusual is that, in the past few years, increasing numbers of its top people are becoming accustomed to making their interior life a part of what they're working on at work. The snippet of conversation at the beginning of this section may be unusual in any company boardroom. Among doctors it is a genuine rarity.

That day in San Antonio, Richard Whittaker, MD, leader of the PLT, summarized the doctors' dilemma: "As a profession we are probably far more comfortable with others' interiors—their bodies and their emotions—than we are, as a group, with our own. We're the doctors, after all, the ones who solve other people's problems. We don't spend a lot of time looking at ourselves."

What began as a series of private, individual coaching engagements has spread to the company's key leadership communities. Members of the office of the CEO—which includes, among others, Rapier and Whittaker—have all created maps of their immunity to change, as has every member of the PLT. The company has begun to consider what it might mean to move further in the direction of becoming a DDO, but it is beginning to create what we would call home.

A physician-led company—especially a fast-growing one like WellMed—depends for its thriving on attracting a continuous stream of doctors who are willing to take on management roles, even as they continue to practice and maintain their identities as doctors. This turns out to be challenging on a number of fronts. Rapier is by now a widely celebrated physician executive, but he would be the first to tell you he had next to no preparation for the role when he started the company.

Medical school and the medical field are not great breeding grounds for building business capabilities ("Most doctors are lousy delegators," Rapier says, "and not the best at holding people accountable, either"). What's more, many doctors face a deep identity conflict when they take on an additional professional role, especially one about which, as you've seen, many may be ambivalent.

To get at this deeper level, people need practices (in our term, their *groove*) that help them get below the water line to uncover the deep assumptions that, unexamined, perpetuate inner conflict and ambivalence. The earlier conversation was part of a structured, facilitated process (by one of us) in which members of the PLT had the opportunity not only to uncover their limitations but also to better understand the way their limiting behavior serves a collective immunity to change. What were their collective hidden commitments? What were their collective big assumptions? You can see their collective ITC map in figure 7-2.

By making this mind-set visible to the group as a whole, and especially by revealing their (possibly distorted) big assumptions, members of the PLT now had the collective opportunity to do something about their limiting mind-set. Nine people were now in a position to take up Bridgewater's favorite question, "Is this true?" Is

FIGURE 7-2

Physician leadership team ITC map

1. Commitment (improvement goal)	2. Doing/not doing instead	3. Hidden/competing commitment	4. Big assumptions
To move from being a "team of leaders" to a "leadership team"	• Not asking right questions (too quick to solutions), not asking "dumb question" • Thinking as individual vs. team, thinking in silos; not creating Big Shared Goals • Focus on owned clinics (vs. contracted) • Focus on what is most comfortable, "where the light is the best" • Too busy to participate • Prioritizing other commitments • Not meeting often enough • Review and reward—individuals over team • Not holding each other accountable • Team not owning the outcome • Don't consider alternatives—we start with the old way • Side-tracking meetings with own agendas • Not mining for conflict • Not connected enough with shared purpose • Waiting for leader to guide, bring up stuff, set direction • Discounting the impact we can have • Not thinking, understanding or deeply systemically as we can—not pushing to grasp realities • Not clarifying • Not believing in our ability to fix major issues • Team boundaries—what is out of line? • Not repairing/engaging boundary violations (avoiding conflict) • Not bringing issues that happen outside PLT but implicate PLT • Not fighting, advocating, and delivering for each other as much or as well as we could • Not taking the authority to act	• To not discovering/having to conclude we aren't up to it, that we are inadequate to the task, to not be seen as ineffective, incompetent • To not experience we can't adapt • To not be perceived by the CEO that we're acting too slowly, wasting time • To not bring things up when the timing is wrong • To not stepping on toes (inside and outside PLT) • To not put ourselves under additional stress, not take on yet more responsibilities and fail • To not be seen as "the heavy, the bad guys" • To not being seen as "too corporate" • To not having to experience unsettling uncertainties • To not being a traitor to my calling • To not losing my identity as a doctor, or even become a "company man" • To not neglecting my "franchise" (silo) • To not "fuzzy" my priorities (by adding even more and bigger priorities) • To avoid uncomfortable conversations and not be too vulnerable • To not be "shot down"	• If the CEO becomes impatient, we must be wrong • We don't have the authority to act; we must be told • The team's needs are not mine • We can't move from incompetence to competence • We don't have the capacity to function at this level • We assume we must be great at it, right from the start (we are not allowed a learning curve as a team) • By becoming a part of the team, you must be less a part of your franchise • Our organization doesn't need a PLT • Someone will tell us exactly what to do if we wait long enough • Being a doctor, I see patients • Can't be a good doctor and be a good leader at same time • Won't be as good a leader as I am a doctor • Value I create as a leader is less than the value I bring as a doctor; my true value is treating patients • As a leader, others will only see my bad side • My changes would not be welcome • We will threaten key relationships, stakeholders . . . would be a threat to ELT • More responsibility must mean more work • That there is ever a better time • Discomfort regarding uncertainty is a hindrance to moving forward

it true that we must succeed all at once, that we are not permitted a learning curve? Is it true that building management capabilities risks abandoning medicine? The PLT had a collective improvement goal to be a genuine leadership team (and not merely a collection of leaders, each looking out for his own area of responsibility). There could be no more important goal for a group charged to lead a physician-led company.

To conclude this series of glimpses into getting started on the DDO path, we present two more examples. As the following organizations work on a smaller canvas (they are as much programs as organizations), they do not take us deeper into the complexities of the lower-left quadrant (the organizational interior), but each teaches its own lessons.

The first—Suncorp's strategic innovation division—comes to us from our developmentalist colleague Jennifer Garvey Berger, sharing work she is doing on the other side of the world. It is an example of a newly created unit in a large corporation, working in a DDO-ish fashion and slowly radiating its approach into the bigger system.

Suncorp Strategic Innovation Division

Most floors in the Suncorp building contain what you'd expect: cubicles filled with people talking on phones; safety and other motivational posters on the walls; sign-in boards to track employees' locations. Someone wandering by mistake toward the quarter-floor that houses the Strategic Innovation (SI) division, however, would see something different. There are no cubicles, only chairs on wheels, desks on wheels, and whiteboards on rails that slide in every direction to create walls, form work surfaces, and even display sticky notes reflecting the thinking of team members. The single permanent wall is covered with paintings created by the group over the past three years, each representing images of strategy, the future, or risk in the visual metaphors that were most resonant for their creators.

This is what home looks like for this fledgling DDO, a special division of financial services company Suncorp Personal Insurance, in Sydney, Australia. Begun three years ago as a strategic investment in the long-term competitiveness and resilience of the business, the SI division had one purpose: to introduce into the organizational DNA a different way of thinking about strategy and the future.

Its founder, Mark Milliner, CEO of Personal Insurance, had grown increasingly concerned about the risk of the status quo for a successful business as well as the threat of "invisible forces of change . . . not only reshaping the insurance industry of the future, but our world of the future." Milliner was also passionate about the need for his leaders to think in new ways about the looming uncertainties. He says that this investment "was about futureproofing our business so that we didn't wake up one morning and find we didn't have a business at all or the world had changed around us."

Suncorp Personal Insurance has a traditional strategy team and an enterprise risk management group to help the business make choices and mitigate risk, but Milliner wanted an internal function that would serve many business needs at once. Not only did he want the new division to think in new ways—to challenge assumptions and help the organization learn about change—but also he wanted the new division to seek out alternative business models and new ideas for meeting emerging needs, build relationships around the world with innovative thinkers who would become strategic partners, expand the capacity of leaders throughout the business to think in strategic ways, and continue to evolve the personal insurance business.

All about the Risk

To meet these goals, members of SI think about risk in unusual ways. Rather than focus only on reducing risk, people at SI consider how a given risk may usher in a new opportunity. In an earlier project, people from across the business began to imagine a series of possible futures that would have a disruptive impact on personal insurance. SI's central task is to uncover and manage options for the company to consider in the event that one of those future scenarios occurs.

This means that members of the team must immerse themselves in future worlds that don't exist—take the perspective of these future customers, imagine their future lives—and then create new possibilities in the present that might provide a bridge to those futures.

This taxing mental and emotional exercise requires capacities most people don't develop in the course of their regular lives. They must deal with many competing perspectives simultaneously, constantly challenge their deepest assumptions, and use diversity and conflict as tools to unlock new ideas. They constantly work together to increase their capacity to make a different kind of sense. As a result, the team is trying to make its work, its structure, and its culture deliberately developmental.

As with the more fully realized DDOs at the heart of this book, the SI team members believe that there is no difference between developing themselves as people and getting their work done. Kirsten Dunlop, executive general manager of strategic innovation, had never heard the term *deliberately developmental organization* when the team was formed. But she was steeped in developmental theory, and she knew she wanted her team not only to think about new things but also to think in new ways. She didn't know exactly how to do this; she calls what team members are doing "leadership in the nude," as they practice on the edges of their own competence and comfort level.

Team members see their own ability to break out of the confines of their previous perspectives as core to thinking about the future of insurance (by thinking about the future in general) in new ways. They believe that the thinking and being patterns they brought with them are too constrained to offer something innovative. This means that development is imperative. Their theory is that a socialized perspective might be too locked in the confines of the current context to do the innovative work that's required. Even a self-authored perspective is likely to be constrained in a single (albeit self-authored) set of beliefs about the world. At SI, workers lean into the self-transforming mind in their work and conversations. And given how unusual such minds are, they know they must support people to develop them.

Regular Reflection

On one early autumn April morning (we are in Australia, remember), the team members gather for a regular reflection day. The twenty-four of them sit in a large circle, with all the whiteboards pushed aside to make the biggest possible work space. In the circle are the *core team*—the twelve members of the division who are permanent members—as well as a group called the *principals*—twelve people who come from the business and are posted to SI for a year. (The latter arrive in groups of three every quarter, and so there are always a few people who are new and a few who are about to cycle off.)

The topic today is the burgeoning tension between the core team and the principals. No one is quite clear what causes this tension, but it's beginning to get in the way of the work and slow the pace of the group. Rather than guess what the issue is or have a vague "team building" session, the SI team employs common practice here (as in other DDOs you've seen): members unpack their understanding by holding a series of fishbowl conversations.

First in the inner circle is a subset of three of the principals, talking about their experience of the difference in the two roles. They talk about their delight that they are getting to do this exciting and innovative work, their attention to the departure of several among them in the next few weeks, and their own anxiety about returning to their previous jobs.

When they pause, those in the outer circle express appreciation for the process of the conversation; they point to particularly good questions, particularly good listening. Some people point out what looks like an area of tension or discomfort.

The next round begins, with a few core team members joining the middle circle and some people pulling back to the outer circle to gain a different vantage point. The conversation deepens, and now people begin to talk about the power differential, about their confusion concerning who gets chosen to be on which so-called option teams, about how they're finding themselves changing so fast that they're dizzy with the effort. Now the tension that previously had been underground begins to bubble to the surface, and the participants turn it around in their conversation so that they can understand it.

In the first round, members in the outer circle were explicitly appreciative; in this round they cast a more critical eye. They ask about the way the inner circle members are enacting their values: How much have they been asking curious questions rather than making points? How much have they been listening to one another? How much have they been uncovering the real conflict? The issue of the option teams fades away as the central issue emerges: some people have a nagging fear that others are selfishly pursuing their own interests instead of doing what the team collectively needs.

This shows up in a topic that one principal calls "the dance between our roles and our personal development." There is widespread agreement that the members are growing and changing, and their previous assumptions about the world are falling away before new assumptions are developed: "We're growing so fast here, with little time to reflect on who we're becoming." They talk about how they're more aware of themselves, of their weaknesses, of their strengths. They are redefining work, redefining leadership. "Now I see leadership is about how attuned you are to the people around you and the context in which you're working," one person says. "It's less about deliverables—which I used to think was the whole point. It's about the journey and not just the destination. I'm noticing what it's like to really notice."

There is widespread agreement that people are changing, but a disagreement emerges between, on the one hand, those who have a sense that the team and its work are primary and, on the other hand, those principals who sense that their own individual growth over the past twelve months is the most important piece. A relatively new member of the team says, "It has to be about me first. I have to slash my floaties [i.e., give up my inflatable swim aids], become more independent in my thinking and action than I've ever been before. I need to feel like I can't swim, so that I have to keep my head up by myself. I have to focus on my own individual development before I think about what's best for the group. I only have a year! First I need to swim before I can think of going back into my team and teaching them to swim."

But someone else counters, "The point of the development is what we're doing for the business. We're getting better on behalf of what the business needs of us—we can't focus just on ourselves."

"That's the point," another member adds. "We're paying attention to our own growth and development for the purpose of doing our work better. If the world were remaining the same, we could remain the same. If the world is changing and the business is changing, we need to change too, or we can't take it forward."

Reflecting on Reflecting

In the first round of the fishbowl, the conversation is fast and furious, and people seem to ricochet off the ideas of their colleagues rather than build on them. By the third round, the conversation has become slower and more reflective, and people listen more carefully. Even though the conversation is impassioned, they reach into the perspectives of those they don't agree with, seeking to understand. They probe and ask clarifying questions: "Have I got that wrong?" "Am I misinterpreting what you said?" They watch the process of the conversation itself, with one member wondering aloud, "Hmmm. Am I just trying to deflect the conversation from a place that makes me uncomfortable?" And they track the changes in themselves, noting, "I could not have thought like this three months ago!" They are aware of the process and the content simultaneously, aware of their own reactions but less captured by them, able to deeply understand and consider the perspective of someone who disagrees.

Vital—and somewhat dangerous—issues are raised. "I'm really reacting to all this self-focus," a member of the core team says. "Professional development isn't for the self, isn't supposed to be self-focused. It's so I can do my job better!"

Someone cries. Someone else gets angry. But these strong emotions are not verboten here, and the group hands around a tissue or steps back to laugh together before pushing deeper into this important and difficult conversation. The ones who have been here for six months or longer find their rhythm relatively easily, even through the tension; the newer ones see what they will be able to do before their time in the group is up.

The conversation begins to weave together the individual and team development ideas, the personal and the organizational. The members close the fishbowl with a conversation about their purpose—individually and collectively, as members of families, communities, and this organization. They reconnect with the idea that insurance is ultimately about creating a sense of hope and security in an uncertain world—a concern they deeply share with their customers. They talk about the way insurance supports growth and risk-taking to create a better future—and it is sometimes the only space of comfort after a disaster. They share their belief in the organization and in the need to find new ways to protect what people most value.

The core team members wonder aloud what they can do to help amplify this shared sense of purpose; the principals talk about their need for personal support and reflection time as well as the stretch the job demands.

By the end of the ninety minutes, the people in the inner circle physically lean in to one another, their tone reflective, searching. The people in the outer circle have pulled their chairs tightly around the middle. They learn that none of their concerns is totally right, and none is unwarranted. They make a new pathway forward, together. The room almost vibrates with the new meaning being created there.

Later in the day the questions raised in the reflection meeting are deepened when the team members learn from their consultant insights from theory and research about power, development, and purpose, and the team experiences and creates developmental practices. They discuss the hidden assumptions that their ITC process has uncovered, and they unpack the team's collective assumptions. They look at the various ways power and connection interact, and they practice listening deeply to the sense their colleagues make instead of the more common practice of listening to build an argument for what should happen next.

A Theory of Practice

This practice of mixing content with developmental practices on the team's reflection days goes back to the beginning. As the team formed, the first off-site wove together ideas of complexity, an uncertain future, and adult development; the members' first practices were about deep listening and honest sharing of feedback. Like the other fledgling DDOs in this chapter, the SI team members used the immunity to change process to discover their personal big assumptions and to find their edge. They also explored the edges of their own development using an individual developmental assessment, as they talked about what they were discovering about the benefits and limitations of their particular developmental stage.

Over time the team has created ongoing practices to strengthen its communities and support its development. Team members have created rituals to welcome new members and to wish farewell to those who are going. They think hard about the theory and practice of transitions, a practice that's vital for a team always in transition. New members take the developmental assessment and learn about adult development—at the theory level and at the personal level. They create art pieces together to externalize the interior.

The principals who leave and head back into the business (now called *pioneers*) are supported with ongoing action learning groups, where they make sense of what it means to think about the world in new ways as they encounter old colleagues and challenges.

Spreading the Word

The strategic innovation team is a tiny island of twenty-four people in a sea of fifteen thousand in the larger company. And yet the SI team is beginning to see some of its practices and ways of thinking move into the mainstream as it transitions from a fringe group to a vital part of the capacity of Personal Insurance to create future offerings and expand its vision of the world.

In SI's short life, it has influenced the larger ecosystem of Personal Insurance to make significant changes in the way people work. For example, the company has experimented with innovative approaches to employees working from home, with resulting extraordinary customer satisfaction, unprecedentedly low levels of absenteeism, and high sales performance. The SI team also led the company to create vital new partnerships (for example, with start-ups to codevelop pioneering and disruptive business models for insurance) and to adapt the model of the core insurance business to prepare for change. Increasingly, the SI team is called on to support innovative thinking throughout the business.

The team stands now at a crossroads as demand for its perspectives and time outstrips its current resources, and its next moves (should it grow? should it create little cells that live inside each area of the business?) will shape not only the developmental nature of the team but also, quite possibly, the developmental nature of the entire business. Will Personal Insurance become a DDO? Will all of Suncorp try this new approach? Perhaps we will learn the ways in which DDO practices create contagious effects that reshape an entire organization.

Or, indeed, perhaps many organizations will follow, as this next glimpse suggests—organizations as big and venerable as Coca-Cola, or as new as a freshly launched start-up.

Flashpoint at Georgia Tech

6:00 . . . 5:59 . . . 5:58 . . . 5:57 . . . The red-numbered digital clock counts down in front of you. You and your start-up team stand before forty smart and committed people who, for the next six minutes, want only to hear some fresh truth from you. What did you do this past week? What did you learn that you didn't know last week? What truth can you now speak regarding customers and your business model? What will you do next week to gain more truth?

Every Tuesday afternoon in the open-space, write-on-the-walls environment of Georgia Tech's Flashpoint—a first-of-its-kind start-up engineering studio (see "What Is Start-Up Engineering?")—ten to fifteen start-up teams within a cohort group gather for the weekly master class. Amid scattered butcher-block tables and Aeron chairs, Flashpoint's most dramatic ritual in a carefully constructed, deeply developmental curriculum takes place: brief presentations by each team on its research from the past week, followed (or interrupted) by questions and feedback. Led by FP director and founder Merrick Furst, a group of seasoned mentors and advisers gives candid, often critical, feedback that is intended more than anything else to be clarifying. "What did you actually ask?" "What did you intend by that question?" "How did they respond?" "What words did they use?" "What do you think they meant?" "What leads you to think that?" "What do you really know for certain?"

Novice and veteran entrepreneurs who want to create scalable, sustainable businesses populate most of the two- to five-person teams. The remaining attendees are product or brand managers and other innovation-related professionals sent by their respective companies to find untapped sources of authentic demand (as Furst would say) and, perhaps even more important, to explore how they might

What Is Start-Up Engineering?

Start-up engineering is a program and framework for finding authentic demand and building scalable companies to satisfy it. Start-up engineers work diligently to identify meaningful pain in customers' lives, to distinguish it from the unmoored market theories entrepreneurs usually begin with and from the solutions customers themselves may imagine they want. These engineers generate theories about customer improvement goals and the constraints that prevent existing solutions from meeting them. They work to find actionable truth by testing to disconfirm their theories, modifying them, and retesting. They prioritize and gauge progress through a framework of understanding, bounding, and reducing the risks that all early-stage companies face.

The start-up engineering process takes approximately six months of full-time, committed work, usually by two or more founders. About two-thirds of the start-ups that implement the program succeed in discovering authentic demand during this period. On the bedrock of this discovery, Flashpoint helps manage start-ups through a process of shaping products and companies that will make money, in a reliable and scalable way, by enabling customers to overcome their constraints and attain their improvement goals.

Source: http://flashpoint.gatech.edu/startup-engineering.

export FP's models and methods to stimulate ongoing innovation in their home organizations.

The personal stakes are high for all participants, because most of them have become strongly attached to (and have invested significant time and money in) a particular idea or vision, which, they discover on a Tuesday afternoon or some other time early in the FP process, is almost certainly wrong. Here's former FP participant Mario Montag—now founder and CEO of Predikto, a three-year old predictive analytics firm that recently raised $3.6 million in venture funding—on his first Tuesday presentation, in which he pitched what he was convinced was a "big idea" in the automobile financing realm:

> I had been working on my idea for about six months, and when I presented it the first time at Flashpoint, I focused very intentionally and in some detail on what I thought was its huge upside and the tasks within it that we could do, thinking this would capture people's attention and get them onboard. It was amazing how quickly experienced entrepreneurs were able to pinpoint a couple of doors I had only opened slightly and kick them down to reveal the assumptions we had made and the associated risks that were all too present . . . Even some of the smaller assumptions, if we couldn't validate them and mitigate the risks, would lead us right off a cliff.

Assumptions that participants hold about customers, their business model, and themselves are challenged all the time at Flashpoint—during master classes, mentor meetings, weekly one-on-ones with Merrick, dialogue with other teams, and through formal and informal use of the ITC approach throughout the process—and sometimes even before the process officially starts.

Kevin Burke, senior global brand manager for the Coca-Cola Company, Glaceau (Vitaminwater, Smartwater), describes his team's first meeting with Merrick during the application process:

> We came in to our first meeting with Merrick with a very focused plan; we had a target audience, product, and approach. We were thinking that Flashpoint would just help us do it faster. So we wrote our plan up on a whiteboard, and Merrick got up and just erased the board clean. Honestly that really scared us. We were so immersed in what we thought the brand was. He said that if we were going to come into the program that we had to think more broadly and had to be willing to talk with consumers and listen in a new way.

That new way of listening and then acting is deeply informed by DDO and ITC principles. Who are your customers as human beings?

What are their improvement goals, hidden commitments, and big assumptions? What does your product or service have to be in order to take their immunities off the table and help them become more of who they are? Whom do you have to become in order to make and deliver your product? What are your own immunities that you will need to overcome? How do we fashion a safe, reliable, and supportive community within FP so that people can absorb and use so much tough love, rather than being run off by it?

Burke talks further about FP's central use of ITC to better understand customers and his own team—and the reaction of his managers back at Coca-Cola:

> Like a lot of corporations, Coke is incredibly strong regarding data, but we all gather it and use it the same way. FP gave us the chance to do it differently. We interviewed people throughout the world and heard the same themes and then saw the big assumptions. The process then showed us what the new products needed to be and how we could make them internally without triggering big assumptions or by being able to respond if they do get triggered . . . What really helps get you immersed and better at ITC is that Merrick just lives it; he uses it even when you meet during his office hours. Where are you now? What's the biggest thing that could kill you? Then he does a map with you related to that thing and you know what you need to do next . . . We've shared ITC with our managers back at Coke, and they loved it. They want us to teach FP tools to more people at Coke. One of our deliverables is to bring this into Coke.

So the developmental culture at Flashpoint may reach further back and further forward than in all the other organizations you've met so far. It reaches further back in a supply chain by using its own practices to more richly imagine the inner worlds of its participants' anticipated customers. It considers a customer's choice to try a new product or service as itself an adaptive challenge for the customer, and it puts entrepreneurs in the position of needing to manage the interior of the imagined customer, even as the organization itself is managing the interiors of the program's participants.

The participants are invited not only to think about the mind-sets of their prospective customers but to identify the self-protective commitments and limiting assumptions they would need to help customers overcome before they can become customers. At the same time, FP reaches forward by instilling in these entrepreneurs a habit of mind they may take with them from the laboratory of the program into their fledgling businesses. In that way, Flashpoint may be an incubator not only of start-ups but also of more organizations with a developmental bent, even perhaps more DDOs.

Is this an accident? Hardly. According to Furst, implementing this new kind of practice, and building a community to support the practice, may be crucial to a start-up's fate, to whether a dream becomes a reality. We'll let him have the last word:

> We walk around with these little theories that we have in our heads about the way the world works. And the world is just way more complicated, way more detailed, and we don't notice that the world is not actually the way we think it is according to our little theories. The way we get disconnected from reality is we think the world works the way our theories are; we build things [products or services] to fit with the way it works according to our theories; and then we are disappointed or surprised when it turns out that our things fit our theories, but they don't fit the world . . . What we found in FP is that it requires a mind-set change to be able to act like a successful founder. That mind-set change is not so easy to accomplish . . . You have to have a set of principles, you have to have a touchstone to ground truth, you have to have practices, and you have to have someone like me hitting you upside the head every so often to remind you . . .[2]
>
> Even when you see the world for the way it is, and even when you know what you have to make, you and your team can't change. And we have to address that also; otherwise, the teams don't succeed. We found a way to create a developmental culture inside the teams that makes it possible for people to take an interest in each other's immunity to change, and it seems to make all the difference in the world.[3]

What Do the Glimpses Teach Us?

We say at the beginning of this chapter that we do not think there is a single recipe or ten-step checklist for starting a DDO, but we hope these glimpses into organizations making their own first steps in this direction give you a sense of certain essentials to keep in mind. An overall impression that comes through for us is the need to work in several dimensions at the same time.

One way to talk about this is that getting a DDO started implicates "head, heart, and hand," and all three must be in play to create the initiating spark. Let's start with the head element. We have not crossed a fundamental threshold until work life engages your interior, until being at work directs your own and others' attention not only to outward behavior but also to what is going on in your head—what you're feeling and thinking, and the underlying assumptions that hold you in patterns of thinking and feeling that may prevent you from being the person you were meant to be.

At the same time, no one would want to work, or be able to stand working, in such a setting unless it invited your interior into the public space of work with the best of intentions, with a good heart. If an organization moves toward becoming a DDO simply because it deems it to be the way to get the most out of its people, then the DDO idea is little more than a new way to control people, to wring more return out of human capital. If there is not a robust, reciprocal enthusiasm for the ways the organization and its people help each other thrive, then the invitation to bring your interior into the shared work space moves toward forced confessional exercises in self-flagellating "self-improvement," and the place will become toxic. No one can speak so enthusiastically and appreciatively, as they do in the examples here, about what is often an intensely uncomfortable experience unless they feel their own struggles are being consistently elicited, and responded to, with compassion.

Bringing the interior into the job, and with the best of intentions, is crucial, but it's still more of a disposition than a visible, sustainable new way of being at work. The spark of creation can come about only through the combination of head, heart, *and hand*—reliable, repeatable practices, structures, and tools with which people and systems build and rebuild the culture every day.

Growing beyond Our Edge: The Organizational Interior

The four-box model is another way of getting at the necessity to keep your eye on several realms at once as a setting—and its leadership— moves, however far it will, toward being a DDO. There needs to be a clear reason—a business opportunity, a challenge, a threat, an unrealized aspiration—that animates the journey in the first place, and it needs to be crucial to the organization (the upper-left box in the model). Otherwise, the first time the journey hits a rough patch (and it will run into rough patches, from outside and inside), the organization will lack a powerful enough counterweight to withstand the forces pulling it back to the status quo.

That strong organizational purpose must then take expression in the working lives of each individual member (the upper-right box). Otherwise, you have lost the trees for the forest ("I love humanity; it's people I can't stand"). Two clusters of questions arise here:

1. Do I, as an employee in this organization, feel excited about and invested in the goal of this new journey? Do I see what it can do for me?

2. Do I experience how I (not only the leadership, not only the company) will have to change to further this journey? Will I experience new demands, expectations, definitions of my role?

Because these challenges inevitably are both technical and adaptive— for the organization as a whole, and for each of its members—the path toward a DDO needs to include the realms in the lower half of the four-box figure. What are the inner dynamics, collectively and individually, that might undermine even a genuine and widespread commitment to advance the journey? How do your groove (your tools and practices) and your home (your trustworthy communities) not only make the interior exterior but also help you—individually and collectively—to change that interior, to develop it?

A fledgling DDO must watch out for a tendency to hold on to only some, but not all, of these dimensions. That is as true for us as it is for anyone. We told you, at the outset, to watch out for our own tendency, as individually oriented psychologists, to overattend to the lower half, and especially to the lower-right quadrant, of the four-box model. That tendency may be reflected in the overall impression the glimpses give you about how to get started. We think the immunity to change approach, for example, is a helpful way to get everyone connected to his growing edge, for reasons we've explained. But we don't mean to suggest it should be taken up without equally vigorous, simultaneous attention to the organizational, systemic dimension.

We gave an early draft of this book to all our DDO exemplars for their reactions and suggestions. Bryan Ungard, of Decurion, was concerned about the examples possibly giving this kind of misimpression. "ITC is not the problem," he wrote. "It is a wonderful model, approach, and method that we intend to continue to use ourselves." But Ungard was worried we were underrepresenting the kinds of hard, essential, complementary work suggested by the lower-left quadrant: "how to deal with power, how to change operations to 'just one thing' throughout, how to shift the culture in the face of external and internal legacies, how to face the inevitable coup attempts, how to face the trade-offs between current competencies and future needs." Our glimpses may tell you less about this dimension because we are too early in the life of these respective stories, but more likely they reflect limits in our current ways of working with fledgling DDOs.

Building Your Home

For organizations taking early steps in the DDO direction, and for our own ways of being helpful to them, what might it look like to more fully engage and elaborate the lower-left quadrant, the organizational interior?

As we have said, every one of the five examples satisfies some threshold requirement on the upper-left side; there is a clear, motivating business aspiration each organization wants or needs to accomplish. Equally clear is the way these aspirations impose new demands and definitions on individual roles (the upper-right quadrant). Recognizing that we are in the presence here of adaptive challenges, it is then our natural bent to move down, into the interior, on the individual side. There may be nothing wrong with this, but if the organization wants to create a culture that will internally, organically meet these challenges (rather than rely on external help and "something extra"), it will need to work on the element of home.

Even the richest set of practices will not be organizationally self-sustaining unless there is a safe, dependable, collectively-ascribed-to "container" in which those practices will operate.

Safe means, for example, that when someone reveals her weaknesses and struggles publicly, she experiences an enhancement of her place in the organization rather than a diminishment. Safe does not mean people can expect to be accepted who are not working to improve.

Dependable means, for example, that workers can count on the practices and the ethos behind them to be a regular, daily experience of how things are done. It does not suggest that workers are never surprised, nor that they can depend on the security gained through mutual collusions and traded-on loyalties ("I can depend on your being on my side").

Collectively ascribed to means that we have all made an uncoerced agreement to operate in this way. It is what we want to do, what each person has decided to do, what everyone wants to do. It does not mean "we all share one mind"; it does not mean a culture of groupthink. It does not mean there are no disagreements, but it means agreeing about what is up for disagreement.

For example, in a discussion trying to get to the root cause of a person's poor decision, there can be all kinds of disagreement as to whether we have really gotten to pay dirt, or whether the person conducting the exploration is doing an effective and respectful job. But there will not be disagreements as to the value of our spending time like this, on what other organizations might consider mere personnel issues. There won't be this kind of disagreement, because this is what we all collectively signed on for.

To be fair to our fledgling DDOs, you can see signs of this kind of evolution already in the Flashpoint and SI examples. No one at Flashpoint is surprised by the kind of grilling to which their business plans will be subjected. The newbies at SI get schooled by the veterans in "how we do things here," and how we do things has a lot to do with cultivating processes that will better enable people to speak honestly, pushing beyond accepted wisdom and due deference. It is probably easier for SI to move quickly in this direction, being smaller, less complex, and more in the nature of a program than a company, but that doesn't make its process less instructive.

One way or another, a safe, dependable, collectively-ascribed-to container for interior work needs to be built by any group, team, division, or whole enterprise that wants to cross crucial thresholds moving in the DDO direction.

Shared Norms, Agreements, and Rules

To our way of thinking, the necessary step in crossing this threshold is the creation of shared norms, agreements, or rules of the road oriented to the work of development.

It's possible for an executive coach or a powerful leadership development program to create shared norms oriented to development that are sufficiently robust to sponsor powerful practices. This is a kind of home, but it doesn't live within the organization. It is what we call a twentieth-century answer. It is also possible for the team or organization to create a strong culture with widely understood and agreed-to norms that have nothing to do with development (for example, a high-reliability organization, a combat unit, a surgical team, a group of air-traffic controllers). And people development can certainly take place in such organizations, but they are not DDOs. They are not deliberately constructed to make an organization and its people each other's greatest resource for development.

For any group wanting to move in the DDO direction, it's helpful to develop these kinds of norms by asking, "What agreements do we, as a collective, need to make in order to provide the conditions for each other to do this kind of interior work? What agreements will enable us, at once, to work ongoingly on our own development (a Better Me), and to support the ongoing development *of our colleagues* (a Better You)?" Looking at the typical features of a DDO in chapter 3 can be one kind of prompt for such considerations. For example, you might ask, "Do we agree that rank will not have its usual privileges?" This means that subordinates should feel responsibility to push back on their bosses when they do not agree or understand, and bosses will welcome, rather than take umbrage at, such behavior.

Nor should a group wanting to move further in the DDO direction consider that, in merely making these agreements, it is successfully banishing counter-normative behaviors. Will higher-ups ever get defensive about the push-back they will receive, or critical of their subordinates who deliver it? Of course! Recall the Bridgewater disagreement about the consultants managing consultants.

And when this happens, there should be no head hanging and self-condemnation ("We aren't a very good DDO," "We don't have what it takes to be a DDO"). The work of building, preserving, and enhancing home is not solely about making the agreements. It is about expecting their continuous violation and then deploying practices (themselves safe, dependable, and collectively ascribed to) to convert those violations into the organization's curriculum. Then violations become opportunities for everyone, in an everyone culture, to learn (as the issue log serves, in the same Bridgewater example).

Unsurprisingly, we think one of the most effective ways for the wayward individual to use the opportunity for learning is to deploy the immunity to change map. For example, if I regularly have a hard time giving or receiving upward feedback despite agreeing to do so, it doesn't have to live long as a source of self-recrimination. I can struggle well with it by acknowledging it is an adaptive challenge and engaging my hidden commitments and big assumptions. Recall the Bob Prince and Nora Dashwood examples from chapter 6; each of their collections of column 2 behaviors ("I don't listen to others" and so on) can be taken as not only counters to their improvement goals but also as violations of shared norms or agreements.

To take our own medicine, in our own evolution in helping organizations moving in the DDO direction, it's fair to say that we have overexercised our forehand (defaulting to our natural bent to lead with the individual interior). In this way we unintentionally have cast ourselves (and the organizations) back into the twentieth-century answer. If we don't help the organizations build their own container for the interior practices, such as ITC and others, we become the "something extra"—good consultants on whom the organization depends. Should we withdraw, the likelihood the organizations will continue in their groove is slim (although individuals may), because we haven't helped them build their own home.

Nor should we beat ourselves up about our (current) limitations. Everyone—the three DDO exemplars, the fledgling DDOs, and ourselves—should be given the chance to grow; and in return for that gift, each of us has the responsibility to struggle well, to work on breaking the earthy crust above so that our new green shoots can find the light of day. In our case, this could involve figuring out our own fear and loathing (the worry box in the ITC map) associated with exercising our backhand, identifying the self-protective commitments (column 3) that make our tendency to prioritize the individual interior over the collective interior (column 2) so "sensible" and "brilliant," and, finally, uncovering and testing the limiting assumptions (column 4).

Work in Progress: A DDO 360 Assessment

To more strongly engage the collective interior and help you consider the agreements you may want to make, it can be useful to have a tool or a picture that lets you know where you are now in your home building and where you want to progress. To help ourselves—and others—better come to grips with the systemwide dynamics in organizations interested in the DDO journey, we've been working on a 360 assessment process to generate data-centered responses to questions such as, How developmentally rich is our culture at this moment? What developmental strengths can we start leveraging now to better develop our people? What are our biggest barriers to being more of a DDO? What gaps should we start closing first? What are the most promising pathways? How do we compare, on the edge, home, and groove dimensions, with more fully developed DDOs? What progress have we made toward becoming a DDO compared with the last time we took this assessment?

In figure 7-3, each of the three DDO dimensions (edge, home, and groove) is deconstructed into six features, for a total of eighteen subdimensions. Home, for example, includes the subcategories *openness about the self, appreciating the whole self, psychological safety, leader vulnerability, view of conflict,* and *view of ex*pertise. Respondents answer a series of questions (see "Sample Questions, DDO 360 Culture Assessment") designed to elicit information about the respondent's experience of each of these eighteen subdimensions.

This information creates a rich picture of the various levels of saturation within and across each of the three dimensions, a picture

FIGURE 7-3
___

Dimensions of a 360 assessment for DDO-ness

Edge: The organization's developmental aspirations

- **Mistake making.** Are errors seen as potentially promoting development?
- **Problem finding.** Are problems identified and generated to promote development?
- **My growing edge.** Are individuals working on their own development?
- **Your growing edge.** Are employees actively supporting colleagues' development?
- **Our growing edge.** Is the organization working on overcoming collective, organization-wide limiting assumptions?
- **Purpose.** Does the purpose of the organization connect to employees' development?
___

Home: The organization's orientation to a safe-enough, trustworthy community for development

- **Openness about the self.** Is exposing one's limitations welcomed as a resource for development?
- **Appreciating the whole self.** Are individual strengths recognized as a resource for development?
- **Psychological safety.** Are teams and colleague relationships psychologically safe spaces?
- **Leader vulnerability.** Do leaders participate equally and fully in developmental activities?
- **View of conflict.** Is conflict viewed as a potential source of development?
- **View of expertise.** Is deference to expertise by role or background minimized?
___

Groove: The organization's orientation to developmental practices

- **Learning supports.** Are job-embedded (rather than external) learning supports routinely used for development?
- **Role-to-person matching.** Are assignments and roles created and modified to spur development?
- **Feedback.** Is consistent feedback on developmental goals given and taken by all?
- **Regularity of practice.** Do practices focusing on development recur regularly?
- **Symbolic tools.** Does the organization have developmental language and articulated principles?
- **Process improvement.** Do employees participate systematically in improving processes to promote development?
___

Sample Questions, DDO 360 Culture Assessment

(On a 1–5 scale from "Strongly Disagree" to "Stronly Agree")

Edge

- "I know my manager's personal improvement goal."
  (Subdimension: My growing edge)

- "This company has a bigger purpose than just making money."
  (Subdimension: Purpose)

Home

- "I feel safe telling my manager when I disagree with what he or she thinks."

- "People here say what they really think only behind others' backs."
  (Subdimension: Openness about the self)

- "My boss is open about it when he or she makes a mistake."
  (Subdimension: Leader vulnerability)

Groove

- "On my team, when something doesn't go right, we take time to talk about why."

- "I'm expected to tell the members of my team if I think we are doing our work the wrong way."
  (Subdimension: Process improvement)

- "In this company, people's official job duties change often."

- "This company expects you to keep taking on new challenges at work."
  (Subdimension: Role matching)

that can be compared to the composite profile of the mature DDOs. Data can also show how a given department or business unit compares to the overall organization's scores.

An Ongoing Process

"How can I get to Carnegie Hall?" the cab driver is asked. The answer? "Practice, practice, practice." It's an old joke.

Bridgewater's Greg Jensen says that sustaining the culture is like going to battle every day—a continuous fight. Charlie Kim, at Next Jump, talks about playing the long game. Christopher Forman, of Decurion, invoking Aristotle, sees building character—in an individual or a group—as a lifelong activity.

What we've tried to do in this chapter—in this book—is to help you, if you're considering the DDO direction by providing you, not a recipe or a checklist, but concepts, tools, and living examples to assist you in taking up a way of becoming, a way of carrying on, that needs to live as long as the DDO itself.

Epilogue

A New Way of
Being—at Work

We wrote this book to bend the world's attention to a new way of being at work. In the past fifty years we've seen extraordinary transformations in our ways of *doing* at work—for example, in the ways we handle, sort, store, send, and receive data and information. As a result of the new technologies, the *doing* dimension of work has undergone a fundamental reorganization.

But even if you're sympathetic to the idea that a business can go only as far as its people will take it, you would have every right to ask tough questions of people who advocate a dramatically new kind of investment in growing your business by growing your people. It might go like this.

> I mean, really. Over these same fifty years have we made *no* similar, game-changing gains in our basic knowledge of human beings, how we learn and grow—and how we resist doing both of those things? Do we have no genuinely new ways of applying the knowledge we do have?
>
> Are we to expect that mere tweaks of the existing paradigms for people development will be enough to unleash unrealized

potential? Are we left with nothing more than hoping that doing the same thing, only harder, will lead to a different result?

Can you direct me to living examples of a significantly different way of being at work—organizations with robustly novel practices, resting on breakthrough science, with a multiyear history of success?

These are fair questions, and they have lacked powerful rejoinders—until now.

But it isn't for lack of trying. Fifty years ago, at the same time the digital age was being born, psychologists thought they were launching a similar revolution on the soft side with the birth of the human potential movement. It was a liberating reaction to the existing psychological paradigms, which were focused on human deficits and disorders. Psychologies of self-actualization, ego strength, and resilience emerged, promising to help us'attend as carefully to psychological strength and health as we had learned to attend to psychological weakness and illness.

By any fair assessment, the human potential movement of the 1960s—like many other bold aspirations of that period—has fallen considerably short of expectations. Its current manifestations— positive psychology, strength-based approaches to assessment, and a view of human happiness fueling one version of the new incomes people seek from work—have an appealing optimism. But they have hardly proven an impressive engine for step changes in the realization of human potential.

The reason is that the human potential movement of the 1960s, and its current heirs, has never had a sufficiently rigorous theoretical base or scientific method. The study of human potential requires a genuinely developmental theory, one that can illuminate the gradual evolution of capabilities. Rather than see strengths and limits as absolute, immutable dichotomies, such a theory would recognize that over time a strength can become a limit that may need to be transcended.

But such a theory, as you now know, does exist. It was born at about the same time as the human potential movement, nurtured in university research labs, and originally focused on the study of child development; now it has become a powerful means for understanding the growth of consciousness and self-understanding in adulthood. Joined to more recent breakthroughs in neuroscience, it is being applied to animate practices and approaches to personal growth that have proven extraordinarily impactful, delivered in one-to-one designs for the benefit of disparate individuals.

What would it mean to make use of this same scientific foundation (whether or not one knew one was doing so) to transform our way of being at work? The answer to that question—the rejoinder to all the tough questions earlier—is what you are holding in your hands. We believe that the companies you have met in this book, taken together, coalesce to present a new image of work. That image, what we call the deliberately developmental organization, is a way for organizations and workers to become each other's greatest resource for flourishing. That image may point the way to the same qualitative leap forward in the unleashing of human and organizational potential as the internet and computer represent for information processing and data transfer.

What you have seen in this book are pictures of real people—Nora, Jackie, Woody—working in real organizations—Decurion, Next Jump, and Bridgewater. They are all—the individuals and their organizations—becoming better versions of themselves. The companies are helping Nora, Jackie, and Woody grow; and Nora, Jackie, and Woody are helping their companies grow; in Decurion's phrase, it is "all one thing."

As you have seen, living out this one thing is hard—but not impossible. When we tell people about the DDO idea, someone always mentions human nature: "It's only human nature to protect yourself, to want other people to think you're better than you really are." "What you're talking about—people letting themselves be this vulnerable at work—is idealistic and naive. It's a nice idea, but it runs contrary to human nature."

This loose concept of human nature quickly gets extended to organizations as well. Apparently, they too have a human nature: "It's unrealistic to think that businesses will devote this kind of time to their people when the going gets rough. The profit motive will inevitably trump all this personal growth stuff."

Well, the people you have met in this book are not fictional characters, and they are not Martians; and they are not holding their breath, operating contrary to human nature for only a brief period. They have been at this for many years. The companies have been at this for many years.

So who defines "human nature"? How many more Noras and Jackies and Woodys—how many more DDOs, operating successfully for how many more years—does one need in order to recalibrate one's definition of what is natural? Probably every genuinely disruptive idea in the world at first seems to fly in the face of taken-for-granted assumptions about immutable limitations. That is essentially what makes disruptive ideas disruptive. They do not disrupt only how we behave; they disrupt how we think.

As the authors of this book, we have had the privilege of learning from Decurion, Bridgewater, and Next Jump. Living with these unusual organizations and their people has disrupted the way we think, and how we feel. We have seen previously independent phenomena—the exterior and the interior; organizational improvement and individual improvement—inextricably linked, and that has made our thinking more whole. The inspiration of their example to bring the less developed sides of ourselves—along with our better developed sides—into our shared work has made us more whole in our humanity.

We warned you, at the start of this book, that meeting the DDOs might involve new ways of meeting yourself, because we've seen the same thing happen in ourselves. Setting out to discover strange lands, we came to reside more deeply within ourselves, in the spirit of Mewlana Jalaluddin Rumi's poem "The Guest House."

This being human is a guest house
Every morning a new arrival.
A joy, a depression, a meanness,
some momentary awareness comes
as an unexpected visitor.

Welcome and entertain them all!
Even if they are a crowd of sorrows,
who violently sweep your house
empty of its furniture,
still, treat each guest honourably.
He may be clearing you out for some new delight.
The dark thought, the sham, the malice
meet them at the door laughing,
and invite them in.
Be grateful for whoever comes,
because each has been sent
as a guide from beyond.

At the start of this book we cheered for the new incomes people seek from work—salaries for the interior self (meaningfulness and happiness) as well as the traditional material benefits. We said there were centuries-old definitions of happiness, one that saw happiness as a *state* (of well-being, pleasure, the absence of pain and suffering). This is the tradition the better-known new workplaces are drawing on when they pay the new income.

But we said there was another tradition, one that sees happiness as a *process* (of our own unfolding, evolving, becoming better versions of ourselves). This definition welcomes more arrivals into the guest house. The pain of struggling well, of laboring toward new life, is not to be turned away, for it may be a guide to becoming the persons we are meant to be.

We wrote this book as an existence proof that there are indeed places for labor that can transform the meaningfulness of the single greatest use we make of the waking hours of our lives. We wrote it to create a spark of hope—and to see what might happen if we together blow that spark into a flame.

Notes

Chapter 1

1. Brené Brown, *Daring Greatly: How the Courage to Be Vulnerable Transforms the Way We Live, Love, Parent, and Lead* (Garden City, NY: Avery, 2015).
2. Josh Waitzkin, *The Art of Learning: A Journey in the Pursuit of Excellence* (New York: Free Press, 2005).
3. Joseph Jaworski, *Synchronicity: The Inner Path of Leadership* (San Francisco: Berrett-Koehler, 1996); and Peter M. Senge, *The Fifth Discipline: The Art and Practice of the Learning Organization* (New York: Doubleday, 1990).
4. Jeffrey T. Polzer and Heidi K. Gardner, "Bridgewater Associates," Case 413-702 (Boston: Harvard Business School, 2013).

Chapter 2

1. Robert Kegan, *The Evolving Self: Problem and Process in Human Development* (Cambridge, MA: Harvard University Press, 1982); and Robert Kegan, *In Over Our Heads: The Mental Demands of Modern Life* (Cambridge, MA: Harvard University Press, 1994).
2. Stanley Milgram, *Obedience to Authority: An Experimental View* (New York: Harper and Row, 1974); Irving L. Janis, *Groupthink: Psychological Studies of Policy Decisions and Fiascoes* (Boston: Houghton Mifflin, 1982); and Paul 't Hart, *Groupthink in Government: A Study of Small Groups and Policy Failure* (Baltimore: Johns Hopkins University Press, 1990).
3. Keith Eigel, "Leader Effectiveness" (PhD dissertation, University of Georgia, 1998). Eigel used a ninety-minute interview assessment measure that we and our colleagues developed (L. Lahey, E. Souvaine, R. Kegan, et al., *A Guide to the Subject-Object Interview* [Cambridge, MA: The Subject-Object Research Group, 1988]). The *subject-object interview* has been used all over the world, across all sectors, over the past thirty years. It discriminates developmental movement between, and within, the levels of mental complexity with high degrees of interrater reliability.

4. Paul T. Bartone et al., "Psychological Development and Leader Performance in West Point Cadets," paper presented at AERA, Seattle, April 2001; Phyllis Benay, "Social Cognitive Development and Transformational Leadership (PhD dissertation, University of Massachusetts, 1997); Gervaise R. Bushe and Barrie W. Gibb, "Predicting Organization Development Consulting Competence from the Myers-Briggs Type Indicator and Stage of Ego Development," *Journal of Applied Behavioral Science* 26 (1990): 337–357; William R. Torbert et al., "Human Development and Managerial Effectiveness," *Journal of Group and Organizational Studies* 12, no. 3 (1987): 257–273; and William R. Torbert and David Rooke, "Organizational Transformation as a Function of CEOs' Developmental Stage," *Organization Development Journal* 16, no. 1 (1999): 11–29.
5. Nathaniel Branden, *The Six Pillars of Self-Esteem* (New York: Bantam, 1995), 22–23.
6. Chris Argyris and Donald Schön, *Organizational Learning* (Reading, MA: Addison-Wesley, 1978), 21.
7. Ibid.
8. We don't mean to imply we are the first to bring this science to the study of organizations. William Torbert pioneered the application of constructive-developmental theory to organizations (see W. Torbert, and D. Fisher, *Personal and Organizational Transformations* [New York: McGraw-Hill, 1995]; W. Torbert, *The Power of Balance* [Thousand Oaks, CA: Sage Publications, 1991]). Frederic Laloux's study of organizations at the self-transforming stage is an important recent contribution (F. Laloux, *Reinventing Organizations* [Brussels: Nelson Parker, 2014]).
9. Frederick Winslow Taylor, *The Principles of Scientific Management* (New York: Harper and Brothers Publishers, 1911).

Chapter 3

1. Carol Dweck, *Mindset: The New Psychology of Success* (New York: Random House, 2006).
2. Karl E. Weick and Kathleen M. Sutcliffe, *Managing the Unexpected: Resilient Performance in an Age of Uncertainty* (San Francisco: Jossey-Bass, 2001).
3. Ray Dalio, *Principles* (Bridgewater Associates, 2011).
4. Edgar H. Schein, *Organizational Culture and Leadership* (San Francisco: Jossey-Bass, 1984).

Chapter 4

1. Each of the DDOs we have studied uses its own leaders as teachers and facilitators for learning-oriented experiences. And each of them makes sure the

leader-as-teacher receives plenty of feedback from the learners. DDOs have found that leading presents an opportunity to practice and grow.

Chapter 5

1. One place to look for confirmation or disconfirmation of that hypothesis would be the other two DDOs. Do they have anything striking to report with respect to this critical business metric? Several years ago, Decurion decided to significantly reduce its central office. All the outside advice told the leaders to hold back the information for as long as possible to prevent early departures and emotional disengagement. Instead, they shared the decision as soon as they made it, many months before anyone would be let go. "Because we were completely transparent in our thinking, the community as a whole took ownership of the scale-down," Christopher Forman says. "Because we continued to support the development of everyone, those who were going and those who were staying, we did not lose a single person we wanted to stay. Not a single person." Bridgewater's CEO, Greg Jensen, says that Bridgewater is at once "a hard place to stay (because 42 percent of people hired leave during the first two years) and an extremely hard place to leave (because almost no one leaves if they make it past the first two years)." A recent review of hires from ten years ago showed that around 40 percent were gone after two years, but around 50 percent were still there after ten years. Bridgewater lost very few people who made it past the first two years.
2. Jeffrey T. Polzer and Heidi K. Gardner, "Bridgewater Associates," Case 413-702 (Boston: Harvard Business School, 2013), 4.
3. Daniel Kahneman, *Thinking, Fast and Slow* (New York: Farrar, Straus, and Giroux, 2013).
4. Ronald Heifetz, *Leadership Without Easy Answers* (Cambridge, MA: Harvard University Press, 1998).

Chapter 6

1. Robert Kegan and Lisa Laskow Lahey, *Immunity to Change* (Boston: Harvard Business School Press, 2009).

Chapter 7

1. Ken Wilber, *Integral Psychology: Consciousness, Spirit, Psychology, Therapy* (Boston: Shambhala, 2000.)
2. "What is Startup Engineering? with Merrick Furst," YouTube video, 8:43, featuring an interview with Scott Henderson, posted by "HypepotamusTV," June 24, 2013, https://www.youtube.com/watch?v=S-U1nqfOUPY.)

3. "Merrick Furst Explains Flashpoint and Startup Engineering," YouTube video, 32:38, from the Atlanta CEO Council's Next Big Idea series, posted by "Flashpoint at Georgia Tech," July 24, 2014, https://www.youtube.com/watch?v=4EdA5pjaTT0).)

Index

Entries followed by *f* refer to figures and entries followed by *t* refer to tables.

Acknowledgments

We happily acknowledge our appreciation—but more than this, our admiration and affection—for the many members of three extraordinary organizations (Bridgewater, Decurion, and Next Jump), who have been, and continue to be, wholehearted learning partners over several years. True to their own principles of transparency, these companies declared nothing off-limits and made every aspect of their operations available to us. We are inspired by their members' countless gestures of thoughtfulness, generosity, and courage in letting us see them in the midst of the intimate work of individual and collective learning.

We especially want to thank Ray Dalio, Greg Jensen, Bob Prince, Zack Wieder, and John Woody at Bridgewater; Nora Dashwood, Christopher Forman, Jeff Koblentz, Bob Lochhead, and Bryan Ungard at Decurion; and Jackie Edwards, Charlie Kim, Greg Kunkel, Meghan Messenger, and Elise Pierpont at Next Jump.

We want to acknowledge the valuable work and good company of Inna Markus Leiter and Claire Lee, who are also members of our DDO research team. Special thanks to Inna, who took the lead in helping our research team to be itself a kind of DDO.

We thank the many colleagues who read and commented on various drafts of our manuscript, while, of course, absolving them of all responsibility for its shortcomings: Dianne Argyris, Jennifer Garvey Berger, Niko Canner, Lorraine Heilbrunn, Bill Hodgetts, Neil Janin, Michael Jung, Bill Lahey, Fred Laloux, Eric Rait, Laura Rogers, Thee Smith, Harry Spence, and Bill Torbert. A special thanks to Jennifer Garvey Berger for generously sharing a rich example of her work with an emerging DDO. Mandanna Farhoodi Moberger prepared the manuscript with care and ingenuity. We continue to appreciate the wisdom and patience of Jeff Kehoe, our long-suffering, never-complaining editor at Harvard Business Publishing.

We remember and celebrate the inspiration of our friend, Jim Fowler who dreamed of "communities of developmental expectation."

Finally, we want to acknowledge each other, and the experience of genuinely cocreating this book. Five collaborating authors could be a recipe for unproductive stress and strain. We like to think the reason it was not has something to do with our learning, at least a little, the lessons of our own book.

—Robert Kegan
Lisa Lahey
Matthew L. Miller
Andy Fleming
Deborah Helsing

About the Authors

Robert Kegan and **Lisa Lahey**, coauthors of *Immunity to Change* and *How the Way We Talk Can Change the Way We Work*, have been research and practice collaborators for thirty years. Kegan is the Meehan Professor of Adult Learning and Professional Development at the Harvard Graduate School of Education. Lahey, also on the Harvard faculty, is a founding principal of Minds at Work, a leadership-learning professional services firm.

Matthew L. Miller is a lecturer on education and Associate Dean for Learning and Teaching at the Harvard Graduate School of Education. **Andy Fleming** is the CEO and a founding principal of Way to Grow INC, the research and consulting home of the Deliberately Developmental Organization™. **Deborah Helsing** is a lecturer on education at the Harvard Graduate School of Education and Director of Training at Minds at Work.